THE
WAR
AT HOME

THE WAR

Editors
Bill Nasson & Albert Grundlingh

AT HOME

WOMEN AND FAMILIES
IN THE ANGLO-BOER WAR

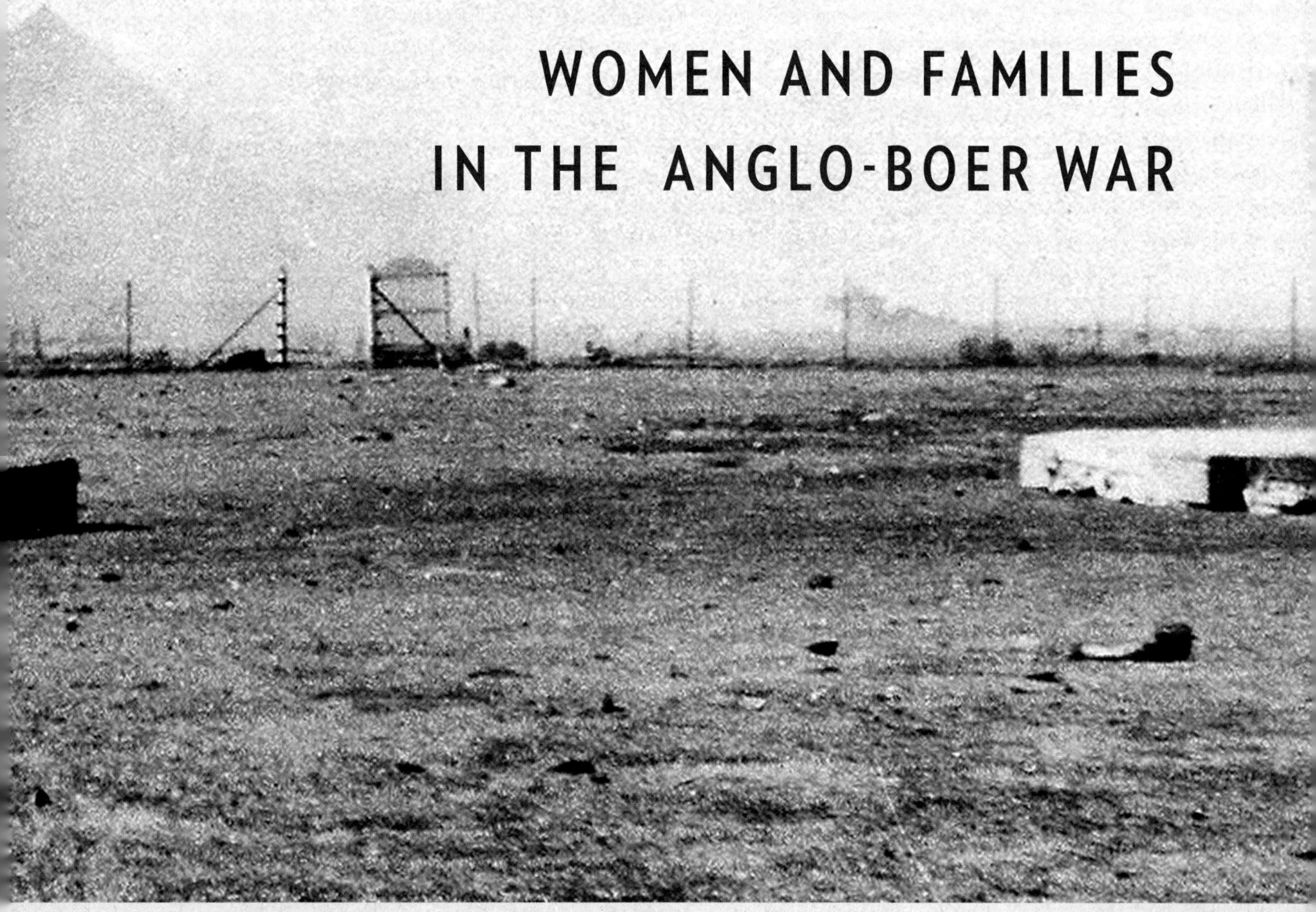

Tafelberg
An imprint of NB Publishers,
a division of Media24 Boeke (Pty) Ltd
40 Heerengracht, Cape Town, South Africa
www.tafelberg.com
Copyright in editing © Bill Nasson,
Albert Grundlingh (2013)
Copyright in text © Individual contributors
Photos © See p. 266
Map © Pete Bosman

All rights reserved.
No part of this book may be reproduced or transmitted in any form or by any electronic or mechanical means, including photocopying and recording, or by any information storage or retrieval system, without written permission from the publisher.

The publisher would like to thank Etna Labuschagne, Vicky Heunis and Johan van Zÿl of the War Museum of the Boer Republics for their help with sourcing of images and other material for the book.

COVER: Pete Bosman
DESIGN: Pete Bosman
TRANSLATION: Linde Dietrich, Chet Fransch
COPY-EDITING: Mark Ronan
PROOFREADING: Lesley Hay-Whitton
INDEX: Sanet le Roux

Printed and bound in Singapore by
Tien Wah Press (Pte) Ltd
First edition, first impression 2013
ISBN: 978-0-624-05899-1
Epub: 978-0-624-05900-4

RIGHT A group of women and their family members are transported to the Barberton camp on rail wagons.

PREVIOUS PAGE In another agonising, disastrous day of scorched-earth tactics, with whatever belongings she has been able to salvage, a woman watches her house go up in flames, courtesy of the British Army.

OVERLEAF Cleanliness in catastrophe: outside the tent that has become their home, Anna Davel and probably daughter perform domestic chores.

Contents

Foreword ... 10
Introduction ... 18
Map of concentration camps ... 21

CHAPTER ONE
Why concentration camps? ... 22

CHAPTER TWO
The defiance of the *bittereinder* woman ... 44

CHAPTER THREE
In the veld with Nonnie de la Rey ... 72

CHAPTER FOUR
Daily life in the concentration camps ... 92

CHAPTER FIVE
A clash of cultures: British doctors versus Boer women ... 120

CHAPTER SIX
'Faded flowers'? Children in the concentration camps ... 142

CHAPTER SEVEN
Black people and the camps ... 168

CHAPTER EIGHT
The 'terrible laughter' of the Boers: Humour in the war ... 194

CHAPTER NINE
The Women's Monument: Planning, design and inauguration ... 210

CHAPTER TEN
The meaning of the Women's Monument: Then and now ... 226

CHAPTER ELEVEN
In Emily Hobhouse's words ... 246

End notes ... 257
Further reading ... 262
Author biographies ... 265
Acknowledgements ... 266
Photographic acknowledgements ... 266
Index ... 267

Foreword

THIS COLLECTION OF ESSAYS, EDITED BY Bill Nasson and Albert Grundlingh, is a significant reassessment of the Anglo-Boer War, portraying the civilian experiences of the war as bleak yet also endurable. Focusing on the plight of women and families, the contributors consider not only their victimhood but also, more importantly, their own human agency. Through a meticulous reading of the written and photographic archival material, the authors provide a detached account, allowing the reader to appreciate the subtleties of the relationships between gender, race and class in the context of a colonial war. The quality of the images and the unfolding details in this book are astounding. Women and young girls are shown with domestic products such as a broom, bucket, chair, blanket and pot. And each person is in their, seemingly, rightful place. At home? But their homes no longer exist, having been destroyed during the scorched-earth policy or involuntarily abandoned.

Homes are now tents – makeshift abodes for these nomads who live in concentration camps. In the photographs, the gazes of these people reflect both their fear and determination – the weaknesses and strengths of those transformed by their predicament.

Much like a cinematographic flashback, the book uses the inauguration of the Women's Monument in Bloemfontein in 1913 as a symbolic foundation. Its centenary is subtly contextualised within a complicated and horrific colonial war and the consequent rise of segregationist nationalism. One of the methods of imperial warfare was the concentration camps, which were designated primarily (yet not exclusively, according to one contributor) for civilians, specifically women and children, whether they were black or white. The scorched-earth policy, which was introduced by the British army in an increasingly professionalised way, had consequences beyond the brutal ordeals of these women and their families. Their incarceration also left a lasting legacy on the history of the country.

Another visible flashback here is the origin of the camps. For political writer Hannah Arendt, concentration camps came into existence long before the totalitarian regimes of the twentieth century made them an important institution of government. They were not the same as prisons. Rather, they were meant to deal with people who were 'undesirables' – individuals who had lost their legal rights and identity in their own country.[1] Hannah Arendt was one of those scholars who mistakenly attributed the rise of concentration camps to the Anglo-Boer War. In fact, as the first chapter by one of the editors also notes, their origins lay elsewhere. Essentially, they were invented in 1896 in Cuba under Spanish General Valeriano Weyler y Nicolau. They came to be refined in South Africa and went on to be implemented worldwide in the following two decades. Indeed, they continue to exist in the present day.

What exactly happened? Civilians – particularly women, children and the elderly – were incarcerated and treated as the enemy because they found themselves encircled by war. For the most part, these non-combatants were becoming accustomed to some state of emergency or martial law because this had been a part of the colonial experience and the rise of a total war. They were subjected to brutal hardships, including loss of freedom,

In the last phase of the conflict, camps such as this one at Merebank, Durban, were established in the warmer, subtropical climate of Natal.

PREVIOUS PAGE The home that the war brought: a street in the British concentration camp at Aliwal North.

separation from loved ones, deplorable and unsanitary living conditions, lack of food, overcrowding and disease. They had to endure under policies that did not originally have the intent to make them suffer or die. Their detention was either administrative or military but not legal, because they were never tried or condemned.

It is important to consider briefly what happened in Cuba. There, in the mid-1890s, the Spanish army's concept of a 'concentration of civilians' led to the invention of camps, bearing the name *reconcentrados*. General Weyler's idea was to separate the civilians from the rebels who opposed Spanish colonisation, under the pretext of protecting them from the scorched-earth policy that was designed to end the Cuban insurgency. They were to be deported and isolated in a type of exile. In other words, individuals were to be removed from their homes and transported elsewhere. Weyler understood that the Cuban rebels were reverting to guerrilla tactics and were being fed, voluntarily or otherwise, by civilians. In order to win the war, Weyler decided to cut those resources by 'reconcentrating', or relocating, the civilian population and dividing the island into zones. In March 1898, an eyewitness, American Senator Redfield Proctor, said that 'it is not peace, nor is it war. It is desolation and distress, misery and starvation' with every 'woman and child and every domestic animal under guard … It is concentration and desolation.'[2]

Mass media emerged during this period, and journalists were able to report on the suffering of the Cubans to a world audience. In addition, the increasingly professional photography of war covered such acts of political extermination.

The Spanish imperial power's defence was based on the belief that the Cuban enemies were barbarians. Regardless, the civilised world was expected to protest and intervene, and the Cubans looked to the United States in the hope that it would recognise their independence. Instead, the Americans invaded the island against the will of its inhabitants and imposed a de facto American protectorate. By 1898 this, at least, ended the forced removals.

For his part, Weyler had implemented a tactic that he had already witnessed on a smaller scale in the United States. During the American Civil War of 1861–1865, he had been Spain's military attaché in Washington and an avid admirer of General William Sherman, who used this tactic against those civilians who were hostile towards the Union forces. Most notably, such civilians in Missouri were displaced and put into what were called 'posts'. The use of extreme force against civilians (which had been intensifying during colonial conquest) could be justified by authorities on the basis of the racial climate of the time, especially if those being conquered were non-Christian. However, in Cuba, the forced removal of civilians, in the context of colonialism and counter-strategy to guerrilla warfare, involved a population that was of European extraction and Christian.

Turning again to South Africa, it should be remembered that British (and American) opinion considered Weyler a 'butcher' and a 'brute'.[3] The *Cape Argus* of 26 March 1897 (a local British-colonial publication) described Spain as a 'disgrace to civilisation'. Shortly after this, the same causes led to the same effects, and a colonial war between the Boers and the British generated yet another system of concentration camps. Aware of what was developing in South Africa, Lloyd George, a Liberal member of the opposition, expressed his concerns to the House of Commons on 25 July 1900, declaring that 'it seems to me that in this war we have gradually followed the policy of Spain in Cuba'.[4] At this point, it may not yet have been entirely the case, but the military failures of General Frederick Roberts and the imminent arrival of General Horatio Kitchener would soon seal the fate of the Boer and black South African population.

This volume of social history is exact and original in its revisiting of this total war – a war characterised by the destruction of farms, the killing of animals, the widespread use of arson and interpersonal violence between men and women. Contributors carefully explore themes such as the complex relationship between charity and Anglicisation: the British authorities only accepted the former because they anticipated it leading to the latter. The authors also enable the voices of the unofficial prisoners to be heard from their hospital beds, their schools, their places of worship, and through their romances and their deaths, thereby giving a picture constantly illustrated by rich documentary and visual sources.

It all unfolds in the summer of 1900. The British have a military advantage over the Boers. They have control of the cities and rail network, but are still far from winning the war in the face of their adversaries. So they begin the classic method of deporting military prisoners to Saint Helena, Bermuda and India. Protection in camps is even offered to those who surrender. Nonetheless, the guerrilla forces continue to generate mayhem for the British army and the idea of internment of families in concentration camps is considered an extension of the scorched-earth policy. The British believe that the only viable solution would be to destroy the farms and the harvest, and to cut off supplies to the Boer troops. Kitchener sets out to resolve the problem when he takes command at the end of 1900. For him, there are no innocent bystanders among the Boer population – and the testimonies of those who resist, discussed in this volume, fail to prove otherwise! Kitchener focuses on dissuading Boer resistance, and insinuates, despite the evidence, that the 'joiners' themselves suggested internment camps for their families. In reality, virtually the entire population is taken hostage. White and black people are all taken as prisoners of war and subjected to harsh reprisals. Moreover, the camps are run by the military with their own clearly punitive goals.

This was the atmosphere, and those who appeared to be victims reacted accordingly. The example of Nonnie de la Rey is of particular interest. She wanted to be considered a prisoner of war in the event of her capture. This would ensure that she would be protected under the first Geneva Convention, or be viewed as neutral under the humanitarian laws that were vaguely in place during the war. Nonnie was a product of the prevailing Boer patriarchal system and she considered herself a 'man', in practice a substitute for her man during his absence. Even if she could not expect the British to respect this decision, she continued to support her husband on commando, where active combatants fought side by side and, at times, women accompanied men. It was for this active role; above all else, that she refused to be incarcerated in the concentration camps. Unsurprisingly, the French, Dutch and Belgians (fuelled by anti-British sentiment) eagerly rallied in support of such an austere and relentless freedom struggle by European Calvinists.

As seen in the pages that follow, the British described the Boers as primitive and unrestrained sensual beings, with a strong sense of family values, who would only submit if their kin were affected. At the turn of the century, reference was made at times to 'Boer herds' or 'Boer flocks', depictions which drew on social Darwinist ideas of human evolution and placed the enemy at a sub-human level.[5] With little choice but to submit, they were enclosed in a camp, which represented a kind of human zoo. There, they were registered, housed in tents, given ration coupons and became names on lists. The process was haphazard.

Neither Roberts nor Kitchener had considered the consequences of their orders. Pushing civilians into cramped quarters with poor sanitation and feeding them on reduced military-level rations could only lead to a disastrous outcome. Already, more British soldiers were dying from disease than in battle, a phenomenon not uncommon in nineteenth-century warfare. In the camps women, children and the elderly were prone to the same fate. Devastating outbreaks of measles were particularly common and later became symbolic of the trauma of camp life.

By the autumn of 1900, high mortality rates were causing a stir among pacifist groups in London, such as the South African Conciliation Committee. Emily Hobhouse, the founder of the South African Women and Children Distress Fund, belonged to this committee. In December 1900, she arrived in South Africa and produced a report on concentration-camp conditions which served as an indictment of the camps. Although not entirely anti-British, this was used to the advantage of the Boers and countries opposing Great Britain (the first translation of the report came from France). Although Emily Hobhouse was expelled from South Africa during her second trip in 1901, her message had been heard in Great Britain. The Liberal Party leader, Campbell-Bannerman, spoke scathingly of his country's use of 'methods of barbarism'[6] and made Hobhouse's report public, an action which led to a subsequent parliamentary inquiry.

The inquiry focused on the desperate situation in white camps. Yet the separate camps established for black Africans were even worse. Their dwellings and plots were also burnt to prevent guerrillas from obtaining resources to continue their resistance.

These inmates worked in the camps and were expected not only to tend to their families, but also to meet some of the needs of the British Army. The high mortality rate in the black camps was largely overlooked by white observers and resulted in little protest and few witness testimonies.

Instinctively, the British tried to deflect their culpability by blaming the unsanitary conditions in the camps on the Boers; their ignorance and inability to be civilised were said to be the cause of the problems. In a complete reversal of the Victorian, British values that glorified the countryside as opposed to industrial cities, the Boers were frequently depicted as primitives living in rural squalor, incapable of cooking the food that was provided and unable to care for their children. To explain this, the authors of this book place the plight of women, children, black servants, white bosses, sick people, caregivers and early humanitarians within a broader reflection on the war. The reader bears witness to the inflicted trauma, the resilience, the helplessness, the loss and the trials of a daily existence. Moreover, a glimpse is provided into the monotony of life that introduced the notion of the 'barbed-wire syndrome' familiar to many prisoners – part of a litany of misfortunes that made these civilian camps the first of their kind in the twentieth century.

As the essays indicate, camp conditions gradually improved during the war. By 1902, nurses and teachers from Britain were being employed to care for the sick and the children. Was this in the tradition of Protestant charity? Was it an aspect of civilising enlightenment? Arguably, not quite. For instance, the English language was to replace Afrikaans, in addition to other cultural impositions. Yet, ironically, the political situation was also changing by then because civilians whose farms had been destroyed were no longer being rounded up and incarcerated. In the middle of that dispersion of civilians and erosion of the last of commando resistance, surrender came.

By then, the British had inadvertently created exemplary victims for the Afrikaners to mourn. The existence of the concentration camps gave more impetus to white Afrikaner nationalism than the rest of the colonial experience. Globally, too, the focus was no longer on Cuba. Although the pro-Boer movement stemmed from opposition to the British Empire and colonialism, its widespread outcry – even if exaggerated at times – against what were viewed as crimes, had a genuine basis.

In the September 1901 issue of *L'Assiette au Beurre* (which was swiftly translated into Dutch), the artist Jean Veber presented several sinister illustrations from the 'reconcentration camps of the Transvaal', as they were then referred to. The drawings included depictions of women mourning the deceased children who lay around them and of British soldiers who hit them or separated them from their children. Alongside the illustrations were captions taken from Kitchener's reports to the War Office in London, emphasising the benefits to Boer women of 'spacious tents where air and freshness are in abundance' and camps where 'jovial mothers' are able to forget 'the melancholy of their predicament'.[7]

In these stark expressions, was there perhaps a risk that extreme forms of propaganda would actually dilute opinions of real atrocities? Would such propaganda not inevitably affect public opinion of the civilians who fall prey to the horrors of war? Would the Boers, who had been victimised by the British, not then seek revenge on black African people because the British had employed them against the Boers? Could one still question ethics within war when combatants were no longer the sole protagonists? Was there ever any possibility of considering the idea of a just or unjust war? After all, from this turning point, the use of concentration camps was going to be part of the machinery of war. The camps of the Balkan Wars and the Great War of 1914–1918 were quick to follow those of Cuba and South Africa.

Therefore, among all the hostile powers of the Great War, the internment of so-called 'suspicious' civilians was common, as was treating them like prisoners of war in breach of international laws. In occupied lands, suspicious civilians were also the victims of reprisals and were, at times, deported and/or sent to work camps. Incarcerating non-combatants as a means of weakening the enemy had always been a strategic method of warfare. And, obviously, the simultaneous capturing of soldiers was far from novel. By contrast, the advent of concentration camps since the events in Cuba and South Africa was an innovation in warfare: ordinary civilians, too, had become victims on the path towards total war. Their camps had become an integral part of the culture of armed warfare.

In many ways, between 1896 (the war in Cuba) and 1918 (the end of the Great War), the Anglo-Boer War also contributed to these changes in the conduct of war during the twentieth century. In South Africa, the deportation and incarceration of civilians had not culminated in mass extermination. But conditions did produce a war against civilians characterised by extreme violence. At the same time, the camp phenomenon was not yet synonymous with the later organised systems of concentration camps. In the Anglo-Boer War, the management of the camps was haphazard and uncoordinated, as this book clearly reveals. Regardless, this was still a total war. Total war requires the incarceration of enemies, be they soldiers captured during battle or civilians perceived and treated as enemies – unarmed soldiers who used their own weapons of hatred, refusal and silence to fight back and prove their resilience.

Clearly, the experience of the Boer people in the republics in South Africa was not that of genocide, as in the experience of the Armenians of Turkey in the Great War. It was that of degradation. The causes thereof were not accidental, inadvertent or intentional cruelty, but rather the essence of war policies in occupied territories, namely, incarceration and isolation. It is on that path that one finds the tragedies and horrors of the victimised women and families of the Anglo-Boer War.

OVERLEAF Boer children carry wood across the Orange river to one of the camps.

ANNETTE BECKER is Professor of Modern History at the Paris West University Nanterre La Défense, and a senior member of the l'Institut Universitaire de France. A social and cultural historian of total war in the twentieth century, she is an authority on the impact of violence upon civilians under military occupation. Becker is one of the founders of the Museum of the Great War in northern France, the Historial de la Grande Guerre, in Peronne, Somme. Her recent publications include a study of the World War I experiences of French poet Guillaume Apollinaire, *Apollinaire: Une Biographie de Guerre 1914–1918* (2009).

Introduction

THE TRAUMATIC IMPACT OF THE 1899 TO 1902 WAR in South Africa on most ordinary Afrikaner people has often been viewed as the defining feature of the bitter Anglo-Boer conflict. The trauma has lingered in popular memory, and not only as a result of the anniversaries that serve to remind us of the conflict. Nevertheless, commemorations, particularly centenary ones, are potentially more than rituals. They may, in fact, give rise to a fresh outlook on history with which to revisit established perceptions of past events and people. With that in mind, the publication of this book coincides with the 2013 centenary of the Women's Monument in Bloemfontein, inaugurated after the end of the Anglo-Boer War, which is now frequently also referred to as the South African War.

Like other recent historical works, this book has been prompted by the present era, which has yielded notable centenary commemorations of events in South African history. The start of the twenty-first century has been marked by commemorations of the 1899 to 1902 conflict; the 1906 Bhambatha rebellion in Natal; the initial founding of the African National Congress in 1912; and the 1913 Land Act. And others will take place in the near future, such as the centenary of the 1914 Afrikaner rebellion at the start of World War I and the centenary of the founding of the now-extinct National Party, also in 1914 – likely to be a muted commemoration, in the light of more recent post-apartheid history.

If one were to compare commemorations, the 1913 Women's Monument and other events would be overshadowed in scope and significance by the 1938 Voortrekker centenary celebrations. At the heart of that occasion lay the awakening of a dormant Afrikaner nationalism, which drew on a momentous past episode to galvanise the *volk*. Such brazen displays of nationalist excess would look out of place in our own, more sceptical age. Yet, it remains an example of how historical commemoration is always viewed through the lens of the present.

Why should the creation of the Women's Monument be commemorated in a South Africa that has changed so much since 1913? Is its legacy still relevant and, if so, what meaning does it hold for ordinary South Africans 100 years later?

To answer these questions the authors of this book explore the shifting sands of memory and consider how the monument – a body of stone charged by emotion – has been perceived at crucial historical stages since 1913. We consider the questions of whom it spoke to originally, what it has been seen to say through the twentieth century, and what it might say now. Alongside its perspective on this particular legacy of the conflict, *The War at Home: Women and Families in the Anglo-Boer War* is concerned with the complexities and contradictions of the war experience of 1899 to 1902, which gave birth to enduring rituals of remembrance.

The War at Home tells readers more than simply the story of this iconic war memorial. Naturally, the 1913 Women's Monument – with its emotional, political, cultural and other memories – embodies a public history of its own. But it also provides a glimpse into the

Clawing skywards into life – the Women's Monument in 1913, towering over the flat Highveld surroundings of the Orange Free State

varied lives and extreme circumstances of a vulnerable civilian society that was directly affected by the shock of a modern total war. The war of 1899 to 1902 was more than one war and more than merely a conflict between armies on the battlefields. Many ordinary rural people – white, black, women, children, families and individuals – experienced the deaths and suffering caused by hostilities beyond the battlefield.

The civilian worlds explored in this book are mainly those of women and families confronted by massive upheaval. Yet, although the collection describes the plight of helpless victims, it also analyses the ways in which the strain of war experience was uneven and often unpredictable. In other words, instead of reinforcing well-worn historical interpretations that reduce the existence of women and families to that of passive suffering, we will examine the vital aspects of civilian endurance – so often overlooked or forgotten.

In confronting the tragedy of the war, the contributors show the endeavours of those who sought to come to terms with the precarious circumstances created by invasion and occupation. Their war was the struggle for a tolerable and decent existence in a complicated landscape of conflicting interests – defiance and accommodation, resistance and collaboration, interaction and withdrawal, fragile certainties and acute insecurities, and hope and despair. If our readers are to remember or commemorate anything about this total war in South Africa, we hope they will gain a sense of perspective when considering what the conflict meant for those who were not under arms.

In the chapters that follow, our contributors look at the powerful implications of gender in wartime, as well as at the personal trials in the countryside of one intriguing and prominent Boer woman who was able to avoid Britain's concentration camps. The camps are, of course, a particularly controversial aspect of the war. For more than a century, their existence has inspired comment and condemnation from scholars, historians, politicians and sentimental Afrikaner citizenry.

We apply a broad-minded approach when analysing the purpose and nature of the concentration camps, and the reasons for their establishment. We also question the common assumption that the development of the camps was inevitable, based on the justification that the war could not have taken any other direction in the calamitous winter of 1901. In the same way, we deal with the evolution and dynamics of the black camps. Contrary to popular perceptions, historical works have documented their existence for several decades. This book suggests that white and black camps were more intertwined and that there was a greater degree of interaction between their separate inhabitants than has often been assumed.

We also record the experience of family life in the concentration camps. Even though there has been considerable focus on the camps, little is known about the circumstances of interned children. To make up for this historical neglect, this collection offers insight into wartime camp childhoods and provides readers with an understanding of how children survived and expressed themselves. It is time to move beyond the narrow view of their presence counting only as a toll of wasted and dead bodies.

In this way, we turn a searchlight on the complex inner workings of the camps. We investigate the everyday life of inhabitants, as well as how the conflicting medical cultures of the confined Boers and the occupying British administration influenced attitudes towards healing and recuperation. Finally, the common link between the horror of war and black or ironic humour leads us to a consideration of the views of those who resorted to comic expression to cope with their extreme circumstances. We also consider the significance of the comic imagination as the ordinary Boer population dealt with the immediate aftermath of hostilities.

As *The War at Home* shows, there were many wars fought from 1899 to 1902. With the fighting front and the home front often being indistinguishable, the Anglo-Boer War was a momentous struggle with many facets and faces, some of which are portrayed here. We invite readers to visit, once again, South Africa's total war.

BILL NASSON AND ALBERT GRUNDLINGH

Hanging on to what was left: Boer families tramp towards the Pietermaritzburg camp.

MAP OF CONCENTRATION CAMPS

CHAPTER ONE

Why concentration camps?

— ALBERT GRUNDLINGH —

Boers in Battle

PREVIOUS PAGE, MAIN IMAGE Getting its tents in a row: the Norvalspont camp, with its parade-ground order, shows the origins of its British Army planning and administration.
SECONDARY IMAGE A melancholic gaze upon a war that carries on . . . Older, as well as younger generations suffered acutely under camp conditions.
THIS PAGE Boer forces on the offensive at Mafeking in the early stages of the war.

When the first shots of the Anglo-Boer War were fired on 12 October 1899 at Kraaipan, south of Mafeking, neither the Boers nor the British could have foreseen the extent of the damage that this war would cause. By May 1902, thousands of hectares of land had been destroyed, thousands of inhabitants of the former Boer republics were displaced and thousands more had died. In addition to the carnage on the plains and *koppies*, the scorched-earth policy and the concentration camps left a deep scar on the physical and psychological landscape of South Africa.

Most of the concentration camps, established by the British from the second half of 1900, were in the two Boer republics, the Transvaal and Orange Free State, but there were also large camps in Natal and the eastern Cape. Towards the end of the war, there were around 50 camps for white civilians and 64 for black civilians. More than 4 000 Boer women and approximately 22 000 children died in the camps. Although there are no precise figures, it is estimated that between 15 000 and 20 000 black people, again mostly children, died in the black camps. All in all, it is likely that more than 40 000 people lost their lives.

What were the direct and indirect reasons for establishing concentration camps? Was the camp system an inevitable consequence of the war, or could it perhaps have been prevented? To what extent did the scorched-earth policy comply with the contemporary rules of civilised warfare? These questions will be explored in this chapter.

When professional soldiers wage war

The British army, and other armed forces in Europe, became increasingly professionalised in the late nineteenth century. War was conducted in a less haphazard manner than the former method of simply overwhelming the enemy by charging at them. And this was one of the more indirect reasons for the concentration camps.

The British Empire was involved in many military expeditions and it was becoming necessary to conduct war in a more solid, comprehensive and varied way. Different expeditions required different approaches, and military planning was adjusted accordingly. Command structures, logistics and strategies were determined bureaucratically and with specific outcomes in mind.

Military professionalism created a distinct culture that emphasised instrumental rationality – the belief that the end justifies the means. This became so entrenched that other considerations were gradually eliminated. Among other things, it led to military

If not the republican Irish, blame the republican Boers: a bridge over the Vaal River blown up by Britain's enemy.

personnel assuming the responsibility of organising the civilian population when hostilities spread from the battlefield to society at large.

As professional soldiers, the military leadership considered that they possessed the competence to deal with civilian matters as well, but gave little thought to their potential complexities. This attitude made it relatively easy for them to implement extreme measures and to justify them. An academic explanation of this mindset maintains that 'militaries, because violence is their business, do not need external ideologies or motivations to encourage excess; and their basic assumptions (the military culture) that develop to handle it may be sufficient in themselves'.[1]

When the civilian population of the two republics initially came under military rule, the way they were treated foreshadowed what would happen later in the Anglo-Boer War. The poor handling of the Boer civilians was not an exceptional case, as similar approaches had been taken by military leaders before.

Professional armed forces had played a part in the *reconcentrados*, the concentration camps established by Spain during its campaign in Cuba from 1896 to 1897. The Spanish forces were under the command of General Valeriano Weyler, who was sent to Cuba in February 1896 to suppress the rebellion that had erupted the previous year. The Cuban rebels had looted buildings, burnt houses, destroyed tobacco plantations and sugar mills, wrecked trains and blown up bridges. Weyler tried to control the revolt by limiting the number of conflict areas, and he divided the island into sectors and fortified them. The rebels may have wreaked havoc, but Weyler retaliated with even more destruction.

Riding but not without resting: Boer forces busy securing one of their camps, or laagers

Weyler's most controversial measure was to move all non-combatants into concentration camps, which consisted of small huts in protected towns. The inmates' houses were burnt and their livestock confiscated. The mortality rate was particularly high and approximately 125 000 people died in the camps. Weyler's methods acquired a stigma of excessive cruelty.

In 1897 a South African newspaper described his actions as a blot on the reputation of the ostensibly civilised Spanish nation. During the Anglo-Boer War, the prominent Cape politician John X. Merriman wrote in a letter to his mother: 'What can an Englishman say of our doings in the Free State, burning, plundering and turning helpless women and children adrift in this weather. Doing as Weyler did when he made the *reconcentrados* in Cuba.'[2]

Similarly, the influential David Lloyd George said in July 1900 in the British House of Commons that the leadership of the British army seemed to be following in Weyler's footsteps.

Besides the events in Cuba, other similar trends in warfare can be observed in the war between the United States and the Philippines from 1899 to 1902, when certain civilians also bore the brunt of the conflict.

Therefore, the camps in the Transvaal and Orange Free State were, among other things, part of a broader pattern of the increased professional nature of armies and military affairs. The trend also manifested in other parts of the world, and featured widely in the press. Although the British military leaders did not deliberately base their policy on Weyler's, they were, nevertheless, generally aware of the direction in which warfare had started moving by the end of the nineteenth century.

ABOVE British forces parade in Bloemfontein following their capture of the Orange Free State capital in March 1900, but the first taste of conquest was not destined to be sweet.

RIGHT Not always worth the paper on which it was signed: copy of the oath of allegiance that republican burghers and Boer prisoners of war were encouraged to sign after the war (From the collection of the War Museum of the Boer Republics)

One of the hundreds of farm houses that were destroyed by scorched-earth warfare.

Little spared when virtually everything becomes a target: above, the wrecked church in Lindley in the Orange Free State; opposite clockwise from top left, British soldiers depart from a farm left in ruins; a dwelling reduced to a shell; a barn is torched; grain bags are set ablaze, confiscated cattle and small-town buildings pillaged and emptied.

In general, the policy was carried out ruthlessly by soldiers who considered it their professional duty to do so and sometimes even derived sadistic pleasure from the task. A British soldier wrote: 'You should have seen the Royal Irish on the loot. They helped the people out with their stuff by heaving heavy bureaus bodily through the windows, putting pickaxes through melodeons and such like wantonness. I heard one yell, "Begory Jim, here is a nice carpet … Oi'll take it home for the ould woman. Lend a hand here!" R-r-r-rip! Up came a handsome pole carpet in strips. And so the work went on, the officers standing by laughing at the costly fun their men were having.'[4]

This vandalism left a deep impression on the Boer women who witnessed it. One of them declared, 'There I stood, surrounded by my little children, while the cruel soldiers plundered my property. Furniture, clothes, food, everything was thrown in a heap and set alight … No matter how much I pleaded with them to save a few heirlooms, they refused to listen.'[5] Incidences like this occurred regularly in the two republics, and the humiliation that these experiences engendered would, in later years, provide a fertile breeding ground among Afrikaners for collective agonising and resentment towards 'the English'.

The British side has argued that the change in the war after the Boers began using guerrilla warfare forced the supreme command to take the women into their care on humanitarian grounds, rather than leaving them defenceless in the veld. But this argument is misleading. The British forces used arson as a military measure because they could not conquer the commandos in the field. The establishment of concentration camps made it possible for the British authorities to remove white and black civilians (mainly women and children) from the farms for military reasons. In this way, the centre of gravity of the war, which had lain solely in the conduct of military operations, shifted to include civilians as well. Therefore it was British war tactics, not humanitarian considerations, that necessitated the camps.

WHY CONCENTRATION CAMPS?   35

Men for whom the fight is over join women and children in enduring a war that continues. The Bloemfontein camp contained comparatively younger men who might have surrendered to British forces or taken the oath of allegiance. The aim of the first concentration camps was the protection through confinement of such surrendered burghers.

Another contributing factor was the British perception of the relationships between the Boers and their wives. The British authorities hoped that the internment of the women in the camps would persuade burghers to desert their commandos to join their wives. Some British imperialists believed that, as well as being strongly attached to their families, the Boers were also unsophisticated, sensual creatures who found it difficult to abstain from sex. They believed that indigenous population groups – for them this included the Boers – had exceptionally high libidos and assumed that retaining the women in the camps would engender vigorous lust in their husbands. There is an example of a homesick Boer early in the war who subtly described how his wife became 'more beautiful' to him every day but, in reality, the Boers' lustfulness was not as great as the presumptuousness of some Britons.[6]

This form of sexual politics did not have its intended effect and the internment of their wives and children did not entice the Boers to leave their commandos. On the contrary, the Boers' farms had already been destroyed and they believed that the British forces were caring for their families. Therefore, they were encouraged to continue fighting; after all, they had less to lose. In this respect, the camps had the effect of prolonging the war rather than shortening it.

Although Kitchener was not responsible for the establishment of the first camps, he played a large part in the expansion of the camp system during 1901. Many historical accounts accurately associate Kitchener with the concentration-camp policy. The motivation for this policy lay in the military situation, but Kitchener's personality also played a role. In general he had a low opinion of the Boer population, describing them as 'savages with only a thin white veneer'.[7] He saw *bittereinder* women, who adopted a defiant and recalcitrant attitude towards military authorities, as further proof of backwardness and

Casualties of war: a mourning woman with children at the grave of a family member in the Bethulie camp.

barbarism. He believed Boers led an isolated rural lifestyle far from the reach of civilising influences. At times he blamed the deaths of Boer children in the camps on what he perceived to be the unhygienic practices of their mothers. He even threatened to charge some of them with manslaughter.

This mindset was characteristic of many British imperialists, and it reveals Kitchener's indifference towards women in general. After his young fiancée had died in 1885, he had little interest in women. He allowed only unmarried men in his inner circle and seldom agreed to see women. In fact, he even thought that the absence of women in his life had helped to advance his military career. These personal traits, which were not rare among hardened British militarists of the time, provide an explanation as to why the plight of Boer women was of little importance to Kitchener. His only concern (and that of those like him) was that policy needed to be carried out. He was not sympathetic towards women and their fate; he considered them to be an alien and inferior species, who merely hindered the execution of his duties.

Many British officers had extreme views on how civilians should be treated during the war. As one officer put it bluntly, 'war is war and humanity is rot'.[8] This viewpoint creates

The fearsome engine of total war in the twentieth century: under the cover of tents and sheets, Boers are transported in railway trucks to the Pinetown camp in Natal.

OPPOSITE, TOP He and his enemy broke bread together, but did not reach an early peace: the costs of General Louis Botha's failed talks with Lord Kitchener in Middelburg, February 1901, would be borne by civilians.
CENTRE Field Marshal Lord Kitchener
BOTTOM Annie Botha, the general's wife with a fashionable taste for large hats

the impression that any measures or actions were deemed acceptable. In Britain, however, the opposition Liberal Party did not agree and became increasingly uncomfortable with the situation. In 1901 it was said in the British Parliament, 'When is a war not a war? When it is carried on by methods of barbarism in South Africa.'[9]

Were excessively cruel measures used in this conflict? In order to answer this question, one needs to look at international standards for the conduct of war established at the time.

At the end of July 1899, about two months before the outbreak of the war, representatives of 24 countries signed the First Hague Convention. The purpose of this convention was to regulate the conduct of war in accordance with certain legal principles. Britain did not sign all the provisions of the Hague Convention, and neither of the Boer republics attended the discussions. Therefore, technically, the Hague Convention did not have a bearing on the Anglo-Boer War because it stipulated that both parties to a war had to be signatories before it could be applied to them. However, this did not prevent both parties from invoking the convention in an effort to justify their respective customs of war.

The Hague Convention was a framework of standards against which war practices could be measured. Of particular relevance to the Anglo-Boer War is the question of whether the transportation of civilian women complied with the existing rules of war. Article 23 of the Hague Convention prohibited the destruction or seizure of an enemy's personal property 'unless such destruction or seizure be imperatively demanded by the necessities of war'. To justify their scorched-earth policy, the British argued that farms were used as military hideouts. But they often burnt farms without proof that they were used for military purposes or that the women who lived there acted as spies. In such cases the actions of the British forces were a violation of the Hague Convention. What followed – the internment of women and children in concentration camps – was a transgression of another order that would have catastrophic consequences.

Women and children sacrificed for freedom?

In historical writing, it is often asked whether events were inevitable and destined to happen, or whether different decisions or actions could have produced another set of outcomes. Although such questions could be dismissed as mere speculation, a consideration of alternative outcomes can broaden and deepen our insight into certain events.

The question is often posed whether the tragic camp deaths during the harsh winter of 1901 could have been prevented. In retrospect, there was an opportunity to steer history in another direction on 28 February 1901 when Kitchener and General Louis Botha met in Middelburg. The meeting arose from Kitchener's desire to prevent a protracted war and Botha's attempt to gain an understanding of the potential peace terms envisaged by the British. According to a message conveyed to Kitchener by Botha's wife, Annie, Botha was convinced that peace was necessary. Although he held that the republics should retain their independence, he was keen to explore other options.

At their meeting, Kitchener tried to persuade Botha not to commandeer the surrendered burghers again, and he undertook not to burn the farms of fighting burghers if their families were not actively assisting them. But such an arrangement would have been difficult to apply practically, and Botha firmly believed that, as a Boer general, he was legally entitled to commandeer the surrendered burghers.

The British also proposed a number of peace terms and offered to install a semi-representative government. However, Botha maintained that a nation fighting for its independence could not accept terms that did not incorporate republican independence – a non-negotiable term. Consequently, after a short correspondence the negotiations came to nothing. Botha maintained afterwards that, where human efforts to achieve peace had failed, the matter should be left in the hands of the Supreme Being.

The time for peace did arrive – more than a year later. The question is whether it was due to providence or the war-weariness of both parties. The war ended when the Peace of Vereeniging was signed on 31 May 1902. Ironically, the terms, which the Boers accepted, did not differ much from the offer that had been made in February 1901. They relinquished their independence and accepted a form of self-government under the British Crown. Other issues, such as amnesty for Cape rebels, compensation for losses and the position of black people, were also broadly in line with the conditions that had been discussed in Middelburg.

The question then arises, what did the Boer leadership gain by continuing the war for another 15 months, especially in light of the deaths in the camps and the lack of any material differences between the two sets of peace terms that were offered? After the failed Middelburg talks, the ferocity of the war intensified and the mortality rate of women and children rose steeply in the cold winter of 1901.

At the root of these problems was the inability of the two military commanders to arrive at a feasible agreement at an earlier stage. Botha prioritised the continuation of the war and insisted on republican independence. The hardened militarist Kitchener did not have full authority during the negotiations and had to consider the wishes of politicians such as Milner (who

The camps were developed with various kinds of shelter, including some solid constructions.

had misgivings about the talks). Subsequently, he continued with his already established methods of arson and transportation of civilians to concentration camps. If the Boers were not willing to be persuaded, according to Kitchener, they would have to live with the consequences of their decision. Neither Kitchener nor Botha could have known in February 1901 how exceptionally cold the coming winter would be. But the plight of civilians had also not been their top priority and was given only cursory attention at the Middelburg talks. The political and military aims of both parties were of greater importance.

Thereafter, the issue of the concentration camps became a political football. In December 1901, after frequent complaints had been made about the situation in the camps, Kitchener told the Boer leaders that if they were concerned then they could look after their compatriots themselves, and he would not expand the camps any further. Botha wrote in a letter that he found it ironic that Kitchener would suggest such a policy at a stage when the commandos lacked the means to sustain themselves. Kitchener had transported the women and children to camps at the start of the guerrilla war – when the Boers were still able to care for them. While the respective military commanders were accusing and blaming one another, the women and children continued to suffer.

If one considers the minor differences between the peace terms of Middelburg and Vereeniging, it can be argued that the camp inmates were inadvertently sacrificed in the struggle for liberation. There had been an opportunity to end the war at an earlier stage: it was not taken because military and political priorities dominated. Although military commanders did not necessarily see it this way, this potential turning point could have made a fundamental difference.

TOP A family life regained, if still in British custody: this *hendsopper*, or prisoner of war who had taken the oath of neutrality, was thus permitted to join his family in a camp.

BOTTOM No shortage of peaceful men along Peace Street, the name given to this road in the Winburg camp

On the other hand, there is plenty of evidence that the women in the camps were predominantly in favour of the continuation of the struggle and encouraged their husbands to keep fighting. The *bittereinder* men, too, had no remorse about continuing with the guerrilla war, and they blamed the deaths in the camps exclusively on the British forces. By persevering in the struggle, the *bittereinders* also ensured that they were not simply overrun on the battlefield by the British shortly after Middelburg, which could have encouraged British politicians to pursue more punitive peace terms than those eventually agreed upon in May 1902. The *bittereinders'* ingenious fighting tactics and astonishing endurance have captured the imagination of people not only in South Africa, but also around the world, and have been admired by several generations of Afrikaners, in particular.

Although there was conflict between Kitchener and Milner about the way in which the war should be conducted to subjugate the republican armies, the British side never seriously considered diminishing its resort to arson – the fundamental reason for the existence of the camps. Even when it became evident that the scorched-earth policy did not have the desired effect, the British remained undeterred. The prevailing opinion among them was that they had burnt so many farms already that sparing a few hundred in 1901 would not lessen the *bittereinders'* resolve.

Mushrooming misery: the Klerksdorp concentration camp

Concentration camps indirectly originated from changing patterns in Western warfare in the late nineteenth century. In South Africa, the basis for establishing such camps was formed by developments concerning the surrendered burghers and the British scorched-earth policy. Civilian women were caught up in hostilities from the outset. Although this was not in keeping with contemporary conventions governing the conduct of war, it did not diminish the British supreme command's resolve and, once established, the camp system was not easily reversed. Moreover, both sides failed to take advantage of the only possible opportunity to terminate the camp system because of their military and political differences.

The dramatic events that occurred on the plains of the Orange Free State and Transvaal were to have notable long-term repercussions. During the 1930s and 1940s, the tragedy of the camps was used as an ideological building block to underpin the robust Afrikaner nationalism of the time. The intense emotions unleashed by the camps were destined to cast a long shadow.

CHAPTER TWO

The defiance of the *bittereinder* woman

— HELEN BRADFORD —

PREVIOUS PAGE Turning their backs in defiance, these women avoid an unwanted photographer's lens while awaiting rail transport to a camp.

THIS PAGE When transported on Imperial Military Railways in the conquered Boer states to more distant camps, such as those in Natal, some women would have to face weeks of travel in exposed conditions.

Boer homesteads were targeted from 1 February 1900, when the vanguard of the British imperial army invaded the Orange Free State and immediately gutted farmhouses and workers' quarters, in what observing local commandos called a *vernielzucht*, or thirst for destruction. This impulse was perhaps intensified by the lifting of the Siege of Kimberley and the British victory at Paardeberg. According to a Russian military attaché, troops on the Paardeberg–Bloemfontein route were pillaging farms indiscriminately, while a *Manchester Guardian* correspondent claimed that the conduct was worse than looting, as it resembled a savage assault on the domestic foundations of civilised life.

Writings on the war invariably overlook this. In South African and other historical documents, descriptions of war revolve typically around clashes between armed men, and representations of male aggression dominate. Indeed, it is rare to encounter women in classic war stories. There are no tales of men seen as weaklings or cowards or of those who are husbands. The prevailing view is not one of British soldiers or black African men descending enthusiastically on places inhabited by women to loot cattle, blind sheep, hang cats, hack the flesh from livestock, set fire to houses and load Boer and black civilians into carts destined for concentration camps. Yet this was the major task of the British army for much of the war in South Africa.

For its rank and file, it was a way of asserting their male power. The Boers, on the other hand, experienced it as a war against women. However, historians who have accepted romanticised Victorian versions of real war as brave fighting between men have overwhelmingly shied away from a depiction of war that illuminates what the imperial army actually did most of the time, namely terrorise unarmed people in places occupied by women.

However, this was how the British imperial army waged wars of colonial conquest in Africa and Asia. Setting fire to homes, looting stock and destroying crops were the standard ways of suppressing resistance. Furthermore, victory achieved by these means enabled Victorian men to become soldier heroes, celebrated as symbols of imperial manhood and the nation.

Lord Roberts's first command, for instance, involved invading and occupying Afghanistan at the end of the 1870s. This invasion badly damaged Indian agriculture through the mass requisitioning of stock, while rebellious Afghan villages were razed. The occupation involved the hanging of rebels, the expropriation of grain and a destructive march to Kandahar, which has been compared to that of northern general William Sherman, in which he laid waste to the southern state of Georgia in the American Civil War. This turned Roberts, nicknamed 'Butcher Roberts', into a national hero and he went on to become commander-in-chief in India and later commander-in-chief in South Africa in 1900.

A broader geographical scope and a longer historical perspective are, therefore, important in analysing methods of imperialist warfare in South Africa during the Anglo-Boer War of 1899 to 1902 and the kinds of masculinity it embodied. Lord Roberts of Kandahar was assigned to this conquest of two African republican states (the Transvaal and the Orange Free State) and was surrounded by staff and generals from his Afghanistan days. On both the imperial and the republican side, the South African War was awash with men who were moving from one colonial war to the next. In the case of the Boers, they had engaged in earlier trekker wars with black Africans over land. In the period leading up to 1899, the experiences of many soldiers of the British Empire included crushing the revolt in Rhodesia, conquering the Sudan and putting down the uprising on India's north-western frontier.

These actions involved the use of scorched earth, looting and inducement of starvation as weapons of war, and this was how many so-called gentlemen mastered tribesmen. They used this tactical arsenal whether natives fought open battles, conducted guerrilla wars or, as in the case of the Xhosa people, were not even fighting at all. Racial denigration of opponents encouraged the use of extreme or total ways of war, and the South African War, too, was seen by many as a war of the British race against opponents who were savages or primitive peasants.

In conventional histories, the so-called gentleman's war, or the phase of conventional warfare that lasted until at least mid-1900, is represented as very different from the harsh phase of guerrilla war. In the former, supposedly little or no destruction occurred. Instead, Roberts urged burghers (republican citizens) to surrender with lenient measures, assuring them that their property and persons would be safe if they swore an oath of neutrality and laid down their arms. In response to this velvet-glove policy, many Boer men surrendered voluntarily.

However, although Roberts's proclamations promised security to most civilians and *hendsoppers*, these and other British promises of leniency were largely disregarded in practice. Why did this happen and why was the scorched-earth policy implemented?

Why the scorched-earth policy?

First, after the Boer invasion and looting in the Cape and Natal in 1899, there was little support for British leniency towards their enemy. British defeat in battles before 1900 undermined the assumptions of imperial masculinity, military superiority and British supremacy. Immediately after these defeats Joseph Chamberlain, the colonial secretary, asked if a force could be sent through the Orange Free State to emulate Sherman's march through Georgia. Thus, retribution through devastation was being considered long before guerrilla war. The War Office declared that international law for European or *civilised* nations could not be applied to the Boers, as they were worse than inferior Africans.

Three days after the Free State invasion, Roberts proclaimed that he intended to confiscate the property of all Boers absent from their farms. Although this extreme proclamation was halted by the British government, there was room for other measures. So when Roberts occupied Bloemfontein, a local ruling stated that, unless they surrendered, all

ABOVE Unwanted visitors making themselves at home, or whatever was left of it. Rimington's Guides or Scouts, an irregular corps of the British Army, eating in a Boer house in 1900.

RIGHT Preserved from possible destruction by invading enemy forces, this organ, owned by P.W.G. Snyman, from a farm in the vicinity of Philippolis in the southern Orange Free State, was carefully buried during the war. It was retrieved after the end of hostilities, restored and put back into use. (Collection of the War Museum)

Seizure and destruction: livestock is confiscated for food by the British and a carriage is wrecked.

men within a 10-mile radius risked the loss of their property. Such threatening of 'primitive' enemies who were challenging British supremacy had considerable support.

Second, confiscating Boer property was an economic as well as a political consideration. It took about a ton of provisions daily to keep 100 men on active service. Supplies from imperial sources had to cross an ocean, pass through busy ports and be transported overland via a single-track railway and wagons. Moreover, the British military logistics system was poorly managed, a problem aggravated by effective Boer raiding. So four days after the invasion, the Boers ambushed 3 000 oxen, 30 000 forage rations and 150 000 soldiers' rations. The advance proceeded only by limiting men to half rations, horses to starvation rations and by recouping losses from civilians. The director of supplies offered soldiers payment for stock; 2 000 sheep and 600 cattle were handed over the next day. Shortly afterwards Roberts instructed officers to exploit local resources to the fullest and to appropriate supplies if they were not for sale or appeared unclaimed.

Long after this debacle, officers troubled by perpetual shortages found the answer in these local resources, for which a large advancing army had an enormous appetite. In April 1900 Roberts ordered that all animals capable of being ridden had to be requisitioned; the invasion was already taking a colossal toll on poorly fed horses and transport animals. In May one of Roberts's commanders, needing food for 11 000 men and 12 000 animals, appropriated crops. For one day's supplies alone, he required 30 000 pounds of mealies, 13 000 pounds of flour, 400 pounds of salt and 2 500 pounds of sugar. He found that farmhouses contained insufficient flour, although meat was readily obtainable. Forces following through this district also conducted farm-to-farm visits to root out resources for hungry men.

As Boer women saw it, they were being robbed of maize, wagons, trekking gear, horses and forage – seizures that amounted to 'wholesale robbery' and 'the utter ruining of the country'.[1] With various officers being told to seize as much as they could, some places were stripped clean of supplies, generating problems for underfed troops in the rear. Flanking columns marching from Bloemfontein to Pretoria fed themselves with great difficulty and Transvaal women observed that troops plundering their farms seemed to be starving. In many ways, the supply crisis is a better key to understanding the character of this war than *koppies* lost and won.

Third, troops went beyond the limits of official policy. Routine destruction occurred as soldiers marched over crops, hacked down fences and lit fires (at times with the contents of houses providing firewood). Food and fuel were essentials in these lengthy marches, penalties for looting were very limited and the power to appropriate was enforced by the threat of guns. Soldiers were mostly young, unmarried and part of an institution designed to turn boys into men: they could prove their masculinity through scorn for domesticity. Hardbitten, irregular colonial units created bands of marauding warriors who descended on farms across the veld with 'blood-curdling cries'.[2] In some instances, injuries (ranging from defeats to alleged atrocities) had been committed against their soldiering manhood, necessitating revenge through pillaging.

The family who lived in this house managed to save a few possessions before their home was blown up with dynamite.

Such destructiveness was not entirely one-sided. Many burghers had engaged in similar vandalism in occupied Natal in 1899. Some Transvalers continued these practices in the Free State. Pillage in a state supposedly their ally called for stern punishment from Boer leaders. Yet looting continued to yield enjoyment for many men of varied ethnic and class backgrounds, on both sides. Deneys Reitz asserted in his 1929 classic war memoir, *Commando*, that vandalism in Natal was not for the goods but rather for the enjoyment of ransacking the property of others. In effect, what was being displayed was the relish felt by men in exerting mastery over the female domain.

Empty houses facilitated vandalism and most farms pillaged on the routes to Bloemfontein had been abandoned for various reasons: rumours of rape had intensified and women were often acutely aware of their vulnerability to sexual violence; loss of cattle was typically economically ruinous; and the prospect of having shells crashing through homes was an added incentive for flight. Thousands of refugees herding stock fled before the advancing troops. British soldiers often assumed that absent men were away on commando and that looting was, therefore, legitimate. Even *hendsoppers* risked destruction of their property if they were absent. Although she had only been away for a few hours, one despairing mother exclaimed that the 'khakis [had] destroyed everything'.[3]

The Havenga Report on rapes

 JAN VAN DER MERWE

Among the personal documents of ex-minister N.C. Havenga, which are stored in the Free State and Pretoria archives, are the records of more than 50 sworn statements given by Boer women and children about the hardships they endured during the Anglo-Boer War. These include accounts of assaults, abuse and pillage conducted by British soldiers.

In one instance, Getruida Jacoba Bruwer told an assistant commandant, C.C. Froneman of Ladybrand, on 28 February 1902 what had happened when a British patrol arrived at her farm the previous month: 'The English soldiers behaved barbarically even though I had little children and was heavily pregnant. They shouted and swore at me, plundered the furniture, burnt the house down and killed the livestock. Then they just left us there. My children and I had to seek shelter under a big tree.'[1]

According to Bruwer, the same patrol returned to the homestead a week later to take her, a Mrs Koen and two other women with small children to a British concentration camp, which was more than half an hour's journey on horseback. The British soldiers forced them to walk and did not provide food. According to Mrs Koen's statement, the women had not eaten much over the previous six days. After hours of walking, she could not continue. The British patrol abandoned the group in the veld, with no food or water. Bruwer recounted how she gave birth to a baby girl in the veld two days later.

Certain statements tell of British soldiers and their black auxiliary troops raping or attempting to rape women and their daughters. Some women managed to fend off their attackers, as was the case with Sarie Margariette Cilliers from the Kroonstad district:

> I was living with my sister Hettie and our children on our farm, Elandsput, when two armed, black, British soldiers arrived on foot on 23 December 1901. One of the *kaffirs*[2] ordered that I go to the cart shed. I did not like his insolence and fled to the house in terror ... I ran to the bedroom but he pursued me.
>
> In the bedroom he hit my head hard. Then he used a sjambok to whip me violently on my arms. After this brutal attack, he threw me to the floor and pinned me down in order to rape me. When he groped me, I screamed. My sister Hettie, who was watching through the bedroom window, rushed to my aid and tried to pull me away. The *kaffir* then let me go. Both soldiers walked away from the farmyard.

One of the most shocking statements is that of Johanna Chatorina Geldenhuys from the Vrede district. She recounted the following to commandant A. Ross on 5 February 1902:

> My 10-year-old daughter, Talita Lootz, and I were alone at the farm on 22 January 1902 when Rimington's patrol arrived. Two British soldiers seized me and dragged me to a room, while a third soldier ripped off Talita's clothes.

The gruesome badge of enemy atrocity in war: an item of bloodied clothing worn by Susan Hattingh of the Smithfield district in the Orange Free State, who was shot by a British soldier. (Collection of the War Museum)

When she was naked, he sexually abused her. I could not bear to see what they were doing to my young child. The two soldiers who were holding me then kicked and beat me. I ended up lying on the floor. The soldier who had abused Talita pushed her away and grabbed me. He raped me, in that room, in front of my daughter. And the other two soldiers stood watching us through the window.

THE HAVENGA REPORT: MYTHS AND FACTS

For decades, there have been misconceptions about the Havenga archival records and questions asked about their true purpose. It was most likely that General J.B.M. Hertzog led the initiative to record these sworn statements. In his biography of Hertzog, C.M. van den Heever confirmed that the Boer general had taken statements under oath from women during the Anglo-Boer War. Hertzog sent these to the governments of the United States and certain European countries for the purpose of anti-British propaganda. Another comprehensive work on Hertzog quotes that the general 'would come face to face with British imperialism in its most stark form. As befits a good jurist, he carefully collected all the English war malpractices as evidence.'[3]

Although the women's statements were recorded by respected Boer leaders, magistrates and commandants, for a long time various untruths were told about the Havenga Report. This may have been partly due to the fact that the records were closed for 25 years. It was said, among other things, that young Nicholaas Christiaan 'Klasie' Havenga (who was 17 when the war broke out) had been instructed by Free State president M.T. Steyn to collect the sworn statements of Boer women and children. It was rumoured that he had been asked to compile a dossier and submit it to the Hague Convention.

But historical sources do not provide any evidence that Havenga ever received such an instruction. Moreover, it is almost inconceivable that a head of state like Steyn, himself a lawyer, would have entrusted someone as young as Havenga with such a sensitive matter. How, then, did the records of these statements end up in the Havenga archival records?

During the war, Havenga served as General Hertzog's notary and personal assistant. It is possible that he was responsible for the safekeeping of the documented statements. These were filed in both the Free State and Pretoria (Central) archives under his collection, and, presumably, for this reason became known as the Havenga Report.

According to Pieter van Breda, who wrote his doctoral thesis on Havenga, he was an extremely private person. Havenga sealed his private documents and requested that they be opened to the public only 25 years after his death. In all likelihood, therefore, the records of these women's statements accidentally became part of his personal collection. Havenga died in 1957, and consequently the records were made public only in 1982.

ABOVE The world of women for those too young to hold a gun or too old to see clearly enough to shoot: members of the Van Niekerk family at the Howick camp.

BELOW This porcelain serving dish, owned by the Oosthuizen family from Fochville, was buried several times on their farm to ensure that it would not be smashed by invading soldiers. (Collection of the War Museum)

ABOVE Dutch family Bibles were a common souvenir for troops involved in the ransacking of homesteads. After the war, some were returned from abroad, such as this one which belonged to HT Heymans and was taken by a Canadian member of the British forces. (Collection of the War Museum)

Resources were also destroyed for military reasons. From March, as their commissariat collapsed, Boer commandos were heavily dependent on local supplies. Boer women were now deeply implicated in fighting this war and invaders recognised this months before deciding that men were guerrillas. Women were told that provisions were being destroyed or confiscated so they would have nothing to give any Boer fighters who arrived.

Finally, various offences elicited punishment. If Boers fought on a farm, the farm could be burnt or stripped of all moveable goods. This was a harsh punishment when many farms, thousands of hectares in extent, served as battlefields. In the adjacent northern Cape, arson was the penalty for local rebellion against British rule.

Impact of scorched earth

Starvation loomed among white women and children, warned a press correspondent who was alarmed by the number of burnt homesteads, a concern with which Roberts's military secretary concurred.

By May, many farms had been destroyed and many urban houses pillaged. The prescient Cape politician John Merriman condemned the destruction and the eviction of powerless women and children in winter. In his view, this was emulating what the Spanish general Valeriano Weyler had done in his *reconcentrados*, or concentration-camp tactics, in Cuba in the 1890s. Boer leaders' assessments revealed panic as Transvalers were warned that everything in occupied areas was being destroyed. By 28 May, the day the republic was annexed by Britain and placed under martial law, confiscation of property had become standard. In the 31 May proclamation encouraging surrenders in the Transvaal, *hendsoppers* were promised only that they would not be imprisoned. The proviso that their property would not be seized had disappeared.

In all, conventional warfare in the Orange Free State was also conventional in a colonial sense. The motives of officers and troops alike were tied closely to acquiring supplies and suppressing resistance, and to their male desires for exhibitions of mastery or revenge. The extremes of *vernielzucht* displayed by a parasitic imperial army shocked numerous observers – and was of profound significance to Boer men.

Not only lambs, but also horses, to the slaughter: one of the thousands of horses killed by British columns

Boer men (February to May 1900)

During the hostilities, General Jan Smuts of the Transvaal declared that the Boers were an 'intensely domestic people',[4] deeply attached to their families and homes. Arguably, Boer men's domesticity was virtually proverbial – their dialect term for 'man' also meant 'husband'. These parochial loyalties were in sharp conflict with a broader nationalist drive. Persuading Boer patriarchs tied to farm and family to identify with the cause of states, embodied by urban professionals like Cambridge graduate Smuts and London-educated President Steyn of the Free State, was a struggle.

This tension was exacerbated by the fact that Boer men were also not regular soldiers – they volunteered to fight. Boers called themselves, and acted like, farmers, republicans or family men. Whatever military skills they possessed, domestic concerns often dominated. For example, the Free State commandant general refused to participate in an attack that coincided with a cattle sale that he was attending and a Transvaler rode home to attend to his sick wife. Boer men were often reluctant to leave their temporary homes, as their domestic needs were frequently attended to by black retainers on commando and sometimes by wives, children and wagons loaded with comforts. At times, the majority could also refuse to fight if they agreed among themselves that the odds against them were too overwhelming.

The invasion of the Orange Free State, and the almost simultaneous reversal of Boer military fortunes, greatly intensified their reluctance to fight. The Boers were being put to flight by an army vastly superior in numbers. Moreover, Boer men were positioned as

Enjoying his command and lapping up an audience, Jan Smuts reads a report to fellow commando burghers.

THE WAR AT HOME

The Van Deventer family at the Kimberley camp. The men of this family had most probably signed the oath of neutrality.

protectors of their families. One Boer man declared that he had gone home to defend his wife from soldiers and his bold black Africans, as he was well aware that the invasion had fuelled black African hopes of the defeat of their own oppressors. White men's nightmares about a black fifth column were aggravated by male concerns about possessions. Husbands, not wives, legally controlled all family property. Men, not women, were traditionally associated with cattle and crops. Numerous Free Staters went home in March because they feared confiscation of their property, and Transvalers were not far behind.

Consequently, commandos melted away. One Free State field cornet had commanded 200 men in early March; by mid-March he led eight, seven of whom were youths. As Smuts observed, 'the great majority thought more of their farms, their families and their private affairs than of the fate of the Republics'.[5] As the idea of sacrifice for *volk* (nation) or state declined, an emergent younger generation of Afrikaner leaders floundered. The most innovative response of these urban professionals or landlord parliamentarians came from Christiaan de Wet, the upwardly mobile backvelder and the new Free State commandant general. As commandos collapsed, De Wet, notorious for his Boer machismo, granted home leave to every man.

More typically, Afrikaner leaders (often steeped in patriarchal customs that differed from those of the Boers) tried to define home as a female domain, and separate men from domestic concerns. They banned women from laagers and tried to pack them off to defend their homes. On the other hand, *mannen*, had to fight like men, regard commandos as a family of brothers and sacrifice property and families for Afrikanerdom. Men reluctant to fight were *bangbroeke* (cowards), and De Wet hoped that 'the British would catch and castrate every one of them, so that they would be old women in reality'.[6] Brute force and the draconian threat of sjambokking underpinned the politics of commando masculinity.

On their last legs: a commando *bittereinder* with horse, the latter still standing

THE DEFIANCE OF THE *BITTEREINDER* WOMAN

Two pragmatic men weigh up the prospects: General Louis Botha, third from left, sitting, with General Jan Smuts to his rear, hold a council of war (*krygsraad*) with officers.

THE WAR AT HOME

Two women bring the comfort of supplies and provide a presence to raise the men's morale, possibly near Newcastle, Natal.

While some fell into line, most black men left their commandos. So did two out of three white men. Some 40 per cent of burghers who had been mobilised at the start of hostilities surrendered between March and July 1900. It was almost impossible to hear a patriotic word, noted a Dutch volunteer, for every man seemed only too glad to exchange war for home. With rumours again rife that the approaching enemy respected neither families nor private property, commandos disintegrated as men retreated to their home districts.

The class aspects of this collapse have long interested war historians who have suggested that the division between die-hard *bittereinders* and the surrendering *hendsopper* burghers more or less matched the division between the landed and the landless. Yet contemporaries did not see a pattern of landed men staying on commando. Indeed, they noticed the confiscation of property and the prominence of wealthier notables among those who fled or surrendered. Wealthy farmers, officers and middle-class men were the first to abandon the cause, they commented, as richer Boers had much to lose. One small Transvaal farmer declared that poor people were refusing to fight because rich people were staying at home. Thus, the influence of class was complicated. Landless Boers typically owned moveable goods and property-owning men had motives to desert. Free Staters fled home to save cattle, and landless men abandoned the cause for a few small possessions.

Generational differences and the differences in men's relationships to women were more significant than class. Patriarchs, scared of leaving their wives and daughters at the mercy of soldiers, abandoned the cause faster than youths. *Penkoppe*, or bullish young men who had no property or paternal obligations, remained to exploit war to assert their virility. Ultimately, the attraction of a velvet glove was less significant than the fear of hostile men threatening the jealously guarded domestic spheres, which were a key part of Boer manhood. Generals could do little to stem the haemorrhage and, with Transvaal forces almost non-existent by early June, President Kruger of the Transvaal teetered on the brink of surrender.

Yet if the Boers were down, they were not out. To explain this, many writers have described brave and inspirational male leadership, singling out the courage of De Wet and President Steyn in restoring the commando will to fight. There is, however, also a less masculine perspective.

Bittereinder women (February to May 1900)

As contemporary colonial historian George McCall Theal observed in March 1900, this was not a European-style conflict because the women were the fiercest advocates of war to the bitter end. 'For independence,' he warned, 'the Boer women will send husbands and son after son to fight to the last.'[7]

What observers like Theal saw was that anti-imperialism was influenced by gender. In the Transvaal, this had long predated the war. And in 1899 Boer women took the lead in opposing British aggression, even threatening to take up arms if men were too timid. Fierce anti-imperialism was also evident among Free State women. The Boer man, noted a Bloemfontein observer, went to town, traded with the Englishman and learnt to tolerate him. On the other hand, the Boer woman, isolated on her farm, nursed an intense hatred of the Englishman.

If these female attitudes were present before 1899, the war deepened them for a number of reasons. Firstly, the imperial relegation of white women to a sub-political status in wartime gave them, ironically, political privileges. Women did not have to take oaths of neutrality or surrender their guns. Nor were women imprisoned for flaunting republican sympathies. Secondly, a war that emasculated many burghers by stripping them of property, arms and protective power over their women created female household heads, female trekkers, female wielders of revolvers against home-invading troops, female

The medical battle front: Boer hospital on a farm

farmers feeding commandos. Accounts of this change in the role of the sexes were admiring – as well as shocked – and often noted that women farmed at least as well as men. This meant a husband could be told bluntly that there was no need for him to be on the farm and that he should go and fight. Thirdly, while Boers were seen as the most prolific Bible readers in the world, the position of men and women in relation to God was not the same. Many a woman, stripped of male protectors, shifted her hope to an Almighty masculine deliverer. If some Boer women preferred their husbands and sons to die rather than surrender, this was partly due to the depth of religious faith in a male Almighty.

Due to their position and their centrality in the domestic farm economy, Boer women often felt the oppressiveness of replacing one male-only colonial state with another, as they faced violated homesteads and the burning of harvests that had cost so much female labour. Women in the Transvaal, panicked by Free State depredations, mobilised other women against looming conquest, adding a violent edge to female hostility towards imperial penetration of domestic domains.

Encroaching hostilities were associated with black men as well as the khakis. Many settler women, who were struggling to replace white men as the source of white authority, found themselves challenged from above and from below. Repressive controls over black Africans had been weakened by the outflow of armed men and the inflow of occupying forces. A common grievance was that black people were not as faithful and deferential as when the *baas* was present, and black African men had begun looting stock. Unlike burghers, who fairly easily maintained the subordination of black men on commando, white women were disadvantaged by their gender in trying to uphold racial authority, especially when occupying forces were obliging them to carry a pass like black Africans. Consequently (and significantly) their status as women fuelled their commitment to racist republican states, which seemed to uphold white supremacy for non-English women. In the Transvaal, elite Afrikaner women singled out the central motive for conquest as the fear of equality between black and white, and miscegenation. Boer men, although anxious about black Africans on their own farms, seemed far less concerned about an overturning of the entire racial order.

As the men flooded home, many Boer women, with stern ideas about what it meant to be a white man, were deeply distressed. Some women invoked the disintegration of republican states to send men back to war. For their own men, they resorted to sexual politics, refusing to feed them, threatening to replace them on commando and taunting them for being less than men by being at home rather than on the battlefield. Tales circulated about wives' injunctions to men to go and fight. 'I can get another husband, but not another Free State,' said one.[8] Men who prioritised their domestic identities, placing the importance of family above that of the nation, were met by women opposed to exchanging their country for a patriarch at home. In demanding that the personal be subordinated to the political, Boer women had the edge on generals – they had the power to make what men had imagined as a refuge singularly unpleasant.

Thus De Wet, with his remarkably successful tactic of encouraging immersion in homes, was not solely, or even largely, responsible for men's return to war. A British officer warned that the ferocity of women had done much to stiffen Boer aggression, while a nurse noted that men shamed by their womenfolk rejoined commandos.

A group of well-off female republican supporters in Newcastle, Natal, ready to do battle

Yet it was not women alone who persuaded men to return to the miseries of war. In the Orange Free State, destruction was personalised: about a thousand men streamed back to fight from the south-east, where reprisals were particularly severe, after experiencing plunder of their farms or arbitrary arrests. So much so that De Wet made the tongue-in-cheek comment that Roberts was the best man he had. In May, responding angrily to Kruger's call for peace to prevent further devastation, Steyn grimly replied that too much property had already been destroyed. Imperial troops waging war on homes, combined with women demanding compliance with racial and gender customs were the key elements underlying the Free State resurgence.

In the Transvaal (as yet unoccupied), in mass women-only meetings and in written appeals, elite urban figures called on women to drive men who were skulking and evading their patriotic duty to return and fight like men. Their more radical counterparts called for women to take up arms, for the formation of an Afrikaner women's corps under a female general and for women to take over male jobs to release combatants. Men who were cowards could be left at home to tend to children. However, the idea of women under arms clashed with dominant ideas of Afrikaner national identity, which centred on male prowess against imperialist aggression. Unsurprisingly, members of both sexes recoiled from the image of women killing white men with Mausers, and many mothers declined to abandon their children for an activity viewed as unwomanly.

THE DEFIANCE OF THE *BITTEREINDER* WOMAN

In any satisfactory explanation of why war did not end with the invasion of the Transvaal, neither women nor the domestic environment should be overlooked. For, by the time the Transvaal generals and Kruger were urging peace on 1 June, the Boer women and Roberts had both made major contributions to the creation of the *bittereinders*, on whom Free State leaders could rely. Gender politics in homes and gendered warfare against homes were more important than macho generals for the continuation of the war.

Creation of a *volk* (June to November 1900)

By September 1900, claimed a German fighting for the Free Staters, the central event of the war had occurred – the birth of a nation of brothers. As farm burning had become standard practice by then, arson and nationalism went hand in hand.

As imperial supply problems continued, farm burning occurred alongside ongoing pillage. In the western Transvaal this, combined with black African raids on farms, drove many Boers back to war. But arson posed a problem of a different order. Why were so many people stripped of shelter and resources that were useful to the imperial army or to commandos?

In some writings, this is not a problem since arson is said to have taken place in a later period. In others, the explanation for scorched earth and concentration camps centres on Boer military tactics, suggesting that arson was an inevitable response to guerrilla war in which the success of the Boers led to draconian methods of reprisal. Concentration camps were supposedly a known, hard and unavoidable tactical expedient for a guerrilla war fought over hostile enemy territory.

ABOVE AND BELOW Raised in the nineteenth century, only to be razed early in the twentieth – farm dwellings are put to the torch.

Some bedding and furniture are saved before a house is burnt down.

Yet the flaw in such arguments is evident from the same war. Although guerrilla war was also waged in the Cape, this did not result in the enforcement of arson and a camp system there. Instead, the successful counter-strategy revolved around martial law and confiscating horses from civilians. The resulting inability to acquire horses and the scrubby terrain as opposed to grass-covered veld crippled Smuts's campaign there. Arson was by no means inevitable, and the deporting of hundreds of thousands of civilians to concentration camps was an extraordinary measure.

An older history is less pious about the origins and intent of arson and claims it had its roots in the intimidating measures of earlier colonial warfare in regions such as Asia. "British officers who had served on the Indian frontier had been accustomed to the destruction of the towns and villages of the tribesmen as a normal act of war", the *The Times History of the War in South Africa* wrote in 1906. Roberts, with his 41 years in the Indian army, turned to this strategy and extended its geographical range *before* September (the date usually cited as the start of the proper guerrilla war). Accordingly, in the winter of 1900 the houses of men still fighting were targeted, especially in the Free State, where they were legally considered to be rebels. Military leaders were targeted first, but other vulnerable people included those who fed or sheltered fighters, failed to report a Boer presence or lived close to disrupted railways. Moreover, indiscriminate arson in the western Transvaal was probably also due to a number of imperial defeats.

Burning houses was very successful. Many *bittereinders* and Boer women balked

ABOVE Tibbie Steyn, wife of M.T. Steyn, president of the Orange Free State.

BELOW Boer women wave republican colours while on their way to a camp. Years later, a camp veteran, Hester Schneider, recalled another such incident while waiting for a train: 'Some of the girls went to town to buy material to make a Vierkleur [the Transvaal republic flag]. When the train pulled out, they lifted up the flag and started to sing the republican anthem. [The British soldiers] walked along the train and said, "We want that flag!"'

at being rendered homeless. Men should think of their *volk* (nation) instead of their self-interest, preached a Free State minister. Again, many thought otherwise, with thousands surrendering or fleeing. Commando leaders threatened deserters with death and forced recruitment. Roberts responded in kind and invoked the death penalty for men breaking the oath of neutrality by returning to war. Burghers who did not take the oath became prisoners of war, as did all new *hendsoppers*. Numerous potential recruits, such as old men and young boys, were detained. New camps were established for the growing numbers of men – and sometimes their families – seeking or obliged to accept internment. Simultaneously, a little-noticed turning point occurred in rural policies. With De Wet reduced to a paltry 2 500 fighters, with Steyn engaged in the near-hopeless cause of re-animating demoralised burghers, and with various branches of the imperial army preparing to leave, occupation columns fanned out across the countryside. Mainly infantry, their prime task was not to fight but to impose a presence and force the Boer enemy into submission by denying subsistence to any who were infiltrating occupied zones. Men should either submit or see their families starve.

One officer objected, as black Africans and well-disposed whites would starve. Another, while supportive of starvation as a weapon, had in mind the starvation of Boer supporters alone. Although Roberts was losing popularity at home as a result of his alleged leniency, he and other generals with experience in colonial warfare were becoming firmly committed to wholesale expropriation. In less than a year, the currents of war therefore carried the imperial army from fighting, to burning white people's houses, to laying waste to two British colonies – all to starve a tiny settler minority. This excess was also fuelled by what ordinary soldiers could recognise as easy targets. Looting, butchery of livestock, invasion and incineration of female spaces was certainly easier than hard plodding after Boer men.

Yet there was also something odd about white female responses to mass arson and mass detention. Women in the Cape, not expected to speak in public, led nationalist protests.

In the ex-republics, exile and house arrest provoked defiance. Isabella 'Tibbie' Steyn, who was house-arrested for refusing to ask her husband (the president) to surrender, declared that women would continue the war to the end. When asked how long that would be, she replied, 'I expect and hope till our last cartridge is shot'.[9] Officers ordering Boer women to tell their menfolk to surrender threatened farm burning rather than house arrest and found that this threat had also lost its potency. Women dragged from their houses declared that they preferred arson to male surrender and women watching their houses burn made biting comments about the manliness of men who fought women.

Victims of arson had long been left to move elsewhere, and destitute people streamed into towns that were already suffering from food shortages. One British response centred on deporting the whites among them to commandos, but this was unsuccessful as either commandos could not be found, or women urged the men to fight on. With a food crisis fast developing in the towns, some officers sent displaced people to the towns. Here, white families with men on commando were often denied rations or storekeepers were forbidden to sell them food. But this, too, had limitations as women set up networks to obtain and share food.

Punitive practices had a gender and a racial character. Since the oath of neutrality was open only to white men, only white men became prisoners of war for refusing to swear it. Only white men were detained to prevent their recruitment. Men were imprisoned while women were exiled or placed under house arrest. In September 1900, this changed. Women were then interned in the emergent Cape and Natal camps, which were for those classified as

ABOVE Ending up under the Union Jack: women and children arrive by train at the Bloemfontein camp

BELOW Still holding republican colours aloft, these women were captured by the British in one of the wagon laagers in which some trekked behind commandos in an attempt to escape being consigned to the camps.

THE DEFIANCE OF THE *BITTEREINDER* WOMAN

undesirables. If white women were sent to supervised camps rather than the towns, this bypassed female resistance networks, lessened local supply problems and removed the problem of implementing starvation pressure to someone else's terrain. Moreover, if arson was no longer an effective threat, perhaps camps would be. As a former inmate insisted, these were punishment camps for wives who refused to ask husbands to surrender. Or as Lord Kitchener notoriously declared, shortly after replacing Roberts, women were outstripping men in their bitterness and commitment to the war, and the only remedy to bring them to their senses would be to confine what he called the worst class to a camp.

What of the Boer men? There is considerable evidence that a mass farm-burning policy actually prolonged the war because, combined with mass imprisonment, it radically reduced options for men. Burnt farmhouses aided the Boer cause, in that the homeless could not flee home. As columns fanned out, so men fleeing to evade capture also lost property, families and homes. In late 1900 there was still a long way to travel on this route of total war with its regional variations. Many had yet to be wrenched loose from their homes, and the lower enthusiasm for war in the Transvaal was attributed to less devastation there. Nonetheless, by eroding the material basis of rural patriarchy, the imperial army was helping to forge a *volk* of *broeders* in the two republics, where an estimated one in three farms had been burnt by late November 1900. Simultaneously, the mentality of men on commando was changing towards a greater nationalist consciousness, greater

LEFT Burghers under arms and brothers in arms: A.G. du Plessis with his nine sons before the war

BELOW Looking down at the Winburg camp, another plague of tents

discipline and a greater lust for revenge. By the end of the year, the number of white men on commando was close to the number mobilised at the start of the war and attacks on the British enemy were multiplying. By November 1900, concluded Britain's *The Times History of the War in South Africa,* the British had lost their grip and the initiative had passed into the hands of Boer partisans.

Laying waste to two republican states through scorched earth and concentration camps was not a consequence of the effectiveness of Boer guerrilla tactics. That view confuses cause and effect. Britain's imperial military, using tactics honed in Asian and African colonies, *created* mass guerrilla war – by unleashing pacification when the few rebels who remained faced popular antagonism and had yet to wage a recognisable guerrilla war. Similarly, with regard to the concentration camps, it is important not to focus on the male sex. Women were viewed as more irreconcilable than men and the punitive dimensions of camps were evident.

Ultimately, the impact of Boer military tactics was a less significant influence than the infusion of the techniques of colonial warfare into the South African arena. The enthusiastic adoption of such techniques, the failure to break Boer women's resistance and the eventual transformation of Boer men into *broeders* was brought about not, by waging war on battlefields, but by imposing colonial pacification on homes.

In 1900 Lord Roberts claimed to have established respectful relations with Boers with due regard for civilian property. His proclamations had had their desired effect in generating surrenders, and steps were taken only against any restive rebels. However, from September onwards his public discourse changed. With the degeneration of the war into guerrilla warfare, he was compelled to use harsh means to end it. The destitution of Boer women and children occurred because their male protectors had abandoned their duty, leaving British command obliged to deport them. In December Roberts declared the war to be effectively over. Yet it continued until 1902 through the successful guerrilla tactics of real Boer men.

But the past can also be seen differently, a view that takes account of the perspective of those undergoing conquest who claimed the existence of a war against women. Firstly, the gentleman's war went hand in hand with warfare denounced by the British Liberal leader Henry Campbell-Bannerman as methods of barbarism. Secondly, many Boer men valued domesticity over the political and military demands of a patriotic manhood. Boer women, on the other hand, constituted the backbone of opposition to British conquest and their attitudes were crucial to driving some Boer men back into war. As *The Times History of the War in South Africa* concluded in the 1900s, 'the women throughout were the more irreconcilable element'.[10]

Thirdly, the draconian reprisals that became more common once both republican capitals were conquered were not an inevitable response to successful guerrilla war but the standard weapons of colonial warfare, applied to intimidate all rebels, whatever their forms of resistance. But colonial pacification failed, in that it created a mass guerrilla war. And it revived men's identification with a nationalist cause. Many now found new ways of being men. As for Boer women, they did not submit, neither in 1900 nor in 1902 when burghers abandoned the war. The 1899 to 1902 war was the single most important episode in creating not only Afrikaner nationalism, but also an Afrikaner nationalism shifting its core to the more irreconcilable sex.

A brave and indomitable woman transformed into a commando fighter, Mrs Otto Krantz, with gun and horse, is caught in an unmistakably mythic moment and mood.

THE DEFIANCE OF THE *BITTEREINDER* WOMAN

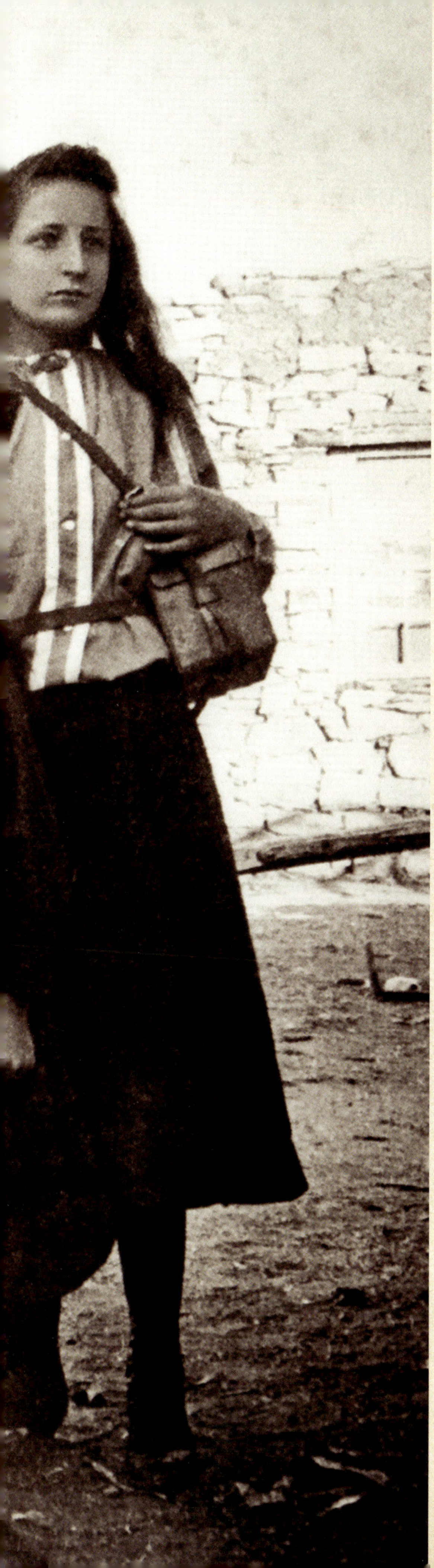

CHAPTER THREE

In the veld with Nonnie de la Rey

ZELDA ROWAN

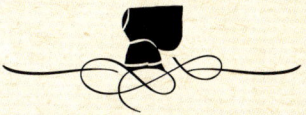

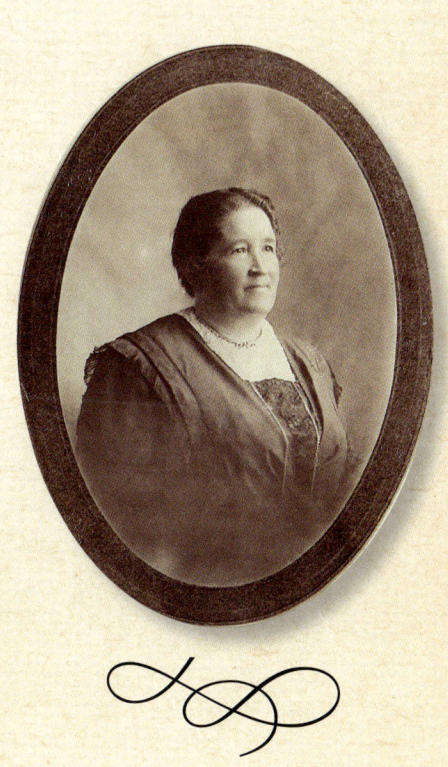

PREVIOUS PAGE, MAIN IMAGE If this is not Mexico or Texas, it must be the Transvaal: children of the De la Rey family of Lichtenburg, having put aside more childish pursuits.
SECONDARY IMAGE Nonnie de la Rey, resourceful wife of General Koos de la Rey

THIS PAGE Women and children in a Johannesburg camp, the fate Nonnie de la Rey sought to escape

Nonnie de la Rey experienced the agony and trials of the Anglo-Boer War first-hand. She lost a son on the battlefield, her farm was destroyed and she roamed the veld with her family for more than a year to evade internment in a concentration camp. Yet, suffering is not the predominant theme in her written account of her war experiences.

Jacoba Elizabeth 'Nonnie' de la Rey (née Greeff) was the wife of eminent General Koos de la Rey. She is one of the few women of the time – and the only spouse of a Boer general – whose writings were published and received international recognition. Her wartime memoir, *Mijne Omzwervingen en Beproevingen gedurende den Oorlog*, was published in Amsterdam shortly after the war, in 1903, and the English translation, *A Woman's Wanderings and Trials during the Anglo-Boer War*, was released the same year in London.

Her tenacity during the war earned the respect of both allies and enemies. From December 1900 until the end of the war in May 1902, Nonnie, her children and three loyal workers survived in the veld. They were not the only fugitive family who lived in the open. It is estimated that, by the end of the war, there were as many as 10 000 fugitive women and children in the Transvaal and between 2 000 and 4 000 in the Free State.[1]

Through Nonnie de la Rey's memoir we get to know a Boer woman who lived in a patriarchal society and was, in many respects, a typical woman of her time. But her assertiveness set her apart from her female contemporaries in several ways. She resolutely took on the dangers and challenges of a nomadic life in the veld while caring for her children and, where possible, supporting and assisting her husband on commando.

She was able to adapt to difficult circumstances and view her experience in a positive way. She was thankful for shared joy, company and resting places, and expressed this gratitude in her reminiscences. She was a formidable woman whose story is particularly relevant in the examination of the perseverance, survival instinct and inner strength of women in the Anglo-Boer War.

Nonnie's life during the war years can be divided into two phases: the period when she lived in Lichtenburg (October 1899 to November 1900) and her wandering years (December 1900 to May 1902). When war broke out on 11 October 1899, the De la Rey family were living on their farm, Elandsfontein. The 43-year-old Nonnie was accustomed to managing the farm while her husband focused on government matters, but now the situation was different – war had begun.

As field general of Lichtenburg, Koos de la Rey departed for the western front (in the present-day North West province) with their two eldest sons, 18-year-old Adaan (Adriaan) and 15-year-old Jacobus. Nonnie visited her husband and sons at the main camp before they were due to advance on Kimberley. There was no guarantee that they would see each other again. Nonnie wrote about the parting: 'Then I said to my two sons, "Adriaan and Jacobus, let your ways be in the fear of the Lord. If I do not see you again upon earth, let me find you again in heaven." And my beloved Adriaan, when I said these words, looked at me.'[2]

Back home at Elandsfontein, Nonnie waited anxiously for every telegram or update from the front. Barely two months later, her husband sent the tragic news that Adaan had been hit by shrapnel during the Battle of Tweeriviere on 28 November, two days after his 19th birthday, and had died in his arms in hospital the following morning. Nonnie was devastated. She later wrote that little had she known that she was raising her son for a cannonball. What Nonnie did not know was that Koos de la Rey had also been injured in the shoulder by shrapnel a few hours before Adaan's misfortune.

De la Rey, who was wounded not only physically but also spiritually after his son's death, made arrangements for Nonnie to visit him at the front. After four days she reached the Vaal River, where she could hear the heavy gunfire at Magersfontein. Her presence soothed her husband's grief. They visited Adaan's grave together and inspected his torn clothing at the hospital. Nonnie moved into an empty house near Magersfontein and cared for her husband until he was strong enough to return to battle.

The next time they saw each other was in March, when Nonnie visited her husband in Kroonstad. He fell ill and she stayed for a few days to support and nurse him while his military secretary, Ignatius Ferreira, handled his administrative work. Nonnie's support undoubtedly helped De la Rey to continue performing his duties under trying circumstances.

In May, De la Rey briefly visited his family on the farm en route to Frederikstad, between Potchefstroom and Krugersdorp, where his commando intended to block Lord Roberts's forces, who were moving from Bloemfontein to Pretoria. Five days after De la Rey's commando had left the Lichtenburg district, black auxiliary troops arrived in the area, captured livestock and intimidated the inhabitants. The group was acting on British orders in reaction to the commandos' presence in the area, and a few days after this incident, British soldiers entered Lichtenburg. Thereafter conditions deteriorated rapidly for those who lived in the district.

Nonnie was gardening when seven mounted British soldiers arrived at Elandsfontein. She fled to the farmhouse, but three men were already wreaking havoc inside and the other four armed soldiers barred her entry to the house. They demanded to know who the owner of the house was. When she answered 'De la Rey', they asked whether she was referring to the well-known general. They insisted that she fetch him from the house, to which she responded defiantly: 'You have been inside, why don't you bring him out yourself? I cannot do so, because he is on commando.'[3] They then continued interrogating her and plundering the house.

Because it was no longer safe on the farm, Nonnie decided to move with her seven children to their town house in Lichtenburg. The house was next to the shop of Ajam Abed, an Indian general dealer, who was friendly with the De la Rey family. Even though

Adopted by the Dutch: this postcard of General Koos de la Rey was sold by the Pro-Boer Society of The Hague in aid of 'the captured women and children in South Africa'.

OPPOSITE (clockwise from top left): The flag as the frock: Nonnie's one daughter (probably on the far right) and cousins, immersed in Boer republicanism; a young Nonnie de la Rey; a group of De la Rey children before the war, including Jacobus (back left) and the son who would die in the war, Adaan (back right)

General de la Rey with a son and a cousin, at war in the veld

the British forces had occupied Lichtenburg, they could rely on him to provide them secretly with food and other necessities.

At that stage Nonnie had only two horses left, one of which had belonged to her late son Adaan. So when British soldiers confiscated her horses, she lost her patience. Not only was she sentimentally attached to Adaan's horse, but she and her family would also have been stranded without transport. She insisted on speaking to General Archibald Hunter, the British commanding officer. She complained about the confiscation of the horses and the incidents on her farm. Hunter had not known about the horses, and he followed it up immediately. A day later the horses were returned to her, and Hunter also assured Nonnie that their farmhouse would not be damaged. But Nonnie did not trust him, especially after it was rumoured that Hunter intended to send her away from Lichtenburg.

Some two months after the British had occupied Lichtenburg on 26 May 1901, they withdrew from the area. The local inhabitants were able to sleep soundly at night for a few months, until General Charles Douglas reoccupied the town in September. Shortly after, British soldiers seized all the sheep on Elandsfontein. By this time, the fear of being taken prisoner and sent to the concentration camps overshadowed everything. Nonnie mentioned their great relief when the British looted everything and then left. On a subsequent trip to the farm, she would discover that one of her devoted shepherds had retrieved 200 sheep and hidden them in a safe place.

When General Douglas moved further away from the town, De la Rey seized the opportunity to visit his wife in Lichtenburg, but he had to leave quickly to avoid being captured. Douglas became determined to track down De la Rey. To show Douglas that she was not starving and perhaps to gloat (because De la Rey had outrun him), Nonnie used the fresh flour her husband had brought her to bake two loaves of bread and sent them to Douglas.

In November, Lord Methuen established his quarters in Lichtenburg and the British forces again claimed her two horses. She insisted on speaking to Methuen and her request was granted after much arguing. When she arrived for the appointment the next morning and found that Methuen was too busy to see her, she kicked up such a fuss that he eventually agreed to meet with her.

Nonnie wrote that Methuen had asked what he could do for her. She requested that her two horses be returned. In history books Lord Methuen is often described as a 'gentleman', and Nonnie's interaction with him supports this. He shook her hand in a friendly way, said goodbye and promised that her horses would not be taken from her. It is likely that he had been impressed by Nonnie's fearlessness.

On another occasion, Methuen visited Nonnie to discuss something that was weighing heavily on his conscience. He had been ordered to burn down the De la Rey residences at Elandsfontein, and was concerned about what would happen to her and the children

The face of British occupation: a detachment of the Kimberley Mounted Corps in Lichtenburg after it was overrun early in 1900, promptly displacing Nonnie

if this were to occur. According to Nonnie's account, Methuen proposed that he leave one building standing. In her response she compared the British forces' mercilessness to God's great mercy, which probably made Methuen feel worse. He chose not to act on the order, but Nonnie did not know if any part of her home would survive the war.

Shortly afterwards, at about three o'clock in the afternoon, Nonnie was ordered to vacate her town house and depart for Mafeking within half an hour. The reason given to her was that she had sheltered her husband when he was in Lichtenburg. She railed against the instruction given by a British messenger:

> Yes ... I did take him in and shelter him; and I shall do it five hundred times more if it pleases the Lord to spare him. I am prepared to go away as a prisoner of war, but I will not do it of my own free will. And you say to Lord Methuen that he knows very well that my husband is only fighting for his rights and doing his best for his country. I will tell you a parable for him. Instead of doing harm to our cause, every step you take against us makes it one hundredfold stronger. Where only one now calls for vengeance, hundreds shall come to be avenged. He can send me wherever he likes, but it will not do you any good. I never thought to be so badly treated in the Queen's name. I could not have believed that because you cannot get the better of our men you would set to work against their women.[4]

The British messenger returned to Methuen without having achieved his goal. Methuen then sent Nonnie another message to say that, although she was not obliged to leave, it would be advisable for her to do so. This convinced her to borrow a team of oxen and pack her wagon within a few days.

IN THE VELD WITH NONNIE DE LA REY

Wanderings in the veld (December 1900 to May 1902)

Nonnie departed from Lichtenburg on 1 December 1900, a rainy Saturday, with her adult daughter, six young children (the youngest was three and the eldest 15) three workers, some dairy cows, sheep, chickens and a wagon laden with other supplies. Nonnie and her grown-up daughter, Ada, travelled behind the wagon in a spider carriage: 'I was beginning my travels willingly, but all unknowing where they were going to end or what the future had in store for me.'[5]

Her destination was not Mafeking, however, but the open veld. The plains and *koppies* of the western Transvaal would be her home for the next year and a half.

Sometimes they were fortunate enough to find farmhouses that had not been completely destroyed by the British. Even if only one room had a roof, it could still provide temporary shelter. On one occasion, they stayed in an empty school; on another they made use of an abandoned shop. If there were no suitable buildings and it was unsafe to outspan in the veld, they would occasionally shelter in caves.

Nonnie grew attached to her wagon as if it were a house or bedroom. It protected them from the wind and rain, and harboured all their possessions. When there were no trees, the wagon provided much-needed shade during the day. She and the children would lie under the wagon to avoid the sun, although this was uncomfortable for the portly Nonnie. In addition to the wagon, they also had a tent.

The length of their stay at a particular spot mostly depended on how safe it was. Sometimes Nonnie was able to linger for a while. For instance, in mid-1901, she found a lovely wooded site next to the Marico River, in the mountains near the present-day

ABOVE LEFT Typical wagon for trekking through the veld – a home of no fixed abode

RIGHT Canvas-covered ox-drawn cart in which to roam about

BELOW Nonnie's nightmare: the grim plight of those held at the Bloemfontein camp

Swartruggens. The British were not likely to pass by, and she decided to stay for as long as possible. Nonnie built a hut for her children, a stable for the horses, a kraal for the sheep and even a makeshift oven to bake bread. She wanted to extend her stay, but General De la Rey was concerned that it would become too cold in the veld, so they resumed their wandering.

The misery and devastation caused by the British scorched-earth policy could be seen everywhere, and Nonnie was haunted by this. The fear of being captured and sent to a concentration camp distressed her. Shortly before the end of the war, she wrote: 'I did not want to be taken prisoner now after having escaped so many times, especially when we were, perhaps, nearly at the end of a terrible war. If only I could get off this time!'[6]

Nonnie had at least two reasons for wanting to evade the concentration camps and choosing to roam around to preserve her freedom. First, she was probably aware of the suffering and hardship in the camps, and knew that she had a better chance of survival in the veld. Second, she would not have been able to aid and support her husband and the Boer cause if she had been imprisoned in a camp. It is possible that she did not realise that the British columns had stopped sending women and children to the camps after December 1900.

When Nonnie had left Lichtenburg, she had taken her livestock and a good supply of other necessities, such as sugar, coffee, rice and flour. But she had many mouths to feed and lived a hand-to-mouth existence. The dairy cows were invaluable because when Nonnie had nothing else to give the constantly hungry children, she could at least provide milk. She kept milk in an earthenware bowl on the wagon and the shaking motion churned it into buttermilk and butter.

They did not often have fruit and vegetables because these rotted quickly and most of the vegetable fields had been destroyed by the fires. However, it had not been as easy to destroy established orchards and on one occasion Nonnie loaded their wagon with fruit when they trekked past an orchard in the Lichtenburg district. Sometimes Nonnie could sow and plant crops in a place where they pitched camp. In September 1901, for example, she sowed maize in the Lichtenburg area. The risk, of course, was that she would have to flee suddenly and lose the entire crop.

Although Nonnie had retained a number of sheep and chickens at the beginning of the war, beef and mutton became scarcer, and by the end of the war she had virtually no sheep left. She had to rely on the kindness of some burghers who provided the travelling party

IN THE VELD WITH NONNIE DE LA REY

A family reunion while on the run: shown here with his field staff is Koos de la Rey with daughter, Lenie, at his side and son, Jan, at his feet, visiting Nonnie in the veld.

with some slaughter animals. Nonnie never mentioned any shortage of chicken, however.

It is evident in her book that Nonnie regularly baked bread, provided she could find or build an oven. When she remained for a longer period in the mountains near Swartruggens in mid-1901, one of her first priorities was to build an oven (it is likely that she constructed it from clay or mud). At the beginning of 1902, she temporarily joined General Jan Kemp's laager at Putfontein (between Lichtenburg and Ventersdorp). She was concerned about the burghers' lack of bread and searched for a serviceable oven, but was eventually forced to use a less-effective structure. She struggled to get the bread and rusks even half-baked but, in her opinion, undercooked bread was better than none.

When her flour ran out towards the end of the war, Nonnie used her coffee mill to make new flour. On commando, maize porridge eventually replaced bread as the staple food, and Nonnie described how they once cooked porridge on an anthill. By the end of the war, Nonnie's coffee supply was running low and she followed the example of the Boers on commando by making a substitute. She roasted diced sweet potatoes over the fire, and produced a mixture in the ratio of one measure of coffee to three measures of sweet potatoes. The mixture was finely ground and proved to be a good substitute for pure coffee, according to Nonnie.

The scarcity of food did not make Nonnie less charitable. Where necessary, she shared

Anna van Rensburg's experiences during the Anglo-Boer War

A year before the outbreak of the Anglo-Boer War, Anna van Rensburg's parents moved from Wolmaransstad to her uncle's farm in the Bethlehem district because their cattle had died from rinderpest.

My parents were just getting back on their feet when the war broke out. The men went on commando while the women and children stayed at home ... I was about three years old at the time.

In 1900 my older brother and I contracted diphtheria. I became very ill and my parents took me to the doctor in Bethlehem ... Soon afterwards my uncle sent word that my dad had to return to the farm, because many British soldiers were approaching.

After that the women fled whenever they saw British troops nearing their farms. The Boer commandos would send someone to warn them. If it was possible to do so, the women always fled behind the commandos. A few of us often fled together: my aunt, her two children, my mom, our neighbour and her three children, and the four of us. Later in the war, the English fired shots at women who fled, so many of them decided to stay at home.

There was a big dam full of reeds near our house. The men had carried iron bedsteads into the reeds and left them standing in the water. Whenever the women spotted British soldiers, we would all hide in the reeds. Children had to sit on the beds the entire day because there was nothing but water all around. We would return home in the evening.

At that point we still had enough food and clothing, and never went without shoes or socks.

Once the men came home for a few days. The women were supposed to do their laundry, mend their clothes and bake rusks for their next trek. Their camp was not far from the house. But British troops arrived unexpectedly and chased the men through the Orange River to Colesberg. The women received no news of them for three months.

After the Boer commandos had visited Bethlehem again, some of the black people started to get cheeky with the women. They harassed the women during the night. Our mothers were very frightened and could hardly sleep.

One evening, Klaas, the male servant who had to sleep at the house, came to tell us that he would no longer do so: 'The Kaffirs told us if they find us at the white people's place, they will kill them and us.' Old Klaas was in tears, but he was too scared to sleep there. Then my mom and aunt fetched some of the maids from the huts to sleep at the house. Those were fearful nights.

In 1901 the British caught many women and sent them to the camps. By that time, the women no longer fled because they had no more draught animals. Oom Nicolaas van Rensburg's wife, another of my aunts, said that she refused to be captured. She kept fleeing, even though she, too, eventually had no draught animals.

She had a very big cupboard. When she spotted British soldiers, she would shove whatever food and bedding they had into the cupboard (the children had to drag it along with a rope).

At that stage she had eight children. Then they would hide in a ditch until the British troops had passed by.

One night when fleeing, she gave birth to her ninth baby under a cart. She said that she didn't even have milk for the little one because of all the hardships. The baby grew up on black coffee.

My aunt was never caught. Once she hid a wounded man. When British troops arrived, she made most of the children lie in bed with vinegar-soaked cloths wrapped around their heads, and declared that they had typhoid fever. The British were terrified of the disease, and they left in a hurry. Meanwhile the wounded man lay under a mattress in the room.

> Anna van Rensburg survived the war and married D.P.S. Brink from Colesberg in 1916.
> Her account was recorded at an old-age home in Carnarvon in 1980, and has been translated and abridged.

her food with other fugitives and Boers on commando, and they shared theirs with her. Nonnie wrote how proud she was of her children, even the youngest boy, who realised that they had to learn to put up with it when there was nothing to eat.

Nonnie had also taken chinaware on her wagon, but most of this was soon broken. Like others in the veld, they used empty jam tins as mugs.

The lack of firewood was a factor Nonnie had to take into account when they travelled through treeless areas in the western Transvaal. Wherever they could, they chopped and collected wood. When this was not possible, Nonnie and her workers looked for anthills that could be set alight, although it was a time-consuming process to cook food in this way. Once, out of desperation, they chopped up the yoke of an ox for firewood.

Like the Boers on commando and the British troops, Nonnie and her party found drinking water in the veld. They never seemed to lack water, but she did complain about the dirty water on Corsica Farm, which lay between Delareyville and Vryburg, towards the end of the war, where many people's needs had to be met.

The commandos were often short of soap, and Nonnie, too, had to look for substitutes. At first she used burnt birdlime instead of soda to make soap, and later she used saltpetre that had been scraped from walls. The Boers on commando used the ash of mealie stalks as a soda substitute, and it is possible she may have tried this but it is not mentioned in her account. She did say that she made starch from green mealies, probably to starch tablecloths and articles of clothing, and the like.

Candles were also indispensable. In the second half of 1901, Nonnie made her own candles when she outspanned in the Lichtenburg district. On one occasion she had started preparing water and fat to make candles when she heard gunfire. They needed to flee but she was reluctant to abandon everything and quickly finished making the candles while the oxen were being harnessed.

Because it was virtually impossible to obtain new clothes in the veld, they had to take good care of their existing clothing. Nonnie taught her children how to mend garments and they often used tanned sheepskin as patches, like the burghers on commando. The burghers referred to these patched garments as 'armoured' clothing. Blankets were used to make dresses and jackets.

Towards the end of the war, the adventurous General Kemp seized a Union Jack and the baize of a snooker table from the hotel in Wolmaransstad that served as a British officers' mess. He donated them to Nonnie to make clothes for her children, which inspired a witty burgher to remark that De la Rey's children were now 'bullet-proof'.[7] Canvas and shoelaces were unravelled to produce thread for sewing, and sheep's wool was used to knit socks and stockings.

Mother and mainstay

It is striking how important it was to Nonnie to keep her household going despite the many challenges they faced. She wrote that people were often surprised at how well the women and children coped in the veld: 'I said, "It does not all go as smoothly as you think," but I often wondered myself when I thought of how we got through day after day.'[8]

Tenacity, adaptability and a strong survival instinct were among the key qualities that enabled Nonnie to survive the time she spent in the veld. She also mentioned repeatedly

ABOVE Women with children try to flee from the enemy with what they were able to salvage, in the company of a few elderly men, who usually took charge of wagon camps.

LEFT This child's dress was bought by Mrs J.B.R. Jacobs from a woman in the Harrismith camp, who had to patch it with different kinds of material to ensure her daughter had something to wear. (Collection of the War Museum)

that her three workers assisted her with daily tasks and were of particular help in difficult times. One of the workers, Simson, was skilled at making fires when they had to prepare food in flight.

Nonnie capably looked after her family in the veld, and constantly supported and made contact with her husband. This probably gave General De la Rey considerable peace of mind and enabled him to concentrate on his war efforts. Nonnie kept her husband's papers and letters safe while he was fighting, and it is largely due to her that so many of his documents were preserved. Ironically, Nonnie had more contact with her husband when she was living in the veld than when she had been at home in Lichtenburg. Because she was able to follow his commando at a distance, they were mostly within reach of each other. At Lichtenburg it had become too dangerous for De la Rey to visit Nonnie regularly. But in the veld he could share supplies that he had looted from the British with his wife and she, in turn, often treated him and his staff to meals. She frequently mentioned how much she enjoyed the company of visitors. There were also times when her exhausted husband would just turn up, have something to eat and rest, if time allowed. She nursed him when he was ill, and they could depend on each other at all times.

Sometimes Nonnie visited commandos in an effort to cheer up the burghers. Whenever possible, she would outspan near the Boer encampments in order to stay abreast of the British troops' movements and flee if necessary. The general warned his family when they were in danger and even rescued them at times. Nonnie had several narrow escapes when travelling with the commandos. Writing about one such incident, she says: 'I had so many children with me and dreaded so much to see them shot dead before my eyes that at one moment I thought it would be better to give in.'[9]

As far as possible, they celebrated festive days together as a family. At the end of 1900, De la Rey and his commandos spent Christmas and New Year with his wife on Zuurfontein Farm, in the Rustenburg area. A year later they spent the festive period together again. On 24 October 1901, the De la Reys celebrated their 25th wedding anniversary. De la Rey had intended to visit his wife that day and had even dressed in tails for the occasion. But his plans were thwarted when a battle erupted, in which he had to participate – dressed in his formal suit. After the battle, he discovered that the two buttons on the back of his coat had been shot off.

Nonnie was not lonely in the veld. As well as her children and the workers, she also had contact with other fugitive families. Near the end of the war, she remarked: 'I was astonished to see how many women and children were still out, and how well they looked, although they were wanderers. We talked about the peace that we were hoping for, though not for a peace that should impair our independence. It was very pleasant that evening to hear the sweet singing of the people as they sat near their wagons.'[10]

The family of her brother-in-law, Jan de la Rey, often travelled with Nonnie and also spent Christmas with them in 1900. Whenever possible, a religious service was held on Sundays and all the women and children, who were still on farms in the vicinity or roaming nearby, gathered together.

There were times when Nonnie stayed at farms of families she knew for as long as it was safe to do so. In December 1900, for example, she was visiting the Kritzinger family at

Koos de la Rey in the family fold during the last months of the war

Zuurfontein. When the British soldiers came close to the farm, they all fled and returned only once it was safer. Nonnie tried to keep some distance away from the British forces, but if she found herself in an unavoidable confrontation, she fought bravely for her family's survival.

It appeared that Nonnie could be resolute when she lost her temper. In May 1902, for instance, a group of British soldiers arrived at Corsica, where Nonnie had been stranded for a period. When they wanted to burn her wagon, she gave them an ear-bashing: 'I was very angry, and I thought, "Do what you like, I shall say what I think and what is right." I told them again then who I was, and said that I was not going to let them burn my wagon. For eighteen months, ever since Lord Methuen sent me out of Lichtenburg, I had wandered round with my children. If they wanted to burn my things they would have to get an order from a superior officer. I was not going to let them do it themselves.'[11] After that, they left her in peace and moved on to another house in the area. A week after this nerve-racking incident, Ian Hamilton, a British general, arrived from Vryburg. After enquiring about her and the children's health, Hamilton notified De la Rey by telegram that Nonnie was still at Corsica and that he had tried to inconvenience her as little as possible.

Poultry truce: defeated and taken captive by Koos de la Rey in the Battle of Tweebosch in March 1902, injured British general Lord Methuen found a chivalrous truce extended to him by his adversary. Nonnie helped him in his convalescence, feeding him on chicken until he was well enough to be turned free to rejoin his side.

The Boer woman and the British lord

Fate sometimes turns the tables. Lord Methuen was wounded on 7 March 1902 in the Battle of Tweebosch, near Stella, and captured by the Boers. It was to be the last significant victory for the Boers in the war.

Methuen lay next to his dead horse when De la Rey bent over him, stretched out his hand and said how sorry he was to find Methuen in such a state. To which Methuen responded: 'Oh, it's the fortune of war',[12] and then asked about Nonnie. Afterwards De la Rey's doctor worked side by side with Methuen's doctor to splint his broken leg.

That evening Nonnie heard about the Boers' success at Tweebosch, Lord Methuen's wounding and his subsequent imprisonment. She confirmed with her husband that this was indeed the Methuen she knew and she then visited him in the morning. It was perhaps a unique moment – seeing each other again after many months in such different circumstances. Nonnie wrote: 'When I had come in he begged me to forgive him for all the annoyance he had caused me, and he asked if I had suffered much discomfort from all that running away. "No," I said, "it all went much better than I had expected. I did not even have to do my best to escape from falling into your hands." "Oh," said he, "I have done my best to catch you." And so we "chaffed" each other.'[13]

Methuen also informed her about the conditions in Lichtenburg and explained the reasons why he had eventually been compelled to destroy her main house on the farm. Methuen asked Nonnie to send a telegram to his wife in England to inform her that he had been wounded and that he was on his way to Klerksdorp. Nonnie, in turn, gave him a telegram for her eldest daughter, Sannie Brugman, and asked if he would send it from Klerksdorp to Pretoria, where she lived. As it was getting late, she wished him a speedy recovery and said goodbye.

That evening, Methuen and his doctor were sent in his spring wagon to Klerksdorp. The next day was a Sunday, and at the morning church service the burghers expressed their unhappiness about Methuen's release. To preserve the peace, De la Rey arranged for Methuen to be returned and consulted the burghers on the next step. After lengthy deliberations and much persuasion by De la Rey, the Boers agreed to abide by the general's original decision. In the meantime Nonnie had slaughtered and prepared a fat chicken, which she sent to Methuen with some rusks, in time for his second journey.

The relationship between Nonnie and Methuen was unusual in many respects. The barrier of hostility that usually existed between Boer and Briton was broken down by mutual consideration and respect. In this way they formed a unique friendship that was to last for years after the war.

A woman in the context of her time

Nonnie was a product of her time. She operated within a patriarchal system that was based on a clear division of roles between men and women. Therefore, she took her role of supportive spouse and capable mother very seriously, and largely found her identity within this role.

The conditions that prevailed during the Anglo-Boer War, specifically the scorched-earth policy and sending women and children to concentration camps, were an assault on the typically female domain. Men spent long periods away from home on commando, which disrupted family structures and broadened women's responsibilities considerably. With the men away, women had to take charge of the farming operations and shoulder the responsibility for their families' safety. Despite her nomadic existence in the veld, Nonnie also managed to look after her family and their possessions.

Men to the fore under female eyes: generals De la Rey and Louis Botha, male leaders of the Boer cause; in post-war years, Nonnie emerged as a notable public figure.

It is interesting to note how Nonnie portrayed herself in her memoir. Her account reveals that she identified with the typical image of a Boer woman. It is evident that she possessed characteristics such as fearlessness, self-reliance, piety, spirit of sacrifice, ability to tolerate suffering, inspiration, hospitality and resourcefulness. She was able to bake bread and make soap and candles under the most difficult circumstances, and she did not shy away from any typically male work.

From this ideal image of Boer womanhood, the notion of the 'volksmoeder' developed and was used in the years after the war to identify and honour Boer women, who

measured themselves against these qualities. This status, for instance, gave Nonnie the platform to enter the public arena in later years and deliver speeches at national festivals. It can be said that there are oppressive elements underlying the *volksmoeder* concept and how it has been used – and often abused – for nationalist purposes. Early in the twentieth century, for example, an ideal image of Afrikaner womanhood was presented and popularised in books by, among others, Willem Postma and Eric Stockenström.

However, Nonnie's memoir was published in 1903 and these books had not yet been written. Nonnie identified herself with an ideal image of womanhood that was a product of her time and this comes across strongly in her writings. It is possible that her memoir unwittingly influenced the later formulation of this ideal image.

It should not be forgotten, however, that Nonnie also possessed qualities that other women of her time might not necessarily have been able to emulate. The most striking of these characteristics were her assertiveness and forthrightness. She did not view herself as a victim and always saw her own suffering within the context of her compatriots' suffering. To

the extent that she could, Nonnie took control of challenging situations and refused to put up with injustice. She was outspoken about the hardship and pain caused by the war, and wrote at the end of her memoir:

> May no other people in the world ever have to endure another such war so long as the world may last. I do not think that it can be forgotten. I cannot say who it was who were wrong, we or our adversaries. But this I can say, that it was terrible to bear. Never could I have thought that human beings could treat each other in such a way. I know well that war is one of the blackest things upon earth, still I cannot depart from all sense of justice and put down every sort of barbarity to war and consider it right. As we were known to the whole world as two Christian nations, I had thought that such things could not be allowed. But I have been taught that suffering and misery can go on increasing to the bitter end, and that in war no deed can be too hard or cruel to be committed.[14]

Nonnie's qualities made her a woman to be reckoned with. She was a Boer woman with a voice, which is why her story is still relevant 100 years after women were first commemorated by the inauguration of the Women's Monument.

ABOVE Boer republicanism being squashed: Jan Smuts is pictured to the left of Nonnie shortly after the establishment of the Union of South Africa in 1910.

OPPOSITE, TOP In the aftermath of the war, the De la Reys visited London to help raise funds for the reconstruction of the ex-Boer republics.
BOTTOM The De la Rey family, finally settled, shortly after the declaration of peace

CHAPTER FOUR

Daily life in the concentration camps

— ELIZABETH VAN HEYNINGEN —

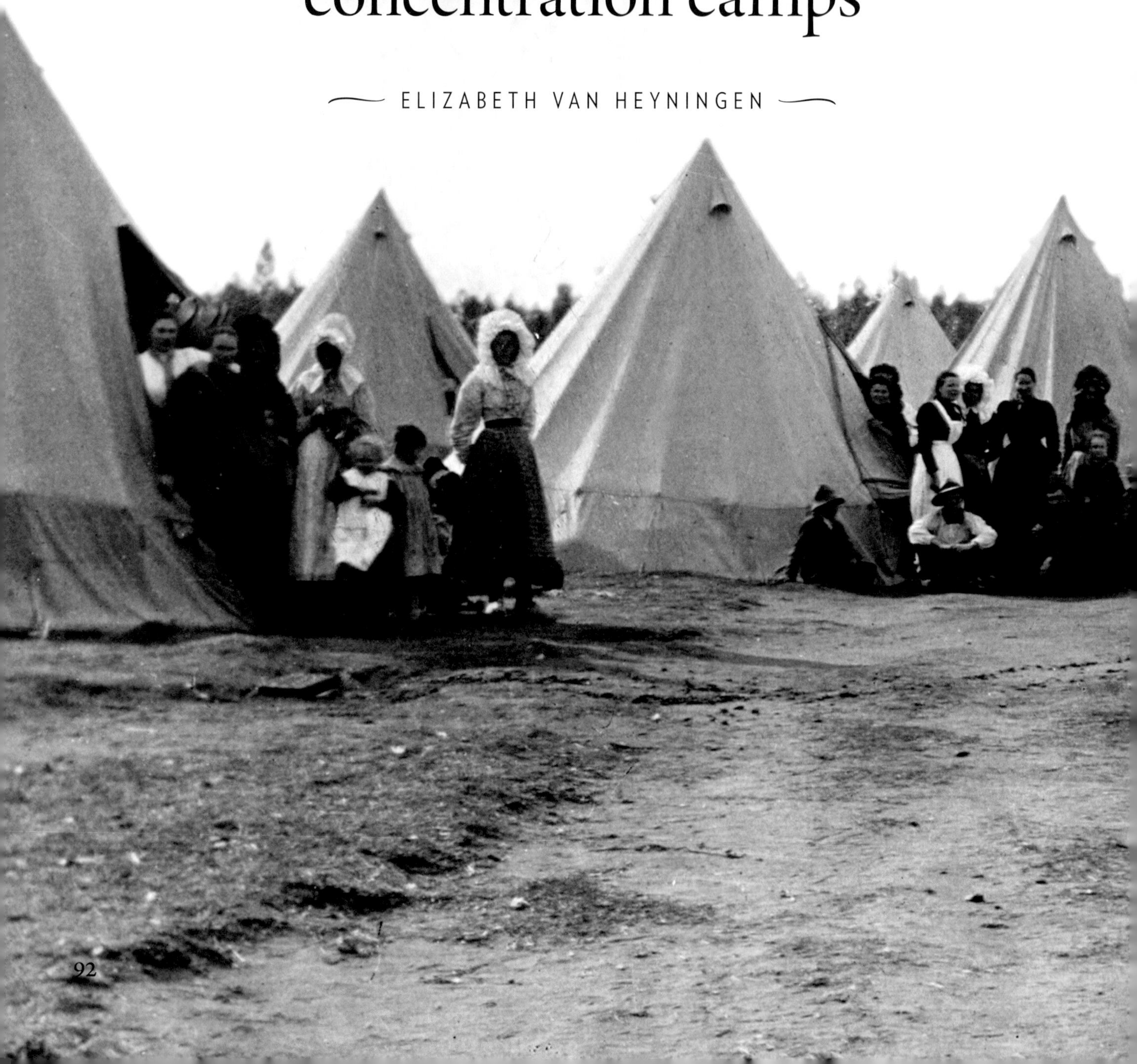

PREVIOUS PAGE In the city of gold, but no riches for these families: a camp in Johannesburg.

THIS PAGE The camp at Winburg, the oldest Boer town in the Orange Free State; ironically, the town was originally named Wenburg (victory town) in the 1830s.

Most of the stories told about the camps describe endless suffering. They tell of the blood and tears of the nation, as commentators said later, grief-stricken mothers and emaciated children buried without coffins or proper graves. The winter months of 1901 were harsh. The weather was unusually wet, the tents were thin and worn, people slept on the bare ground and many were sick. In addition they were adjusting to the loss of their homes and the unfamiliarity of camp life. It is hardly surprising that misery dominates the descriptions of camp survivors.

But these snapshot images of camp life tell only part of the story. The concentration camps were actually small towns of 3 000 to 5 000 people, much larger than the nearby villages of a few hundred. This close congregation of large numbers of people meant that their needs were great, in particular the need for more effective services. The effects of this rapid, unplanned concentration of country people had similar consequences to those of urbanisation throughout the ages, with epidemic disease decimating the population. One might argue that the British ought to have planned for this but, in the confusion of wartime, they did not. The more enlightened British were well aware of their failure. Lucy Deane of the Ladies' Committee, sent to investigate the camps, commented to her sister:

> It is a huge object-lesson to the world in what not to do! For if the children hadn't been so massed together, the death rate from those terrible infectious diseases would not have been so great. We brought the women in to stop them from helping their husbands in the war and by so doing we have undoubtedly killed them in thousands as much as if we had shot them on their own doorsteps, and anyone but a British general would have realised this long ago, at the beginning, for we could not feed them properly, or house them properly and often we couldn't even doctor them properly. We just created out here 33 London slums of the worst description![1]

However, in time, as routines were established, the health of the camp population improved and life took on new rhythms. Then, for many, the greatest ordeal was the dreary monotony as they waited for the war to end.

There are also misleading impressions about life before the establishment of the camps. It has been said that everyone waited on their farms for the arrival of the British. Far from it. The British march to the north was preceded by rumour and fear. No one knew what to expect but many, like Margaret Marquard in Winburg, dreaded a 'reign of terror'.[2] Masses of people fled before the advancing armies and not all of them were republican burghers. The families of Cape rebels crossed the borders from Griqualand West into the Free State and the Transvaal; the Natal border was even more permeable. Republicans also sought refuge in Basutholand, Bechuanaland, Swaziland and Mozambique. President Kruger encouraged his people to leave their farms and move deep into the Transvaal, but more cautious leaders realised that such a mass migration was not possible and urged the Boers to remain on their farms. Nevertheless, by the time the British arrived, the villages and towns were already overflowing with refugees, not all of them *hendsoppers*.

ABOVE A mournful rite of passage for the bereaved: a group make their way to a graveyard at the Pietermaritzburg camp.

OPPOSITE Women at the Aliwal North camp display the mute desolation of personal loss – the portrait of a deceased loved one is visible on the chair.

In the second half of 1900, relative calm was restored for a few months and the British attempted to establish a civil administration in their newly annexed colonies. But this was short-lived. As the Boer commandos revived and began to gain a grip on the country, farmers faced a more difficult dilemma than they had in 1899 – they knew that if they rejoined the commandos, their families were likely to suffer. When Lord Roberts crossed into the Free State, he began to burn farms as retribution against the commandos (although the number that he destroyed was far smaller than some literature suggests; it was approximately 500 out of a total of 30 000).[3] Many of the Boer men took the decision to continue the fight even though they were aware of the consequences. As 'old Izak' gravely explained to Margaret Marquard, the women and children must endure, it was the same in all wars.[4]

No one had anticipated the ruthlessness with which General Lord Kitchener would pursue his campaign when he became commander-in-chief on 29 November 1900. Neither the British secretary of state for the colonies, Joseph Chamberlain, nor the high commissioner, Sir Alfred Milner (Lord Milner after 24 May 1901), could have predicted that an entire countryside would be devastated. They were not personally responsible for planning for the families who had lost their homes, and Kitchener was so secretive about his actions that even the War Office had little idea of what was going on. (This is partly why the revelations of Emily Hobhouse, the British liberal humanitarian, were so important, for she was the first person who could provide the British public with detailed information on what was happening in the erstwhile republics.)

As is often the case with military activity, the drives themselves were haphazard. The British moved slowly in the first months, hampered by lengthy transport convoys. They gathered Boer families, who were forced to travel with them for days, sometimes weeks, before they could be sent to camps. These families were not permitted to take much with them and

they suffered sorely from hunger and cold. In some cases, soldiers would return to a farm three or four times, gradually removing or destroying stock and buildings, before rounding up the inhabitants. Many women slipped away into the veld, sometimes protected by loyal black retainers or commandos.

The experience of Bessie Grobbelaar of Schotland West, near Kroonstad, illustrates this.[5] Her father, who had never favoured the Free State's support for the Transvaal war against the British, decided to rejoin De Wet's commando only in February 1901. The family, which included a number of other women and children totalling a group of 37, fled into the veld with a pot of *vetkoek*. Bessie was 18 years old and missed the comforts of home, longing for a cup of decent coffee, as they had had neither coffee nor sugar for a year. 'I yearn so much for coffee that tears are running down my cheeks,' she wrote later. She was constantly hungry and mentions food often in her account of this period. Like Nonnie de la Rey, the best known of the fugitive women, the women in Grobbelaar's group struggled to make soap and to keep up standards, such as bleaching and starching their *kappies*. They were not alone: neighbours from the Kroonstad district came and went, and Bessie's father and brothers kept an eye on them. On 2 August they were finally taken by the British and they did not reach a camp for 10 days.

Adjusting to camp life

Arriving in a camp was another trial for the families. The processing that took place further bewildered these tired, and often ill, people. Their names were entered in registers, then they were issued with ration tickets and given tents, if they were fortunate. They found themselves among strangers and it took time to re-establish networks of family and friends, which were central to their identities and their place in the world as they knew it. In more orderly camps they were able to adapt more quickly but at times, especially in the early days, hundreds arrived together to find there were no tents and the superintendent was overwhelmed by his job.

The new inmates were confronted by an alien and hostile environment. Country people, who had been accustomed to living by the sun and the seasons, were now governed by industrial time and regulated by rudimentary gongs. They rose to the ringing of a bell and their privacy was invaded daily by camp staff demanding that they air their tents and send sick children to hospital. The British staff, chosen partly for their loyalty to the imperial cause, seemed cold and unsympathetic. Many people yearned for a little kindness. The major complaint was about the food, a monotonous diet of flour, salt, sugar, coffee and meat. Records make it clear that the Boer complaints about the meat were often justified. They still received fresh meat but it was, at best, little more than skin and bone. They found tinned bully beef nauseating and the frozen meat, which began to arrive in 1902, was often of questionable quality. Many families became ill and people died. It is hardly surprising that the Boers bitterly resented the camps.

Yet there is a broader context to this situation. The British did not originally set up the camps with the intention of changing Boer life. The first camps were scrambled affairs and the camp administrators were unable to keep pace with the inflow of burghers. But the

TOP Nicknamed 'Slippery Joe', and with good reason – the constantly scheming Joseph Chamberlain, Britain's secretary of state for the colonies, who believed in all of South Africa being part of a Greater Britain.

ABOVE This ration ticket was issued to a certain Dr L.G. Martinius, who worked at the Brandfort camp hospital.

ABOVE A severe snowstorm struck the southern Orange Free State on 10 June 1901, creating a new crisis for living conditions in the camps at Aliwal North, Bethulie, Norvalspont and Springfontein.

LEFT The novelty of snow for children from the Aliwal North camp

ideology behind the camps changed, perhaps partly unconsciously as people often act on unexamined assumptions. The war itself was justified by the British as a fight for justice but, also implicit in the conflict, was the conviction that British civilisation was superior. Almost every British official took this superiority for granted – for example, Kitchener, notorious for his vilification of the Boers, and Superintendent Strange of Kaffirfontein Native Refugee Camp (Bloemfontein), who commented proudly on Britain's magnanimity in setting up camps for black people.[6] However, there was a more complex network of ideologies underlying this crude assumption.

DAILY LIFE IN THE CONCENTRATION CAMPS

This civilisation, as the British understood it, had evolved largely during the course of the nineteenth century. The British middle classes, who had risen to political dominance in the first half of the century, had a powerful influence on social norms and cultural practices. Their ideas were shaped by both religion and scientific advances. These changing ideas were not uncontested, and an example of the intellectual clashes that occurred is the fierce dispute about evolution. In a rapidly modernising Britain, debates about topics such as gender, childcare, health and sexual standards were hotly contested and had significant political implications. In Britain the reformers targeted the working classes, who often lived in miserable conditions. But the working-class voice was becoming stronger so transformation was not straightforward. Consequently, the colonies became useful settings for working out these ideas because the repercussions did not fall on the British electorate.[7] While no one spelt this out explicitly, the closed societies of the camps were perfect laboratories for this kind of social experimentation, and zealous doctors, teachers and other officials soon realised this. They were abetted in their project of *civilising* the Boers by the authorities.

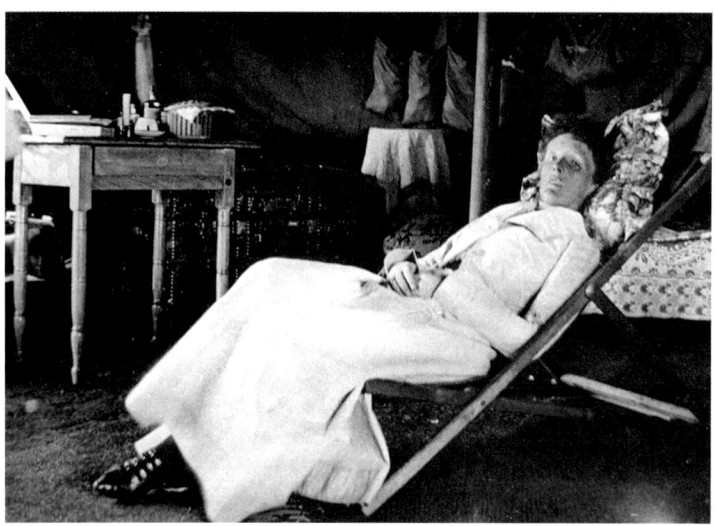

Daughters of Empire on their mission to civilise Boer women and children in modern British ways: below, a Scottish teacher relaxing in her tent in Bloemfontein; bottom, camp nurses and doctors in Pietersburg.

From the beginning, Lord Milner was very much aware that the Boers were now British subjects who were likely to attain political independence within a few years (by 1900 it was unprecedented within the British Empire to withhold political rights from white subjects). Most of the other colonies of settlement, with the partial exceptions of the Cape and Quebec, were ruled by people of British descent, largely espousing appropriate British values. The Boers needed a crash course in elements of British civilisation and the camps were a good place to start. Lord Milner was supported, not only by camp officials, but also by the women of the Ladies' Committee, which was appointed by the War Office to investigate the camps.

Although women were excluded from political power, the British recognised that they had a powerful influence in shaping social and cultural values and many played an active role in public life by the end of the nineteenth century. Indeed, the appointment of the Ladies' Committee could be seen as an example of this.[8] Conventional gender prejudice often led the British to refer to all the camp inmates as 'he' and to make provision only for men; nevertheless, the Boer women were also within their sights for reform. It is important to recognise that this kind of process was at work if one is to make sense of, for example, the extraordinary statement of the Transvaal director of burgher camps that the British nurses 'have created

Making the most of a botanical backdrop: the Faure family from Smithfield in an unidentified camp

a very favourable impression, being physically strong and attractive, and presenting by ocular demonstration, to the inmates of the camps, examples of British womanhood. The moral effect of the association of these earnest noble-minded and cultivated ladies, with the people of the veld ... cannot fail to be productive of much good in many ways.'[9]

Reforming the Boers took many forms. Education was the most obvious vehicle but this went far beyond the instruction of children in English. Sport, of course, was regarded as a means of inculcating manly British values. Celebrations, such as concerts, Christmas and the (postponed) coronation of Edward VII in 1902, were also used. Industrial order was taught through the spatial organisation of the camps (in rigid lines) and the imposition of daily timetables. As the British became more controlling, almost every aspect of daily life served their purposes. While many Boers found the endless surveillance and the routines restrictive, not all of them rejected the changes. Some burghers recognised the value of effective sanitary practices and embraced middle-class respectability.

Daily life

Most people lived in the camps for at least a year. The worst period, the winter of 1901, is the time that is predominant in popular memory. But life did improve. The once-despised routines provided a degree of order and Boer families became more accustomed to them. Superintendents quickly realised that people needed to keep active to prevent demoralising depression and they began to introduce a variety of activities.

There were a surprising number of able-bodied young men in the camps as unemployed men were considered particularly undesirable, due to the belief in the adage that the devil makes work for idle hands. Nearly a third of the adults were men and a great majority were young.[10] Testimonies of women give the impression that they were *hendsoppers*, men who

Fair weather for some who were more fortunate: Durban's Merebank Camp, where inhabitants found the climate milder and less taxing than weather conditions in the Orange Free State and the Transvaal

had thrown in the towel. In one sense this is probably true. Thousands of men, captured by the British, were given the choice of taking an oath of neutrality and going to the camps or being sent overseas to Ceylon, Bermuda, St Helena or India. It is not surprising that so many chose to take the oath because they could at least help their families in the camps. It is possible that many of them were deeply ambivalent, like Pieter Jacobus Strydom.[11] He was a lieutenant in the Orange Free State artillery, who was taken prisoner in Green Point and then sent to Brandfort camp. Strydom was lonely and unable to express himself publicly, so he kept a diary recording his intimate thoughts. For months he found it difficult to admit, even to himself, that he had taken the coward's way out, in the hope of reaching his beloved wife in Johannesburg. By the end of the war, he bitterly regretted his decision to take the oath of neutrality and, when news of the surrender arrived, he was appalled that the republicans had lost all they had fought for.

Strydom's diary is interesting on a number of levels. He kept his diary in English, like many educated Afrikaners before the war, and, although his English was not perfect, he was sufficiently skilled to be given the responsible job of issuing rations. For this he probably earned a reasonable wage, as issuers were paid between five and 10 shillings a day (doctors were also initially paid 10 shillings a day). In this way it was possible for the men to supplement family rations by buying extra luxuries in the camp stores. A closer look at Strydom's account of life in the camp clarifies why routines were important, however alienating they may have been.

In the gruelling winter months of 1901, Brandfort was known as a 'bad' camp, with a record mortality rate from measles. The superintendent, somewhat unusually, was a Cape Afrikaner by the name of E.J. Jacobs. At first it seemed as if he was just doing his job, but the Boers disliked him intensely. Strydom wrote of him: '… to me personally he is very considerate and friendly, but that is all I can say in his favour, I think him as unfit for the

position he holds, as a man could possibly be. In the first place he does not seem to take any interest in anything, secondly, he is a man utterly without pity or feeling for anybody, and seems to be too bitter, and prejudiced against the Dutch.' The assistant superintendent was even worse, a zealous officer who 'makes life a burden and unbearable to anybody who has the misfortune to come in contact with him'. Lower-ranking officers were even more incompetent. Although the camp was inspected regularly, nothing improved. Then Inspector St John Cole Bowen arrived.

If any British man can be described as a hero of the camps, it is Cole Bowen. Everyone, including Emily Hobhouse and the Ladies' Committee commented on his calm competence. Cole Bowen, an Irish military man, had originally been superintendent of Norvalspont camp and was later promoted to inspector. He managed to gain the trust and respect of the Boers, even though he was loyal to the British cause and a great believer in order. Strydom wrote of him:

Displaying more than a touch of class: previously well-off, and still well-dressed, Boer women at the Merebank camp

> What a blessing his coming was – [it] can only be known and appreciated by those who were on the spot, and who had to indure [sic] the hardships of the life in the camp at that time. About two days after his arrival, changes for the better commenced. Large ovens and tanks for boiling water were put up, so that the people could get their bread baked with less trouble. Corporals were appointed on the lines, and in fact the whole workings of the camp were brought under a better system and rules were laid down in every department; the rushing and crushing to receive rations etc. were put a stop to, so that everybody could come at his turn and get what he had to receive at once without waiting and fighting for it,

He came, he saw, he reformed: Inspector St John Cole Bowen (right, with walking-stick), praised by Emily Hobhouse, among others, for his work in improving camp conditions

DAILY LIFE IN THE CONCENTRATION CAMPS

Workshops like these at the Norvalspont camps kept Boer men busy with small crafts and trades.

it was wonderful to see what one man, (who understands his business), could do in a short time – many were the secret blessings from thankful hearts called down on Inspector Bowen, (as he is called in this camp).[12]

Jacobs disappeared and was eventually replaced by Captain J. Dwyer, whom Strydom described as 'the right man in the right place – it is hardly necessary to say more about him, a gentlemanly straightforward man, whose main object seems to make this camp a model camp and to make everybody happy'.

As well as the daily sanitary chores, there was a good deal of skilled work for the men to do. Those with carpentry or leather-working skills found themselves in great demand. The bleakest of the carpenters' tasks was making coffins but, in time, they also turned out beds or *katels* for families to sleep on, and desks and benches for the schools. When the scrawny cattle were available for slaughter, the hides were tanned and *velskoene* produced. Less skilled men were used for brick making because, in 1902, solid buildings began to replace the marquees and tents. Kroonstad camp alone produced 100 000 bricks a month.[13] Other men worked in the vegetable gardens, the produce of which transformed the health of the camp inmates.

It is unjust to label all of these men as *hendsoppers* because many were experiencing the same conflict as Strydom. But there were degrees of collaboration and some men allied themselves willingly with the British cause.[14] The camp police were trusted by British

Boer National Scouts, who switched sides to ride for the British

officials and were much vilified by the women, so they may have fallen into the category of *hendsoppers*. The motivation to join the curiously named 'looting corps' was understandable. These men were recruited to round up Boer cattle and were allowed to keep some of their booty. Apart from the financial advantage, riding in the veld gave them their freedom and perhaps a sense that they were retrieving their masculinity and honour.

The camp men were also a major source for the recruitment of National Scouts, a Transvaal unit consisting of renegade Boers that was established by the British around October 1901, and other such groups, and their numbers were not insignificant. By the end of the war, approximately 5 000 Boers were fighting for the British. As far as the camps were concerned, these Boers were of dubious value: their recruitment deprived the camp of necessary labour; they could be arrogant, disruptive and upset routines; and, above all, they angered the women whose men were prisoners of war or still on commando. The camp superintendents were expected to support the recruiting officers but *hendsoppers* disrupted the placidity of camp life. Eventually camps were set aside for these people's families or they were separated from the main camps.

It was more difficult to occupy the women. Of course, they had their daily chores, which could be arduous. Washing by hand is hard work and although some camps provided hot water and washing troughs, judging from the photographs women often had to go down to the rivers and crouch on the banks to do their laundry. Given the endless dust storms that swept through the camps, penetrating everything, and the numbers of babies and toddlers to be kept clean, the work must have been endless. Queuing in the rain or the hot sun to collect rations was also tedious. A number of women were permitted to bring servants into the camps, usually the staff children who had grown up in Boer homes. This job could be foisted onto them or their own children, who were sometimes kept out of school for the purpose, although this practice was discouraged. The children ate the sugar before they got home, Cole Bowen complained when he was superintendent of Norvalspont camp.

For a long time, cooking was a struggle as there was very little fuel. At first the women were allowed to roam the veld in search of dung and wood but these resources were depleted quickly. Eventually wood or coal was delivered to the camps but it was difficult to cook with the limited rations. The British advocated soups or stews but the shortage of vegetables and fuel made this difficult. The Boers often resorted to making biltong. Unsurprisingly, the culture-bound British were horrified but, regardless, many tents were hung with drying meat. There is no mention of spices in the records but they may have been available in village shops, as long as stocks lasted. Although there was plenty of salt, the food was tasteless, unless it was prepared by a skilled cook. It is no wonder that, when vegetables were introduced, Bessie Grobbelaar remarked: 'We really enjoyed the onions, which we cooked with sugar.' The single luxury was coffee and its aroma scented the air. The Boers preferred to roast and grind their own coffee and the British soon accepted this. There are very few complaints in the official records about the quality of coffee in established camps, in contrast to the comments about the meat.

Shopping provided some relief from the monotony. In many cases the women were given permits to go to nearby towns, where they could visit friends or buy forbidden Dutch medicines (the patent medicines still sold in South African stores). All the camps had their own shops. In the Transvaal camps Poynton Bros was given the monopoly while in the Orange River Colony (ORC) a variety of traders were allowed to compete. Prices were regulated and profits were siphoned off to pay for special items such as sports equipment for the camp children (by the end of the war there were soccer fields and tennis courts – and in some camps even swimming baths). Occasionally alcohol was traded illicitly because the camps were supposed to be dry, in theory. A rare occurrence took place in Harrismith, where a particularly enterprising trader imported such luxuries as fresh fruit and fish from the coast. This man, Cardova, was soon ousted by

No surprises whose hands are idle when it comes to domestic work... The mundane but essential chores of daily life being performed by women and children – cooking, fetching water, stacking firewood and doing laundry.

DAILY LIFE IN THE CONCENTRATION CAMPS

indignant local traders on the grounds that, under old Free State law, Indians were not allowed into the Orange River Colony.

Ginger beer was in demand and the Boers themselves sometimes produced and sold it. The British disapproved, as they did of any independent enterprise, but found it difficult to forbid such a minor self-indulgence. Although there is no mention of shops in women's testimonies, it is easy to imagine clusters of women chatting at the counters as they bought sardines, Quaker oats, jam, tinned butter or even, on the odd occasion, a piano accordion.

Shopping may have provided brief pleasure, but it was not enough to keep boredom and depression at bay. Reading between the lines of well-known testimonies, like that of Miem Fischer, it is clear that women often despaired. When Fischer was relocated to Durban, her melancholy comes through in her comments about the weather. She found the Durban heat in February unbearable after the crisp Highveld air. It was 'oppressively warm. The heat is nearly unbearable. It gives a feeling of unmentionable lethargy,'[15] she wrote on 25 February. A few days later there was a 'harsh wind, filthy nauseating weather' and the 'foul cigarette air' gave her a headache.[16] She also recorded the daily deaths in the camp, even though they were not excessive in Merebank.

Religion was a vital source of comfort, and the British often commented on the women's common practice of singing hymns and psalms. There were even moments of exaltation. When Revd A.M. Murray of Weenen visited Pinetown camp in May 1902, he conducted a series of revivalist meetings 'during which the Holy Spirit broke through and many people, both old and young, were led to Christ then and during a meeting afterwards led'.[17] However, the women's faith was often tested by the deaths occurring around them.[18] Religion

Many camps, like the one at Jacobs, Natal, provided stores, such as Levisohn & Cohen's (shown here), where those Boers who had money in their pockets could buy various daily supplies.

108 THE WAR AT HOME

More 'Highveld' than 'high' tea: gatherings in the camps would have been punctuated by the clunk of tin mugs, not the clink of china.

is more than faith; it is also a form of cultural practice. The Victorian deathbed culture was not confined to Britain.[19] The women clustered in the tents of the dying children, to the dismay of men like Revd A.D. Lückhoff. He insisted that 'friends and relatives abstain from all long-faced despondency, with total absence of any cheer and hopefulness.' 'This [has a] bad effect on patients; if anyone [is] seriously ill, they "hands up" and cluster around to await the end, lest perchance they miss seeing "zoo 'n prachtige sterfbed" (such a beautiful deathbed),' he explained in his moving diary on life in Bethulie camp.[20] One reason Lückhoff's diary is so enlightening is that his brief comments combine his deep compassion for the suffering of his people with a remarkably modern understanding of how demoralising their old-fashioned values could be.

In addition to faith, great comfort was to be found in friends and family. The British deplored gossip but, nevertheless, the women would get together in the tents at night. Bessie Grobbelaar's family met every evening for hymns, prayers and to talk about those outside of the camps. 'In the evenings our neighbours visit us in our tent. Tannie Lenie Swarts is the joker. We mostly talk about our poor people in the veld,' she wrote in her diary. Once or twice they discussed the possibility of escape. One of the Grobbelaars' new acquaintances was Nonnie Vermaak, some of whose family were still outside the camp, and Bessie and her friends believed they could seek refuge with them. They planned to escape one dark night by slipping between the blockhouses. But Mieta Rheeder advised

A time-honoured and cherished symbol of domestic normality, this small bowl was sent to Mrs S.H.L. Barkhuizen in the Bethulie camp by Miss C. Barnard of the Springfontein camp. The plate was buried for the duration of the war.

DAILY LIFE IN THE CONCENTRATION CAMPS

Scrubbing away on washday at a Johannesburg camp

against such foolhardy action: 'She says it is too dangerous – the Tommies will shoot us and we don't know the area since our family lives in the Kroonstad district. She told us to stay where we are and to be content, that we should not put our children at risk of being killed.'

One of the constraints posed by historical writing in the Victorian period is that sex is rarely mentioned. Yet these were camps filled with young people. In Brandfort camp, for instance, the average age of the adults (over 16 years old) was 35, and 663 of them were single. The British sometimes described the Boers as immoral. It is hard to understand what gave rise to this critical view, as the Boers were not a promiscuous people, but it is possible that young people were freer in their relationships than the British were accustomed to. Widowed men and women sought partners to help support their children and single people sometimes found partners.

Marriages took place, but not all relationships were formalised in marriage and occasionally illegitimate births are recorded in the registers. There were also cross-cultural relationships. British Tommies were banned from the camps but there are several accounts of soldier grandfathers marrying Boer women from the camps.[21] Officers usually sought the company of British staff but they also sometimes formed friendships with young Boer women. However, because such liaisons were frowned upon, few records of such events have survived. There is only fragmentary evidence suggesting cross-cultural relationships. In Bethulie camp the errant and alcoholic Dr Barrett was accused of visiting the tent of local assistant Johanna Louw at night. On one occasion

TOP Bringing in an important life source – water carts at Norvalspont

BOTTOM By their bonnets shall you know them: these younger Boer women, retaining their traditional *kappies*, received training as assistant nurses at the Springfontein camp.

he told orderly J. Wessels that he was in love with her, and referred to her as 'my girl'.[22]

In terms of workload, single women bore fewer of the household burdens but they had relatively few employment opportunities. However their one option was to work in the hospitals. It is estimated that, by the end of the war, several thousand young women had worked as probationers, or assistant nurse aids. The growing number of these positions testifies to their value – Klerksdorp camp hospital had over 50 by the end of the war.[23] Their wages ranged from one shilling and sixpence to six shillings a day, a useful contribution to family income. In time, the British medical staff, who frowned on the more primitive Boer medical practices, recognised the invaluable opportunity to reform the Boer family by training young women in medical and household skills. Doctors often initially complained about these women and the difficulty of communicating with them, but by

DAILY LIFE IN THE CONCENTRATION CAMPS

The deathly gaze towards nothingness: Boer family with a sick child at the Bethulie camp

the end of the war they had become so enamoured with this project that Dr Pratt Yule, the medical officer of health for the ORC, had set up an elaborate training programme for nurse aids, examined them and issued them with certificates. At the end of the war, a handful were employed as private nurses.

Unfortunately, there are few personal accounts of Boer women who nursed in the hospitals, with the notable exception of Bessie Grobbelaar. And testimonies like hers should be read with a degree of circumspection. Unlike Strydom, whose diary was personal, they were written partly for public consumption. They are formulaic and they tend to have a triumphalist element as the women usually recorded only those aspects of life that described their suffering or defiance.[24] According to Grobbelaar, working in the hospital was a means of protecting the children from callous British medicine. Since they were refused food, she gave them soup or beef tea to drink when she could. The measles epidemic was probably at its height when she was there because she provided a graphic account of the effects of a type of gangrene of the jaw that was usually fatal. She was relieved, as she found the nights lonely, that in Brandfort camp the mothers were allowed to remain with their ailing children.

The camp officials gave considerable thought to the children because, by 1900, Britain was taking a more concerned stance about child welfare. It has been said that Edmund Beale Sargant, who had taken charge of education in the new colonies, planned a school system for the camps while chatting to the superintendent over an 'evening glass' in Norvalspont camp. His plans were not completely fulfilled because schooling was never compulsory, but nevertheless the British invested a good deal in education. Teachers were recruited from all over the British Empire and many were highly educated. Lily Rose of Pietermaritzburg camp, for instance, was trained in infant education at the Froebel Institute in London, where she would have received the most advanced instruction available.[25] Teachers were usually in their early thirties and came to the camps partly out of a desire to contribute to the war effort, but also in the hope of adventure and, possibly, a husband. (In this they were often successful.) They also genuinely cared for their charges and this affection was frequently returned.

Anna van Rensburg's memories of the Harrismith camp

According to my mother we were captured in May 1901. One afternoon an Englishman arrived on horseback and ordered the women to get ready because they would be collected the next day. My aunt would have chosen to flee and hide somewhere that night, but it was May and bitterly cold. My mother wasn't prepared to take the little ones outdoors in the cold. So the next day we were loaded onto mule wagons.

The British didn't allow us to take many possessions along; my mother could take only a small suitcase of clothes for us. Before our capture we had mostly worn two dresses, and the boys two sets of clothes, one on top of the other – if the British caught us, we would at least have some clean clothes. My mother wanted to take a chair along and each time she put the chair on the wagon, they (the British soldiers) threw it down again. But when the wagon departed, she climbed onto the back with the chair.

Apart from us, there were already three other families on the wagon. Then they picked up some of our other neighbours as well. There were mainly boys on the wagon. My mother told me that an Englishman, who rode behind the wagon, remarked 'Oh, it's all boys.' Whereupon she said, 'Yes, 20 years from now, these boys will shoot you people to blazes.' [*Ja, oor 20 jaar skiet hierdie boys vir julle dat julle bars.*]

That evening the women had to carry their belongings from the mule wagons to the ox wagons, which would be used for the rest of the journey. When my mom arrived at the ox wagon with a bundle of bedding on her head, she found an Englishman lying on his stomach, eating a loaf of bread and a tin of jam. His legs were up in the air, a horse's rein wound around each foot. My mother flung the bedding down next to the wagon, which startled the horses. The Englishman was dragged off by the bolting horses. He clung to the grass for all he was worth. Later they looked for the 'lady' who had frightened the horses. My mother said, 'I didn't see a lady anywhere.'

Then we were transported to Harrismith. There were many round tents on the slope above the town that were used to house the women. There were lots of women and children, but I don't know exactly how many.

The women went regularly to a big corrugated-iron building to receive rations. My mom told us that the mothers with little children could manage on the food they were given, but ones with older children, and particularly boys, found it hard. We were given bread, mealie-meal, condensed milk, tins of jam, coffee and sugar. Some women also received packets of Maizena to make food for the babies. We seldom got meat, and when we did it was very lean. At times, some of the women threw the meat into the faces of the men who distributed the food ...

All kinds of diseases started spreading among the people. Whooping cough, measles, chickenpox, and the worst – typhoid fever. Many, many women and children died from that. The British erected huge tents that served as hospitals, and there were British nurses and doctors from England. The adults and children who were sick with fever were only supposed to get soup and milk, but the healthy people who visited the patients secretly brought them milk porridge and other food.

I remember that my mom used to bring me milk porridge in a small cup. She hid it in the pocket of her dress and fed me in the hospital. I was seriously ill. One evening my mom expected me to die during the night. So, once again, she brought the linen nightdress she had made when I had diphtheria. But, once again, I recovered.

My mom gave birth to a baby girl in the camp, who reached the age of four months and then died. Before the baby died, my mom had had pictures taken of us five children at the photographer's studio in Harrismith. I still remember it well. Yes, much grief was endured there.

> Van Rensburg's memories of camp life during the Anglo-Boer War were recorded at an old-age home in Carnarvon in 1980. The account has been translated from Afrikaans and abridged.

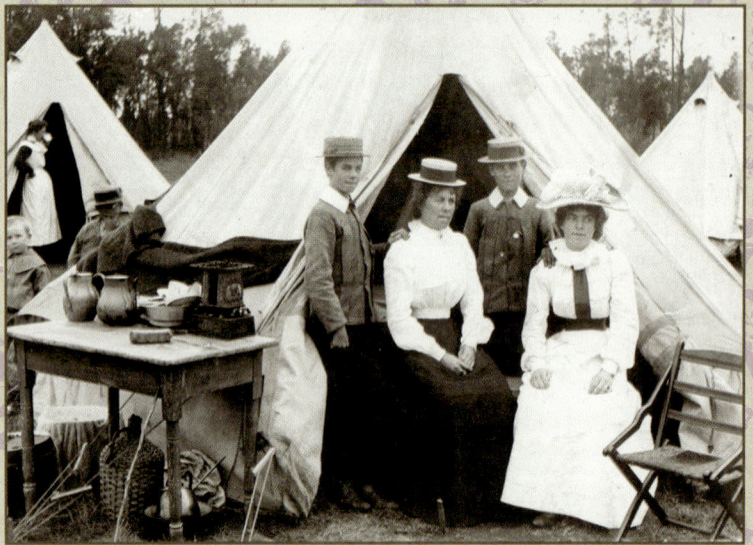

ABOVE A solitude of tent flaps: the Vredefort camp

LEFT AND IMMEDIATE RIGHT Families pose with a small number of valued household possessions at various camps

FAR RIGHT Observed by Lisbeth Richter at the Bloemfontein camp, Mynie Fleck holds a child inside a bell tent, standard-issue accommodation to British forces in South Africa.

DAILY LIFE IN THE CONCENTRATION CAMPS

Not far from the diamonds, but only dust to be found here – the camp at Hopetown, near Kimberley

Inevitably, education was of an anglicised variety. A shortage of books meant the children were taught through action songs, such as the English nursery rhyme 'Ring around the Rosie', which first appeared in print in the 1880s. 'It is now not an uncommon occurrence for the children to play their games in English and to join in round games to the accompaniment of well-known old English rhymes and songs,' the ORC chief camp superintendent reported in 1902.[26] There was also a strong Scottish influence in nineteenth-century South Africa, and this was evident in the camps. When Revd Robertson, the Dutch Reformed Church advisor to the ORC camps, visited Bloemfontein, a child was asked to sing to his wife. To her astonishment, 'the little one struck up "Far Awa frae Bonnie Scotland"'.[27] Although some burghers resented this enforced anglicisation, many embraced the opportunity for their children to receive a schooling that was not available on the isolated farms. Strydom certainly approved, noting that 'the children are nearly all attending school at least those whose perants sees [sic] the necessity of having their children educated, some there are who does not avail themselves of this splendid opportunity from some foolish feeling of prejudice or other I don't know what to call it'.

Growing boys were particularly irked by the confinement of the camp. Twelve-year-old George Brink (later General Brink who commanded the 1st South African Division in the East African and Western Desert campaigns during World War II) was in a privileged position as the son of the Vredefort Road superintendent. He and his friends found an outlet for their energies by helping to drive the Scotch transport carts to and from the station. Once out of sight of the camp, they engaged in 'glorious' races. A young German taught him to handle a mule team so that 'within a short while I was able to handle any mule team with the best and won many a hard fought mule team race. It was all great fun and the outings we thus had revived our spirits so that we were no longer greatly concerned about the duration of the war.'[28]

OPPOSITE Treats on the way: Bloemfontein camp children eagerly await the arrival of Hannie Blignaut and helpers (top); some pounce on the biscuits that have been brought (centre), while others, with more restraint, receive sweets and biscuits from Irene Fraundorfer (bottom).

DAILY LIFE IN THE CONCENTRATION CAMPS

ABOVE A recreational gathering at Pietermaritzburg where one musical woman (seated to the left of the table) even managed to get a guitar into the camp.

BELOW The small freedom of clearing the rope: the high jump at a sports day, Vredefort camp

Organised sport was another way of absorbing male energy. Bored young officers stationed nearby took a keen interest in this aspect of camp life, supplying footballs and forming teams to compete with the men. Strydom played croquet, unexpectedly, but he also enjoyed football. 'We had a football match today, married men versus single, in which we poor married men got a good beating four goals to nil,' he wrote on 30 April 1902. On another occasion, his team played against the Army Service Corps, again losing by four goals. Sport was a quintessential British activity and was introduced throughout the empire because it was believed to instil notions of manliness and fair play. Inspector W.J. Bentinck, previously superintendent of the Klerksdorp and Vereeniging camps, certainly held this view and he promoted sport with enthusiasm. 'They have made the Britisher what he is and can also make the Boer the same,' he reported on one occasion.[29] Even the young girls were provided with skipping ropes while the older ones played tennis, along with the teachers and nurses (the British staff also suffered from the poor food and confinement of camp life).

Music, usually ignored in war records, permeated camp life and brought comfort and pleasure to the Boers and British alike. There are few accounts of the Boers' own music in the camps but many of the men joined bands. Strydom took charge of the band in Brandfort camp and, before the camp closed at the end of the war he became bandmaster, for which he was paid the fee of two shillings a day. The women could share in music, and pianos or harmoniums were much sought after. Few were as fortunate as Lottie Theron, who had been able to bring her piano into the camp, but most

118 THE WAR AT HOME

camps acquired some instruments over time. For example, Krugersdorp had a number of instruments and the musical club regularly entertained the inmates.³⁰

The British also used music for their own purposes. Like it or not, the Boers soon became familiar with the British national anthem, which was played on every ceremonial occasion. As described earlier, younger children learnt through song, and older ones also sang British tunes. George Brink recalled the pretty Du Plessis sisters, one of whom favoured a song about birds: '"Come birdie come and glee with me, I have a green cage all ready for thee." … We boys soon invented a chorus for this song and when the Misses du Plessis came to realise that we were pulling their legs, they didn't call the birdies any more.'³¹

For the Boers, music was also a means of affirming their own identity. 'They sing psalms and hymns, on and off all through the day,' a young English teacher, Lily Rose, commented. As both sides were Protestants, the enemies shared more than they often acknowledged and the Moody and Sankey hymns sung by the Boers were familiar to many of the British.³² *Volksliedere* were discouraged but it was difficult to prevent psalms from being used for political purposes. Mrs A.M. van den Berg recorded an occasion in Merebank camp when 16 December was commemorated by two groups representing General Botha's and General De Wet's parties. The two parties vied with one another by singing psalms praising the Lord, the Botha party singing Psalm 146 and the De Wet group singing Psalm 134. When a *hendsopper* attempted to remove the republican flags that they were wearing, some women struck off his hat and marched round the camp singing Psalm 134.³³ This is another example of the triumphalism that is so common in women's testimonies but it does indicate the way in which religion, politics and music fused in the expression of Afrikaner identity.

Camp life was grim, especially in the early days. The women, men and children in the camps had to face hunger, exposure, illness and death – and more. The thousands of deaths, mostly of young children, caused unmentionable grief. The harshness of camp life was felt most acutely by women whose husbands were prisoners or still out fighting and those who had young children to care for. Often unwell themselves, many of these women were scarred forever by the loss of their children in the camps.

But the story of the camps would not be complete if the women are only viewed as victims and their situation seen as wholly bleak. If the history of the camps is to be wholly understood, it is worth exploring the multi-layered experiences of the camps. As Emily Hobhouse observed, even Lord Kitchener could not stop the course of nature. Deaths occurred in the camps, but so did births and marriages. Adults still loved, cried, prayed and worked, and children still found ways to play.

Although perhaps not happy, the Botha and Oosthuizen families are portrayed as alive and well at the Bethulie camp in this official photograph taken to confirm to husbands that the occupying authorities were taking care of their kin.

CHAPTER FIVE

A clash of cultures: British doctors versus Boer women

— ELIZABETH VAN HEYNINGEN —

PREVIOUS PAGE, MAIN IMAGE A medical fraternity that brought modernity: hospital medical staff at Brandfort, a camp that suffered from a particularly high mortality rate.
SECONDARY IMAGE Graves of over 1 700 inmates who died at the Bethulie camp

THIS PAGE Another life that ebbed away tragically young: Gysbert Johannes Vermeulen, aged 12

THE MOST BITTER EXPERIENCE TO EMERGE from the camps was the deaths of children. In both the white and black camps, children died of the infectious epidemic diseases that have ravaged society for centuries. At the time of the Anglo-Boer War, the world was beginning to understand the nature of disease but medical science was not sufficiently advanced to provide effective therapies – antibiotics would not be developed for another 50 years.

In the black camps, the majority of the deaths that occurred were child fatalities. Similarly, approximately 22 000 Boer children also died in the war, leaving a legacy of grief and a diminished Afrikaner population. As a result, the management of disease in the white camps became a battleground between the doctors, who understood the causes of epidemic diseases but could not cure them, and the Boer women, who had little knowledge of modern science but drew on their traditions and the veld to make a host of remedies to manage the symptoms. Relationships between the women and the doctors were further strained by the gender bias that was present in medicine at the time, which emphasised the omnipotent role of the male doctor. For the Boer women, care of the sick was integral to their role in the home and an aspect of their feminine identity.

By 1900 Britain had significantly improved the control of the infectious diseases that, before the nineteenth century, had ensured that cities survived only through constant migration of people from the countryside. Since the Middle Ages, to live in a large town in Europe seemed to guarantee an early and unpleasant death. Most deaths were caused by diseases such as smallpox (virtually the only disease for which there was an effective therapy), plague (by 1900 this was no longer a curse in Europe, but had spread to the rest of the world), typhus (also known as gaol fever and caused by lice), cholera (from 1832), typhoid (the incidence of which had increased in the second half of the nineteenth century) and tuberculosis (another growing scourge). In the 1830s it had been discovered that clean water supplies greatly improved survival rates and this triggered the sanitary revolution of the nineteenth century – two decades before Louis Pasteur had begun to identify disease pathogens.

These advances reduced the adult mortality rate but not that of children under the age of five. In 1900 the British infant mortality rate was 156 per 1 000 live births, and was increasing. Many children died of diarrhoea, often called infant or summer diarrhoea (possibly rotavirus). But another cause was a mysterious 'wasting' condition, whereby children failed to thrive and gradually became emaciated. The variety of terms

ABOVE The cemetery at the Brandfort camp. This camp was notorious for its high child death rate from the measles epidemic that hit hard during 1901 and 1902.

OPPOSITE Nothing ahead but her grave: Miss Strydom holds the body of her youngest sister at the Bloemfontein camp.

that doctors had for this condition is an indication of their futility in treating it. The names included wasting, inanition, atrophy, marasmus and tabes mesenterica.

Britain's changing demographic pattern – in which life expectancy was gradually rising – contrasted with that of the Boer republics. The demographic pattern of most pre-industrial societies was one in which a high birth rate correlated with a high infant-mortality rate. An analysis of the limited census data available suggests that the Boer republics were no different. The Boers on the farms, with their large families, were accustomed to the deaths of some of their children. But the excessive number of camp deaths and the circumstances in which they occurred make any rational explanation for the deaths seem unpalatable – even unforgivable.

The causes of death in the camps

There is no mystery about the main cause of death in the camps. Most children died of measles, or measles-related complications. Measles damages the mucous membranes of the body and, therefore, related respiratory ailments such as pneumonia and bronchitis were also common causes of death. Measles was a common childhood malady until a vaccine was developed in the 1960s. Camp doctors were familiar with the mild

form that they usually encountered in Britain, which became endemic in city populations of over 250 000 as the virulence of the pathogen decreased. They could not explain why it was so lethal in the camps; some were inclined to attribute it to the degeneration of the Boers as a result of their isolation.

But the Boers were not unfamiliar with measles. There is mention in historical writing of earlier epidemics and the name of Bloemfontein's resort, Maselspoort, is probably a reference to one such outbreak. The most vulnerable group were children between one and 15 years old. Adults did not generally succumb to the disease (although we do not know how many contracted it) and neither did babies, who may have received some immunity from their mothers.

As well as being common, measles is one of the most serious human diseases. It is caused by a highly infectious virus, which is related to rinderpest. In 1900 there was no scientific knowledge of viruses and, therefore, the pathogen had not yet been identified. As was the case in Fiji in 1875, without immunity mortality rates could reach 50 per cent or more. And there was no cure or treatment apart from warmth and attentive nursing. Cross-infection could be contained by quarantining patients but that recourse was almost

ABOVE Like the poor and hungry Oliver Twist of Charles Dickens's classic social novel, the plea of these children in the Bloemfontein camp is also for 'more, please' as young women prepare some food for them.

OPPOSITE, TOP The ever-present and nagging issue of food: distribution of vegetable rations at Norvalspont
BOTTOM Symbol of scarcity: ration card issued to Elizabeth Landman at the Ladysmith camp (Collection of the War Museum)

impossible in wartime South Africa. Good nutrition was important for managing the disease, especially an adequate supply of protein. Modern research has demonstrated that the potency of the virus increases with overcrowding. Therefore, it is clear that the camps provided ideal breeding grounds for this life-threatening infection.[1]

Yet measles was not the disease that the camp authorities feared the most. The Anglo-Boer War was 'the last of the typhoid wars', and infectious diseases killed many more soldiers than were lost in combat. Typhoid (then also called enteric, now known as salmonella) was the cause of many British soldiers' deaths in Bloemfontein, where most water sources were contaminated. The camp authorities did not want to make the same mistake as the negligent military and they were determined to keep it out of the camps. They were fairly successful. Mortality rates from typhoid were high (it was one of the major causes of death in adults) and it was rife in places like Bloemfontein but it never reached the epidemic proportions that it had among the British troops.

The struggle against typhoid was different from the fight against measles. Typhoid is caused by the salmonella bacterium, which was identified in the 1860s. Although it could present with a variety of symptoms, there was an effective diagnostic test and even a vaccine. This had been developed at the Netley Military Hospital in Britain just before the war but the British army did not use it much because it was regarded as experimental – a decision for which British troops paid dearly.

The conditions necessary for the spread of typhoid were also well understood. Typhoid is a disease of poor sanitation: it is spread in water, faeces and polluted soil, and even by flies. Undoubtedly, the fly-infested camps – in which diarrhoea and dysentery were

THE WAR AT HOME

rampant and dust storms blew – provided ideal conditions for its spread. But rigorous sanitary controls could prevent its spreading. This was one reason why the authorities were vehement about cleanliness in the camps, but this obsession was also a source of contention with the inmates, who resented the intrusiveness of the controls. Treatment for typhoid consisted of careful nursing and, above all, a bland and restricted diet because death often occurs from perforation of the intestine. Boer mothers, watching their children waste away, misunderstood the reasons for limiting meals to milk and eggs, and believed that their children were being starved.

Although these types of diseases (and respiratory ailments) were the major killers in the camps, the range of other illnesses that occurred gives us an indication of the poor state of health of the inmates in the early months. The most significant of these was scurvy and its prevalence was inevitable, given the lack of fruit and vegetables in the diet. The absence of vitamin C leads to the dissolution of collagen in the body, which causes tooth loss, extensive bleeding and opening up of old wounds, resulting in a painful death. Relatively few people in the camps actually died of scurvy but it was widespread and undermined the health of the inmates. Dr Pratt Yule, the Orange River Colony medical officer, suspected that only scurvy could explain the 'intense constitutional depression' that followed the epidemic diseases.² Eventually lime juice was introduced and, later, vegetables were included in the rations.

In the Lowveld malaria affected the general health of the camp population. Children also died of other childhood illnesses such as whooping cough, scarlet fever and meningitis (especially common in Mafeking), and several of these were exacerbated by measles.

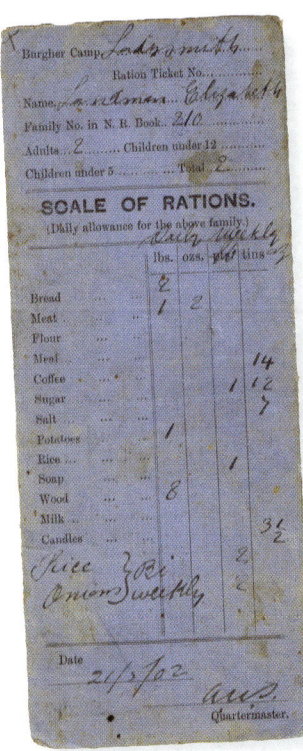

A CLASH OF CULTURES: BRITISH DOCTORS VERSUS BOER WOMEN

128 THE WAR AT HOME

ABOVE A universal reality of camp life: mourners at the Bethulie camp graveyard

OPPOSITE, TOP Tents of the Welsh hospital at the Springfontein camp – a philanthropic initiative funded by Christian humanitarians in Wales. Its medical staff included a British-educated Indian doctor, Umedran Lalbhai Desai.

BOTTOM Stiffly starched: nurses of the privately funded Second Irish Hospital

The most common causes of infant deaths were diarrhoea-related infections, and adults fell victim to typhoid, cancer and heart disease. 'Senile decay' accounted for a number of deaths of the elderly.

It is likely that the camp inmates suffered from many unrecorded complaints that were not lethal but would have weakened them. Colds and influenza were probably common in the winter of 1901. Judging by post-war accounts, many children had worms and similar parasites, and their poor diet would have resulted in ubiquitous tooth decay.

Some diseases are rarely mentioned in historical accounts, perhaps as a result of Victorian convention. As it was taboo to speak of sexual organs, women's ailments like cystitis, which must have arisen, never appeared in the records. References to puerperal fever are fairly uncommon even though doctors were particularly alert to its possible occurrence after childbirth, especially because they viewed Boer midwifery as unsanitary and uninformed.

Tuberculosis is also not often referred to in historical documents, although it was a scourge in Europe and the United States, increasing in Cape Town and widely discussed. Our understanding of the ailments that attacked the Boers in the camps may be only partial but the information is, nevertheless, more detailed than what we know about the pre-war Boer republics. The sources provide a fascinating glimpse into the health of a society in crisis.

Conflicting practices of medicine

As one historian has explained, 'culture creates the treatment if not the disease'.[3] The conflict between the British medical staff and the Boer women in the camps was influenced, not only by the medicine that they practised, but also by their social identities and cultural beliefs. The camps gave rise to residual bitterness among Afrikaners and this can be better understood if we realise that there was more involved than the tragic deaths, however traumatic they may have been. In addition, attempts by the British to control the deaths were perceived as an attack on the Boers' whole way of life.

By the end of the nineteenth century the British medical profession was held to be the moral and scientific arbiter of society. Leading Victorian commentators like Thomas Carlyle and Charles Kingsley accorded doctors the right to preach on social matters far beyond the field of health. Medical practitioners had achieved this position with some difficulty. Nineteenth-century Britain was still driven by class, and this affected medicine. At the top of the hierarchy were the London physicians, who, until about the mid-1800s, often had status but surprisingly little practical knowledge of the human body. But the camp doctors were not drawn from this group of men.

The camp doctors were surgeons and many were trained in Scotland, where their education was derived from the remarkable Scottish Enlightenment of the eighteenth century. They had originated from the emergent middle classes and had struggled to establish themselves in British society. George Eliot's character Dr Tertius Lydgate in

OPPOSITE Medical staff with one odd woman out: Dr Ella Scarlett, under a rakish hat and in khakis, was the Norvalspont camp doctor who also served on the Ladies' Commission on camp conditions.

BELOW Apprentices in Anglo-Saxon healthiness: nursing sisters Wessels (left) and Van Niekerk (right), trained by hard-headed Matron Bullin at the Springfontein camp hospital

Middlemarch is a wonderfully perceptive depiction of such a man – high-minded, clever, ambitious but financially insecure. By 1900 much of this struggle was over but there was by then a surplus of qualified practitioners in the United Kingdom. The doctors who volunteered for the camps were looking to the future and hoped to find employment in the new colonies. And a number of them managed to become district surgeons after the war.

One of the most important aspects of their education had been training in public health. They were heirs to the revolution that had demonstrated that mortality rates in Britain's industrial cities could be reduced by clean water supplies and good sanitation. This message was reinforced by Pasteur's germ theory and the work of Joseph Lister, the pioneer of antisepsis, who showed that hygiene was the key to combating lethal bacteria. The argument that cleanliness saved lives became ingrained into Victorian consciousness and acquired moral connotations. To be clean was to be virtuous, to be civilised, to be British. Dr John Ross of the eastern Cape, a descendant of Scottish missionaries, wrote in a handbook published in 1887:

> Attention to the laws of health is a public as well as a private duty … People must be taught that attention to public health is a moral duty, that cleanliness, avoidance of excess and health preservation go hand in hand with mental and moral training, and that morality consists as much in a hearty submission to the precepts of health as to the observation of creed.[4]

Camp doctors not only clashed with the Boers, but also with the superintendents. This conflict was usually about status and whose priorities took precedence. Dr John Hunter squabbled constantly with Captain Joseph Viner-Johnson, superintendent of the Kimberley camp, and made demands that infringed on Johnson's authority. Although unusually arrogant, Hunter reflected the views of the late-Victorian medical profession when he told Viner-Johnson: 'I am and will be always willing to consult and defer to your opinion when possible in your official capacity as Superintendent, and also as being an older man with a larger experience of the world, but I will certainly not submit to any interference from a layman in hospital or medical matters. I also wish to draw your attention to the fact that the care of the sick takes precedence of all.'[5]

Yet these doctors faced a dilemma. Confronted by the 'faded flowers', as Emily Hobhouse called the wasting children, the camp doctors could do very little. As 'agents of empire', supporting the British mission in the camps, they should have been able to cure the children. But they could not. In a defensive reaction, the doctors blamed the Boers themselves. Even today, the aspersions that the British cast on the Boers arouse a visceral anger in many Afrikaners. To understand what happened, it is necessary to disentangle the elements of this hostility.

Scapegoating or blaming someone else, usually an alien element in society, for infection is a feature of most epidemics. In the nineteenth century the British blamed various parties for the outbreak of disease: the Irish peasantry for the famine deaths; the Indians and Chinese for cholera and the plague pandemic of the 1890s; the British working classes for high mortality rates in industrial cities; and the Cape Muslims for smallpox in Cape Town in the 1850s and 1880s. In the camps British doctors felt helpless in the face of the growing number of deaths and it was inevitable that they blamed the Boers for the deaths of their own children. In addition the British naturally believed that their enemy, the Boers, would be in the wrong. Such is the propaganda of war – one does not fight against people who are in the right.

The scapegoating involved vilifying two aspects of Boer life: their personal hygiene and mothering abilities. The first criticism has created the most anger because Afrikaners resent the suggestion that they were a 'dirty' people. The aspersion arose partly from the British officials' perception of Boer medical practices, which they viewed with distaste. These perceived deficiencies were written about in the published Blue Book reports, officially issued by the War Office for the information of Parliament but also distributed to the public.

An aspect of modern biomedicine that affected camp medical policy was the growing importance of the hospital. Before the recognition of the role of germs in infection, hospitals were lethal places. Only the poor, who could not afford home care, entered them. Florence Nightingale is widely associated with the reform of the hospitals and she created sanitary places where well-trained, middle-class 'ladies' cared for the sick. Although Nightingale and her followers did much to reorganise hospitals, they remained conservative in other ways. She did not challenge the gender relationships of the day, and nurses were subordinated to doctors. Although nurses were, in one sense, modern women, they were also expected to be docile and obedient to male authority.

But the transformation of hospitals, which began in the 1850s, took decades to be

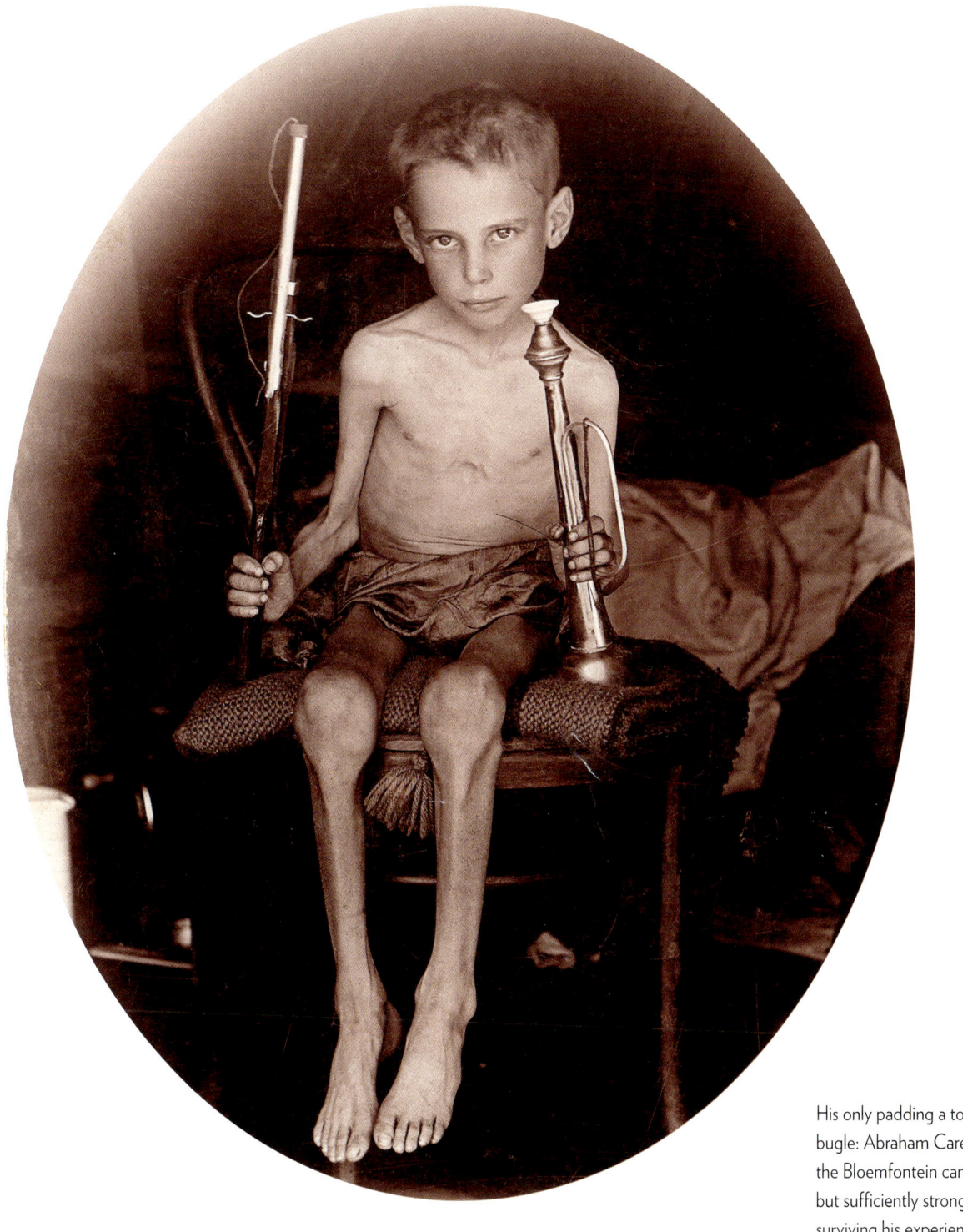

His only padding a toy gun and bugle: Abraham Carel Wessels at the Bloemfontein camp, emaciated but sufficiently strong to end up surviving his experience

accepted. As late as the 1890s, the British working classes still resisted hospitalisation, and hospital practices, such as restricted visiting hours, seemed cold-hearted to many people. The middle classes continued to be nursed at home, by private nurses if necessary, until surgery was sufficiently advanced to require sophisticated operating theatres. Therefore hospitals remained places that were entered reluctantly until almost the end of the century. Women, in particular, felt disempowered in hospitals because they were not permitted to take care of their own children. For the medical professions, however, hospitals enabled them to control the management of the sick more effectively.

The camps provided ideal laboratories to demonstrate the value of modern British

Looking crisp and out in force: medical staff at the Winburg camp

medicine. Enforced hospitalisation ensured that the sick received regular medication, correct dosages and appropriate diets. The doctors regarded this as vital care for typhoid patients because in the tents they could not prevent infection or stop the women from feeding patients with unsuitable food. Also, measles patients fared better in hospital, as the hospital marquees and buildings were more insulated than the overcrowded, leaking tents. Although the records are not adequate enough to demonstrate incontrovertibly the superiority of hospital care, the case of the Mafeking camp suggests that this played a role in reducing deaths.

In Mafeking, measles was introduced by a group of families from Taung who entered the camp in August 1901. The disease spread through the camp like wildfire and Mafeking achieved the unenviable reputation of being the camp with the highest mortality rate from measles in a single month. The investigations that followed revealed that although the senior camp doctor was conscientious and hard-working, he was a poor administrator. The camp was severely understaffed and many of the children who died from measles were in the tents and had not seen a doctor for over a week. The introduction of an efficient medical administrator brought the epidemic to an abrupt end.

The advantages of modern biomedicine were not obvious to most camp inmates. The British regarded their resistance as particularly unenlightened, although they knew that such opposition had also occurred in the United Kingdom. Some of the republican Boers in the camps were educated people. Professionals like Dr John Bernard Voortman, who had served first in a Boer ambulance and later in the Bethulie camp, were often British trained and shared the medical ethos of the British doctors – if not their political mission. But these men were in the minority and most of the camp inmates were rural peasantry with limited education. They had survived for three centuries in a harsh and isolated African environment by drawing on medical knowledge inherited from seventeenth-century Europe and experience from the landscape around them.

Despite some major scientific advances, seventeenth-century medicine had been largely based on the tradition acquired from classical Greece, which had become modified in its passage through medieval Christian Europe and the Spanish Muslim world. In essence, this ancient Galenic system was concerned with bringing the 'humours' of the body into harmony by controlling its secretions and excretions. This tradition had been considerably modified and the Boers inherited fragments of the system, with little understanding of the philosophy that underlay it. The Boers do not seem to have practised bleeding (unlike Jeremiah Goldswain, a British 1820 settler in the eastern Cape) but regularly practised the sweating out of fevers. Louis Tregardt recorded this in his diary and it also happened in the camps – the British complained about the Boers closing up the tents and covering patients in rugs.

Some form of herbal or natural medicine is generally practised in every society, no matter how advanced it might be. With limited access to pharmaceutical products, the Boers turned to the world around them. Their knowledge was most likely acquired through both experience and interaction with indigenous people, and they created a large range of remedies. Some

BELOW Washing at the Standerton camp hospital

BOTTOM The Norvalspont camp hospital, laid out in neat lines

A CLASH OF CULTURES: BRITISH DOCTORS VERSUS BOER WOMEN

ABOVE Opposed to the camp hospitals, many Boer women clung to traditional cures and induced the sick to sweat out their ailment, closing tents and covering victims with warm bedding.

OPPOSITE Boer women used wild plants, like saffron (top) and *kakiebos* (centre) to manufacture their own traditional home medicines.
BOTTOM Curing by numbers: portable medicine box in wartime use by the Red Cross

of these have been passed down orally and others have been recorded by local museums. However, the main reference source is a volume entitled *Volksgeneeskuns in Suid-Afrika* produced by the South African Academy for Science and Art.[6] Its compilation is an indication of the continuing importance of traditional Boer remedies to Afrikaner ethnic identity. It also reflects the pride that Afrikaners take in the qualities of initiative and self-sufficiency.

It is usual for people to assume that folk therapies are derived mainly from plants and herbal infusions. The introduction of *Volksgeneeskuns* refers, for instance, to *Digitalis purpurea* (foxglove), *Sutherlandia frutescens* (cancer bush) and similar well-known and sometimes effective plants. In the camps, however, the Boers had little access to such vegetation. Many of the remedies were derived from the fynbos biome of the western Cape and there was no *buchu* on the Highveld. The terrain of the camps was often arid, unfamiliar and rendered barren from the search for fuel. One of the few references in the camp literature to herbal medicines is the mention of using eucalyptus – an alien gum tree that is native to Australia and an intrinsic part of South Africa's landscape. Nevertheless, the Boers used a range of other products, from household chemicals to animal parts and excrement. In *Volksgeneeskuns*, for example, there are 54 remedies for snake bites, including brandy, other spirits, the flesh of live or dead fowl, garlic and onion. It is also suggested

136   THE WAR AT HOME

that the bite be cut open and Condy's Crystals (potassium permanganate), turpentine or various infusions be applied. The remedy of drinking human urine was perhaps the most distasteful to the modern mind.

There are 71 remedies for measles listed in *Volksgeneeskuns* – another sign that the Boers were familiar with this disease. *Volksgeneeskuns* lists sources but not dates so it is impossible to know when or where the measles remedies were applied. Some of the therapies suggested are familiar, sensible and harmless. Aletta van den Berg favoured saffron while Mrs S. de Kok advocated *kakiebos* (*Tagetes minuta*), a plant introduced into South Africa from Argentina only during the Anglo-Boer War. Sour milk, warm wine, sorghum beer and sulphur are cited regularly. Some recipes are precise: 'Smear hard fat onto red flannel, grind cloves and scatter one teaspoon on the flannel, scrape camphor onto it and one knife point of red powder and a couple of drops of turpentine and castor oil. Spread evenly and place on chest.'[7]

On the other hand, more than 22 of these remedies contain goat dung. By far the most popular formula, provided by 15 people, states: 'Take fresh goat dung from the cattle yard. Add water to it. Let it cool. Drain the mixture well and give half a cup every hour to the feverish person until he breaks out in a sweat. Then give half a cup of warm wine.'[8] Aletta van den Berg insisted that the dung should come from a goat on the veld or a mountain, not the farmyard. She mixed her *mis* (dung) with *wonderessens*.[9]

Emily Hobhouse dismissed British criticisms of remedies like these. She was familiar with similar folk practices among her father's parishioners in Cornwall. She explained that investigation had shown that the green paint smeared on a child (Dr Kendal Franks, a military doctor commissioned to inspect the camps, had been appalled) was merely eucalyptus. But Hobhouse was being disingenuous. Alice Gomme, a notable British folklorist, was fascinated by accounts of Boer medicine when they were published in the British Blue Books. Although these reports were intended to portray the primitive nature of Boer life, she compared them to similar practices in England. The British working classes and country people were as reluctant as any Boer to expose their sick children to fresh air or water. She observed that

> when some of my own children were ill with measles, a nurse I had in the house told me that children with measles should not be washed nor their bed-linen changed for the first week; and that the sun should be excluded from the room, otherwise they might be made blind for life; and that in her mother's time the children would be put to bed in their clothes, and these would not be changed until after the third day.[10]

On another occasion the leg of a man suffering from blood poisoning was saved by the careful application of fresh cattle dung. The nurse who recounted this story to Gomme had obtained her knowledge from her grandmother, a village doctor. It was 'much resorted to by villagers for miles round the place where she lived in Yorkshire'.[11] The contentious green paint, Gomme suspected, was used in lieu of a green liquid made from plants, the origin of which had been long forgotten.

A CLASH OF CULTURES: BRITISH DOCTORS VERSUS BOER WOMEN

Our information on the use of herbs and animal excrement comes mostly from British sources. Therefore, it is impossible to know how much these remedies were favoured, although *Volksgeneeskuns* certainly suggests a broad popularity. But their use may also reflect the fact that there were limited products available to the camp Boers. Patent medicines were considered to be more important and the Boers brought these with them from their homes, bought them in camp stores or smuggled them in from nearby villages. The women's testimonies refer to them regularly.

Patent medicines have been widely utilised for many centuries. Initially the Boers in the Cape used Halle medicines, originally produced and distributed by an orphanage in Halle in Germany. The opening paragraphs of the diary of Louis Tregardt were devoted to an explanation of the value of these medicines, especially '*Essentia dulcis*'. By 1900 Halle medicines had been replaced by *Huis Apotheek*, which came in a box with instructions for the use of the various items. Many women could not read and, in these cases, the family relied on the appearance of the bottles and their places in the box in order to identify them.[12] Old people, it has been claimed, 'knew exactly when green bitter medicine (*groen amara*) or white emetic would be more appropriate'.[13]

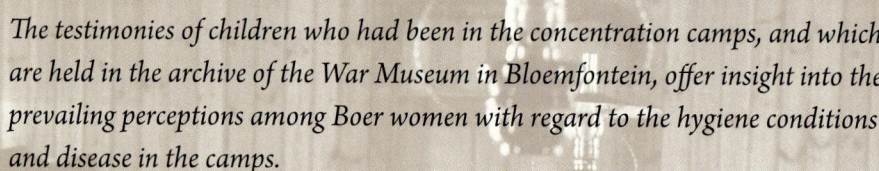

The testimonies of children who had been in the concentration camps, and which are held in the archive of the War Museum in Bloemfontein, offer insight into the prevailing perceptions among Boer women with regard to the hygiene conditions and disease in the camps.

Johanna Elizabeth Opperman (née Van Strÿp), an orphan, described the conditions in the Irene camp: 'The camp was divided into six sections. One whole section had to share a single [zinc] bath that stood in a tent. There was no soap or disinfectants. My aunt never took us to bath us there because she was afraid that we would catch infectious diseases. We were washed in a small basin in our tent.'

S.L. Prinsloo, another child inmate, wrote as follows about children dying in the camp: 'The general view was that if a child went to hospital, he or she wouldn't return. I had measles. My mom positioned herself at the door of the tent. When she saw the nurse who was coming to investigate whether there were ill people, she told me, "Get down under the bed." I had to lie there until the nurse had gone past.'

According to **Susara Magrieta Susanna Holder** (née Coetzee), her mother was so desperately worried about her sick children that she would follow just about any advice: 'All of us had whooping cough, and one old lady told her, "Take your children to the river and let them sit in the running water." My mom replied, "Ag, tante, I've already lost two children and I don't want to lose these ones too." Mom later took us to the river anyway, and she reckoned that we got better.'

The British doctors were critical of these medicines, partly because they knew that many women handed them out indiscriminately, but also because several contained opium. The Ladies' Committee attempted to ban them from the camps. It is likely that the British were aware, however, that opium products and other, more dubious, patent medicines were widely available in Britain. One such opiate, Godfrey's Cordial, was a popular remedy to soothe children, and Chlorodyne, recommended to the teachers coming to the camps, contained laudanum, tincture of cannabis and chloroform. But such undesirable ingredients could be excluded more easily in the controlled environment of the camps.

The daily habits of the Boers were under fire as well as their practice of medicine. Obviously camp conditions made it difficult to maintain standards of hygiene and the British were well aware of this. As the camps developed, better latrines were introduced and night toilets were put closer to the tents. Clean water became readily available and, as health improved, the task of keeping the camps clean became easier. But the hygiene issue is obscured both by camp propaganda and by perspectives from a very different era.

We live in an age in which consumer advertising advocates that homes should be as sterile as operating theatres and the faintest human odour is regarded as reprehensible. It would be impossible to reproduce or even comprehend the odours of the past. It may be difficult to imagine, but the magnificence of the court of Louis XIV at Versailles came with a complete absence of sanitation and personal hygiene. Cape Town was a dirty, smelly place in the late nineteenth century, even after domestic running water became available and an effective sewerage system had been established. Relatively few people had bathrooms and middle-class homeowners in Woodstock fertilised their orchards with human excrement. Men often chewed coarse tobacco and spat in the streets and on public transport. There were spittoons in gentlemen's clubs and Paul Kruger even had one in his home.

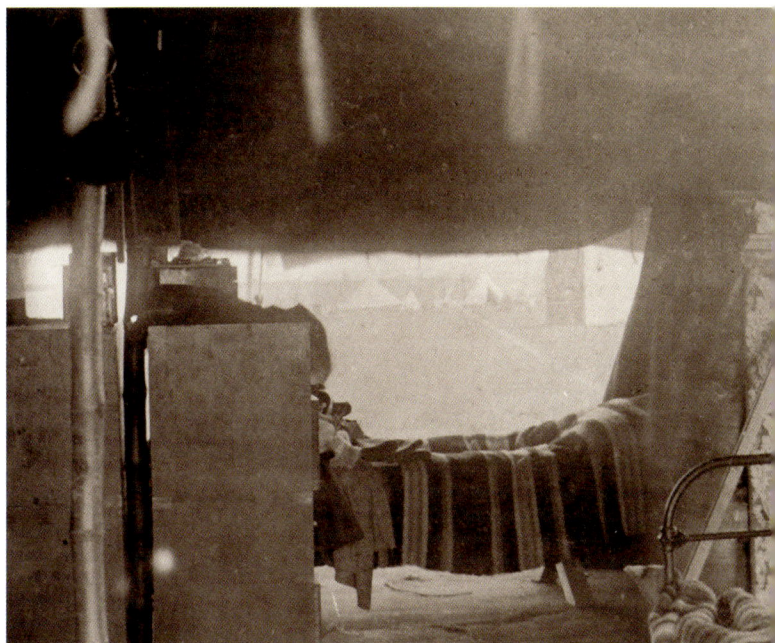

A rare glimpse of the inside of a tent in one of the camps.

A lack of sanitary infrastructure and the acceptance of a less sterile environment continued into the twentieth century in civilised Europe. In 1960s Britain, some working-class homes still lacked bathrooms and country people in less developed parts of Ireland sometimes had no toilets at all. It is unreasonable to believe that the Boers were any different from many other societies of the day in their approach to cleanliness. They were excoriated by the British for behaviour that was commonplace as a result of wartime propaganda, combined with the very real fear of typhoid epidemics. British diatribes need to be distinguished from the day-to-day realities of camp life and the struggle to maintain effective sanitation.

The critical attacks on Boer women's maternal prowess came from a different quarter. By 1900 the British were becoming concerned about their infant mortality rates, which were not decreasing. The concern about sickly infants became part of a larger debate about the

TOP Nursing sisters at the Springfontein camp deciding on a spot for their tent with the aid of some army officers.

ABOVE Hospital staff, including two black assistants, in front of their work place in one of the camps.

degeneration of the British working classes after the war (giving rise to a well-known commission of inquiry on the poor quality of military recruits). From 1900 the medical journals are filled with articles debating the causes of infant deaths. As well as the identification of pathogens, discussion focused increasingly on the ignorance of British mothers, their failure to feed their children properly and the problems associated with bottle feeding. When they attacked the incompetence of Boer mothers, the British camp doctors were joining in this debate and working through some of the issues that would be at the forefront of British medical thought in post-war years.

The British authorities considered these to be women's issues and, by 1900, believed that their own educated women could play a role in educating the Boers. In this regard, the teachers and nurses who were selected for service in the camps were chosen as representatives of their nation as much as for their training. Most of these women were from the middle or lower-middle classes. They were mainly in their early thirties, unmarried and professionally qualified. They were expected to represent the best qualities of British womanhood. Many did so. They worked hard, performed their tasks conscientiously and shared the discomfort of camp conditions with the Boers – they lived in similar accommodation and shared rations. Some became ill from hard work and a number died. Sadly, the dedication of these people has been forgotten and is largely unstated in post-war history.

In the women's testimonies, the nurses were usually depicted as heartless, careless, slovenly or incompetent. It is difficult to reconcile the conflicting sources, although it is clear that some of the nurses were unsuitable. Alcoholism was sometimes a problem experienced by both nurses and doctors. Nurses could be abrasive and ill-tempered, like Nurse Madeleine Allen of the Heilbron camp and Sister Adcock in Bloemfontein. Dr Neil Pern was relieved when Adcock left and wished he could get rid of Mrs Ilbery as well. Nurse McLeod seemed to have quarrelled with everyone. As a result she was transferred from camp to camp until she was finally dismissed.[14]

The apparent callousness of the nurses may have been the result of poor communication combined with a lack of empathy. The British nurses did not speak Dutch or Afrikaans and neither they nor the teachers had much understanding of the ordeals the Boer women had endured. One of the Kimberley nurses remarked that the women she had encountered were more warm-hearted than she expected. She found them 'amusing' because they were singing hymns all day.[15] On the other hand, the nurses sent by the Dutch government could speak the language and were highly regarded, like Sister Bakkes in the Winburg camp, who was loved and seen as a ray of light.

Aloof but on the same level: the British nurses, like other officials, such as the camp administrators, generally shared the same spartan conditions and rough environment as the inmates.

The history of the high mortality rate in the camps has been muddied by misunderstanding – the product of a sense of superiority and lack of understanding on the one hand, and ignorance, depression, fear and anger, on the other. Most doctors and nurses worked hard to reduce disease and death. Their failure stemmed from the lack of planning for the camps, something for which they were not responsible themselves. Under the circumstances of poor accommodation, overcrowding and inadequate nutrition, some form of epidemic disease was inevitable. But it was a tragedy for the Boers that the attack came in the form of measles, which was highly infectious, lethal and difficult to treat. Even with modern medical knowledge applied in the camps, mortality rates rose to levels that were unprecedented in the Boers' experience. It is hardly surprising that the Boers rejected methods that seemed callous, coercive and ineffective.

At the same time, when Emily Hobhouse dismissed Boer medical practices as those of simple country people, she had the political motive of gathering sympathy for the Boer women and the hardships they were experiencing. Similarly, doctors like Franks chose to emphasise the uncivilised nature of Boer remedies in order to demonstrate the superiority of British civilisation. They were most likely aware that modern science had also not penetrated British society very deeply. But the camps were ideal showcases in which the seemingly dangerous medical methods of the Boers could be contrasted with the modern sophistication of middle-class Britain. In castigating the Boers, the doctors in the camps had a message, not only for the Boers, but for their own people as well.

CHAPTER SIX

'Faded flowers'? Children in the concentration camps

SE DUFF

PREVIOUS PAGE Children in their school classroom at the Bloemfontein camp. In the words of early-twentieth-century American poet Theodore Roethke, these pupils 'have known the inexorable sadness of pencils'.

THIS PAGE Grim prospects lie ahead for this group of refugee children waiting to be taken to one of the camps, where the greatest incidence of deaths was among the very young.

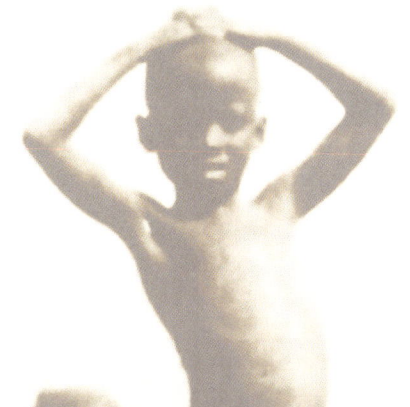

In April 1902, 12-year-old Machteld Nel was moved from the Potchefstroom concentration camp with her mother and siblings. They were taken to the newly opened Jacobs camp in Durban. Machteld was a niece of J.P. Schutte, a member of the Transvaal Volksraad, who had accompanied Paul Kruger into exile in the Netherlands. In a letter to her uncle and aunt, Machteld acknowledged that their new accommodation was 'much healthier than at other places' and also more comfortable because they lived in houses rather than tents. But most of the letter was devoted to a description of the camp's surroundings. She wrote excitedly: 'Aunt, we can see the sea from here, and I have already visited it twice – it is a wonderful thing to see.' She added that 'Mum has also been up to the bluff where all the ships arrive'.[1]

Machteld and her family had been held for almost a year in the Potchefstroom camp, where they had all contracted measles, struggled to find enough food to eat and witnessed the deaths of several family members. Her mother wrote despairingly to Machteld's uncle: 'Oh brother, death rules us here, and there are so many dead and I cannot name them all.'[2] Machteld's father was being held in a prisoner-of-war camp and the location of various members of their extended family was unknown. In contrast – even though Machteld's mother and brother were ill, and their cousins missing – their move to the better-run Jacobs camp felt like a holiday, especially because it was close to the sea.

Machteld told her uncle and aunt what she was going to do during the day: 'Uncle, a school has been established here – Andries attends already and I think I shall also go on Monday.'[3] This was one of the many camp schools established for the Boer children. They formed part of Lord Milner's strategy to anglicise Boer society by teaching English to children in the camps. In the eyes of the British authorities, Machteld and her siblings shifted from being simply refugees that should be kept away from the conflict (her brothers were seen as potential Boer soldiers) to being malleable future subjects of a South Africa under British control. White children became valuable to the colonial authorities.

Indeed, the value of interned white children has extended into the twentieth and twenty-first centuries. They have been central to the ways in which the Boer concentration camps have been remembered. The photograph of an emaciated Lizzie van Zyl, who died in May 1901, a few months after her portrait was taken, has become emblematic of Boer women and children's suffering in the camps. It has also become symbolic of the British neglect and mismanagement that led to the deaths of approximately 27 000 people in the camps (around 22 000 of them under the age of 16), and of the Boers' inability to prevent such

suffering among their own families. It should be noted, however, that the mortality rates of children in the black camps were as bad as, if not worse than, those of white children. Between June 1901 and October 1902, it was estimated that 5 160 of the 6 345 deaths – more than 80 per cent – recorded in black African camps in the Transvaal were children. Between September and December 1901, 3 093 of the 3 832 reported deaths in the Orange River Colony's black camps were children.[4]

After visiting the Bloemfontein camp in January 1901, Emily Hobhouse wrote: 'I can't describe what it is to see these children lying about in a state of collapse. It's just exactly like faded flowers thrown away.'[5] Her description of Boer children as 'faded flowers' is precisely how the interned white children have been remembered. They were the innocent, suffering victims of adult selfishness and incompetence. This powerful view of the Boer children's experiences remains prevalent in the present day. Writing in March 2013, a journalist from *Die Burger* argued that little has been written about children's toys during the Anglo-Boer War because children died at such an astonishing rate in the camps that toys were not part of their day-to-day existence.[6] This is fundamentally untrue and there is ample evidence to suggest that children did play in the camps.

But this perception of the camp children as victims is not a recent phenomenon. From around mid-1901, the South African and British publics were acutely aware of the

146 THE WAR AT HOME

personal grievance against the British was not unusual among girls of the same age. John Fourie, a resident of Aberdeen, noted in his diary in September 1901:

> Mrs Niel P. Fouché and family (women and children only) had to appear before the Commandant this morning, because they did not open the door on Saturday night, when the Tommies were hammering at it. When Mrs F. asked who it was, they would not answer, and when they broke the door a little daughter of Mrs F. about 12 years of age through [sic] at them with an axe.[21]

Although there are very few recorded examples of civilian children physically attacking soldiers, this incident demonstrates that when children – particularly Boer ones – entered the concentration camps, they often did so with awareness of the politics of the war and with strong views about its legitimacy. This was also influenced by the presence of Boer children on the battlefields. During the first half of the war, many Boer fighters were accompanied by their wives and children on commando. These Boer children, in addition to the boys who joined the republics' war effort as soldiers, were witnesses to the conflict. Therefore it is not surprising that many Boer children in the camps believed that they were participants in the war, not merely innocent victims.

The scorched-earth policy was seen as punishing Boer women and children for the republics' refusal to surrender. Even though Boer children often engaged in small acts of resistance against British authorities (described below), they, and the interned black children, suffered physically and psychologically in the camps. In many cases, this simply buttressed the children's hatred of the British, and their own sense of being equally involved in the conflict.

Trauma in the camps

The names given to babies born in the concentration camps memorialised Boer women's sorrow in the camps. The baptismal records kept by the Dutch Reformed Church demonstrate that babies were given the names of their parents and grandparents. This may have been a defiant attempt to maintain Boer society through a naming tradition, but it was also influenced by the distress of women in the camps. When visiting the Bloemfontein camp in early 1901, Hobhouse was asked by a new mother to name her baby: 'I suggested "Dolores," or, what I thought would be better still, "Hope". But the sad, sick mother can see no hope, and chose "Dolores" for her little child.'[22]

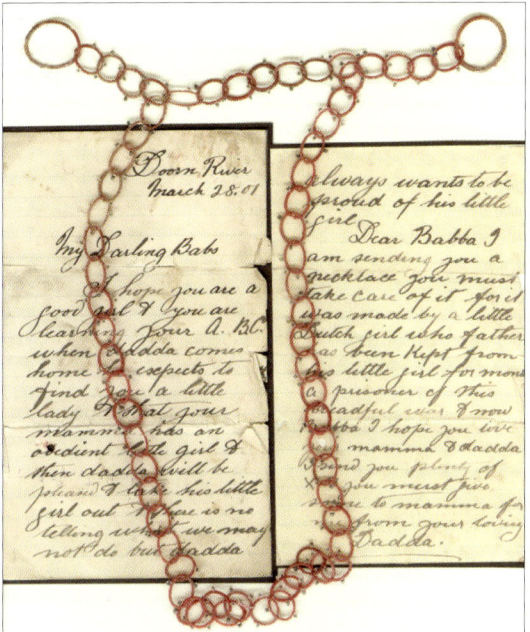

This necklace was made by a Boer girl and given to a humane British soldier, who sent it to his daughter in March 1901, urging her to treat it with care, as it had been made by 'a little Dutch girl whose father had been kept from his little girl for months, a prisoner of this dreadful war'.

To be surrounded by death, as Machteld Nel's mother wrote, is deeply painful for any person, but for children who had lost their siblings and their parents, the experience of the camps constituted a psychological and physical trauma. Children could not be shielded from the deaths around them. They participated in funerals, often carrying the coffins or, when coffins could not be made, the shrouded corpses of deceased children. As a young girl, M.E. Kilian, a survivor of the camps, watched her mother die in their tent. Afterwards, she wrapped her corpse in a sheet and arranged for it to be removed: 'A weak breeze caused a corner of the sheet to flap, as if she was waving goodbye to us. I held the baby, as we six orphans stood there.'[23]

Exceptionally young combatants taken prisoner of war by the British. Pieter Willem Pieterse (front row, third from left) was aged 11 and shunted from camp to camp.

Compounding this, some families were split up when they were moved to the camps. Revd E. Farmer, who visited the black refugee camp at Krugersdorp, reported that 'families are separated … there is no knowing if fathers or mothers, sisters and even wives, certainly many husbands, are alive or safe'.[24] Orphaned children were looked after by relatives, former neighbours or even strangers whom they had met in the camps. New families were formed when mothers or older sisters took care of those children without families. It is little wonder, therefore, that Boer children were occasionally accused of being rowdy and unruly, with 'objectionable language and habits'. This was worsened by families' cramped living conditions. One despairing mother commented, 'I have not even room to punish my boy when he is naughty.'[25] Camps were enormous and, to children, frightening places where they were easily lost, and where busy mothers or older siblings could not be as attentive as they were normally. Children suffered injuries, ranging from fingers caught in furniture to falling into open fires. They were dirty; they had infestations of fleas and lice; they wore ragged hand-me-downs; and food was scarce.

Children's lengthy separation from their parents and siblings led to their additional hardship of not being able to recognise close relatives – particularly fathers who had been away on commando or interned in prisoner-of-war camps. One woman admitted that she didn't recognise her own father when he returned from Ceylon and collected her and her siblings from the Pietersburg camp. Another was frightened of the 'strange uncle' who returned to them.[26]

There were also boys in prisoner-of-war camps. Lenie Boshoff-Liebenberg spent part of the war in the Klerksdorp and Howick camps, and her younger brother, who was then

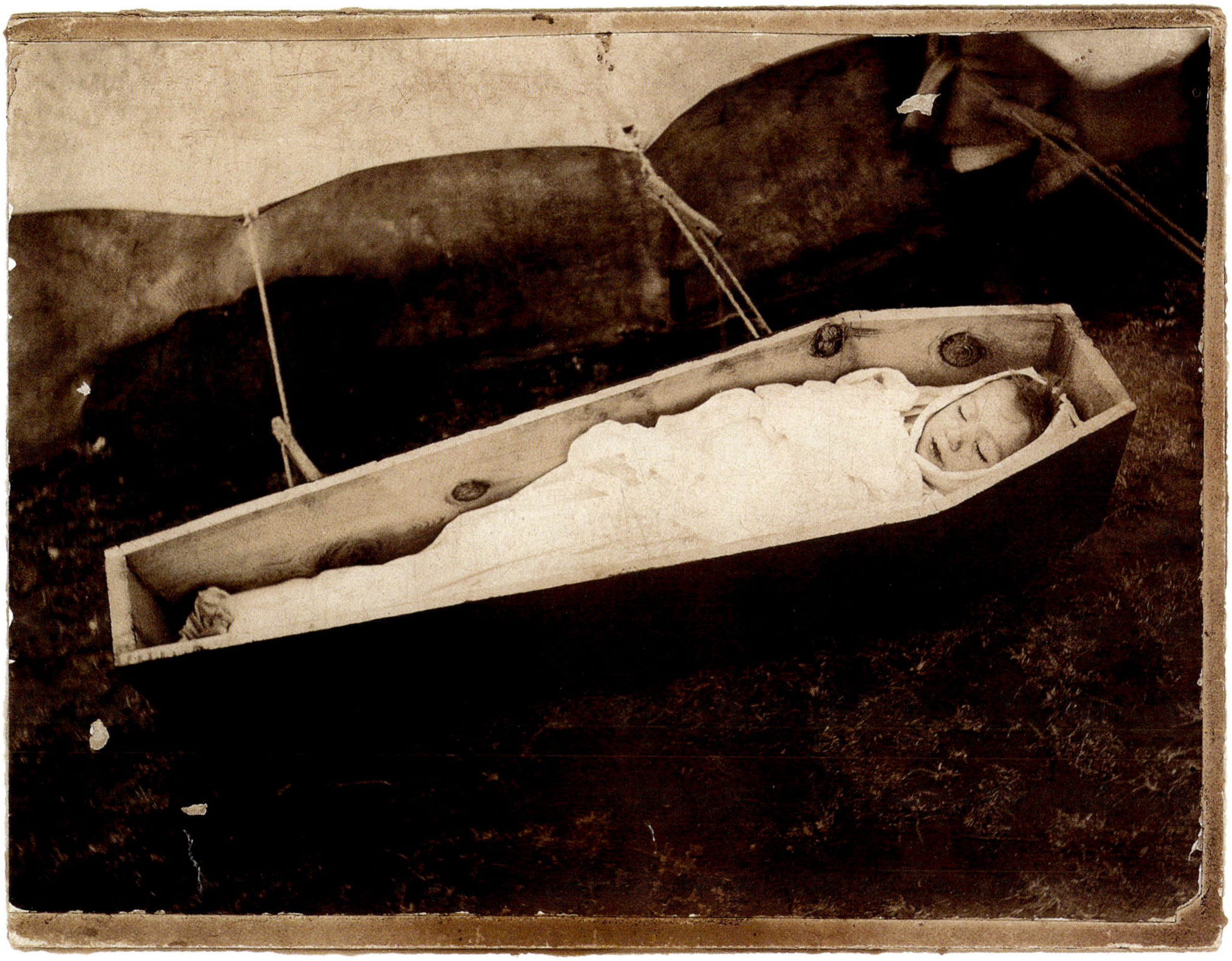

One of the most haunting and enduring images of the war: the body of three-year-old Japie Berg of the Bloemfontein camp lies just outside the tent in which he died, awaiting burial. Although his fate would be used as sentimental folklore, what his corpse signifies is not allegorical but real. He was a simple victim of the war at home, dying a cruelly premature death. The screw was his favourite plaything, which he had asked his mother to give to his father.

12 years old, ran away to join his older male relatives on commando in 1901. The following year, he and other prisoners of war were sent to India, where he got sunstroke. Much of Lenie's rage against the British stemmed from the fact that her 13-year-old brother had returned profoundly altered by the experience: 'After he returned, he was not the same Isak anymore. No, everything was strange.'[27]

Children also experienced trauma before arriving in the camps, which contributed to their compromised health. Not only did children witness their homes, possessions and livestock being destroyed by British troops, but they also withstood journeys to the camps that were lengthy, uncomfortable and badly provisioned – they sometimes went without food for days at a time. Many travelled in open wagons or train carriages and there are several accounts of young infants, some of them born on the journey, dying of dehydration and heat exhaustion. Margaret Marquard wrote:

> The Fourie people were brought to town in one party, on open wagons, without having granted them the opportunity of getting food prepared for the journey. Once on the road a little tinned beef was given, and once a plate of flour to the women to make something for the younger children … When they got to some bad pools of water there was no restraining the children: they would drink, hungry and thirsty as they were. Of these 20 children nearly every one took very ill with dysentery after reaching town: the only child of Piet Fourie, about two years old, died on Wednesday 3 October.[28]

She refers a few times to children being responsible for collecting their siblings and property before being moved to the camps. For instance, in late 1900, Mrs Jan Geldenhuys travelled from her farm to Winburg to do some shopping. There, she was detained by British soldiers and her 'little girl' was sent 'out with two natives and two carts to fetch the other seven children'. They were all destined for the Bloemfontein camp. In a similar case, widow Cronjé from the Senekal district was not permitted to leave Winburg, and was directed to send her young son and 'native out with the cart and mules' to collect her remaining three children.[29]

Although these incidents were distressing to these children and their parents, it gave them unprecedented agency and power over their siblings, servants and other adults. Wars turn societies upside down. Women take up employment and the socially marginalised are allowed positions of authority – as was the case with children.

Capture the children: Life in the concentration camps

The suffering of children was only one – albeit significant – part of camp life. We know that children also played, worked and went to school. There are records of Boer children having fun in the camps and these accounts help us to understand some of the dynamics of camp life. One camp survivor explained: 'For me, as a child, the camp was wonderful, and the Tommies were very good to us.' Her family did not go hungry because her two unmarried aunts were permitted to leave the Volksrust camp to earn money in town. With these funds, as well as those of her wealthy grandparents, the family was able to buy food and other provisions. She was also the only child among a group of adults and had the undivided attention of her grandmother, who had raised her since her mother died before the war.[30]

In this case, wealth and, possibly, being politically well connected, cushioned a white, middle-class girl's experience of camp life. Social divisions outside of the camps were replicated to some extent within them.

One of the most visible groups of young people in the camps were white, educated middle-class girls in their late teens. These young women, many of whom spoke English fluently, often took on positions of significant authority in their own households and the camps. They spoke on behalf of their parents; they earned money, usually through washing and sewing, which could be used to buy food, clothing and other essentials; and they became nurses and, later, teachers. Their education and the confidence gained from shouldering responsibility meant that these girls could mediate between Boer inmates and the British authorities. Lenie Boshoff-Liebenberg, whose wealthy middle-class family received slightly better treatment on account of their social standing, organised a petition demanding better rations, particularly for sick children. She took it to the camp superintendent, who agreed, after some argument, to provide inmates with more meat.

Boshoff-Liebenberg's mild insubordination was tolerated because she – and similar young women – were of the same class as the British men with whom they dealt. The British did not deal so leniently with similar resistance from children who were less well off or

The simple joy of childhood fantasies: porcelain dolls from the Netherlands sent as Christmas gifts to children by Dutch republican sympathisers (top) and a toy tea set belonging to six-year-old Helena Burger at the Winburg camp (bottom).

Children had to shoulder a share of the burden. Here, boys carry firewood to their family tents at the Bloemfontein camp.

well connected. Perhaps this is why there are many references to young boys from poor families running away from the camps. Hobhouse referred to three boys, two of them aged 13 and nine, and none of them with wealthy parents, who had escaped after a British soldier had – apparently jokingly – threatened to send them to the prisoner-of-war camp in Ceylon for being naughty.

Hobhouse was particularly alert to class difference, and distinguished between 'ladies of refinement and wealth, and … the wives of poor men'. She was especially concerned about the daughters of these wealthier families, who would normally have attended schools like the Huguenot Seminary: 'I want very much to take the best class of young girls out of camp and place them in boarding schools. The mothers cannot bear to see their girls, month after month, idle in these camps. The life seems to be very demoralising owing to its purposelessness, and this camp in particular is quite bad for young girls.'[31]

She identified four middle-class girls, between 13 and 18 years old, in the Bloemfontein camp who were willing to go to school. They were sent to the Midlands Seminary in Graaff-Reinet (a branch of the Huguenot Seminary) for six months. While Hobhouse was interested only in assisting the daughters of wealthy families, and most of the girls whom she sent to school had well-off parents, others were equally concerned that the majority of camp children were living in idleness. Yet evidence demonstrates that children were certainly not 'idle'. They helped their mothers and other women, queued for rations, caught fish and small animals for food, swam and played games. One man remembered children pretending to be on commando. Boys in the Barberton camp played marbles

Developing educated young subjects of the British Empire: two school classrooms at the Bloemfontein camp

using the stones from fruit, pebbles and other small objects. From time to time, there were also organised activities. On Christmas Day in 1900, the Bloemfontein camp held a sports meeting and concert. On King Edward VII's birthday the following year, there were three-legged races, a high-jump contest, a tug-of-war and a choral competition. In December 1901, the camp superintendent organised a picnic for the children of the camp.

In spite of all this activity, Hobhouse, the British authorities and even the Dutch Reformed Church were concerned that children were not productively engaged. When writing about efforts to reform South Africa's education systems after the war, Lawrence Richardson observed that there was 'a desire on the part of many to "capture the children" by using schooling to form a new generation of white South Africans who were happy subjects of the British Empire'.[32] This thinking was evident during the conflict as well. The first officially sanctioned concentration-camp school was opened in the Norvalspont camp in February 1901. Under Edmund Beale Sargant, the director of education for the Transvaal and Orange River Colony, schools were established in the majority of camps in the Transvaal and Orange Free State, as well as in two Cape and six Natal camps. Between November 1901 and May 1902, the numbers of children in the Transvaal camps more than doubled and grew from 7 689 to 17 213. In the Orange Free State, almost 10 000 of the 13 000 Boer children in the camps were attending school.

A game played everywhere in the world, including concentration camps: marbles belonging to J.G.B. Fourie from the Brandfort camp

Given that the teaching medium in these schools was English – even though most of the teachers were Afrikaans-speaking – and that

160   THE WAR AT HOME

An outdoor gathering of a large group of children in an unidentified camp

attendance was never made compulsory, the popularity of the schools seems puzzling at first. The purpose of the schools was to

> end the 'retrogression' of the Boers, making them outward-looking and open to 'progress' and 'modern civilisation'. 'Next to the composition of the population, the thing that matters most is its education', said Milner, '… Everything that makes South African children look outside South Africa and realise the world makes for peace.'[33]

School buildings were hastily constructed and ramshackle. They did not have desks, books, chalk, blackboards and other basics. They were soon overcrowded with children varying enormously in age and ability. The high attendance rate was due partly to parents' eagerness to send their children to school. In some camps, superintendents went from tent to tent explaining to adults why their children should learn English and attend classes regularly. However, the children also enjoyed going to school. It is particularly telling that many camp survivors could still, in old age, recite the poems and songs they had learnt in the schools. One woman remembered that she liked school so much that she refused to go home: 'I remember to this day how I leant against the school's wall and cried because I did not want to return home, but wanted to go to school. How proud I was of what I had learned and I can still remember one recitation which we were taught.'[34]

In the chaos and disorder of camp life, the schools provided children with routine, stimulation and the undivided attention of adults. Even if they could not understand their teachers, they were still entertained by, and interested in, their lessons.

Similarly, many children attended the prayer meetings, Christian Endeavour Societies, catechism classes and Sunday Schools established by the Dutch Reformed Church. Although parents tended to insist that their children attend these activities, it is striking how many children went regularly to Sunday School. In the Howick camp, the Sunday School was 1 200 strong, the Merebank camp's Sunday School employed 130 teachers for 2 650 children and at the Wentworth camp there were 35 teachers and 1 298 children. Like the British authorities, the Dutch Reformed Church viewed the camps as an opportunity to bring more children into the church. With this – literally – captive audience, the ministers encouraged religious revivals as a means of whipping up religious enthusiasm among children, especially adolescents. During Pentecost in 1902, there was a revival in the Pinetown camp. At one prayer meeting for young people 'the power of the Holy Ghost was present and many there assembled were powerfully overcome by the knowledge of their sinfulness'.[35]

The circumstances of the camps contributed to the success of these revivals, like high-school attendance. During a chaotic, overcrowded and psychologically traumatic period, the revivals offered young people a means of making sense of their predicament and provided hope for the future.

The British authorities tolerated the presence of the Dutch Reformed Church's ministers in the camps because they provided education, were not disruptive and did not question the authority of the superintendents. They did not permit ministers and teachers to enter the camps for black people because it was believed they would only 'unsettle' black refugees. The schools in the Boer camps were established to prepare white children for a united post-war South Africa within the British Empire. Black children were also to be made ready – in their case, for work. Schools were not established in black camps. One official explained that 'to educate natives upon the level of white education would be insane … our first duty should be to instil in them a sense of the value of labour'. Another official agreed that educating blacks would 'reduce the available number of farm labourers' and even 'upset the social structure of South Africa'.[36] Accordingly, black children were put to work alongside their parents.

These children did earn some money for their work, and the labour was justified partly on the grounds that they were contributing to their families' earnings. But the real reason for encouraging children to work was the demand for domestic servants, particularly in Johannesburg. Superintendents of camps near Johannesburg were notified of the

TOP LEFT Children being fed soup at Bloemfontein camp

ABOVE Group of cheeky-looking small boys at laundry time, Norvalspont camp

RIGHT Stoic and upright, even when seated: the Viljoen family next to their tent and wagon at the Middelburg camp

'FADED FLOWERS'? CHILDREN IN THE CONCENTRATION CAMPS

RIGHT A war of shortages, but not necessarily of African servants. Here a young girl helps a Boer woman at the Bloemfontein camp with laundry.

BELOW Children of canvas caught on paper: the gaunt-looking Venter children

need for black servants in Johannesburg, and girls and boys were sent to two agencies established to channel these children from the camps into domestic work. In this way, 276 boys and 133 girls were employed by Johannesburg households.

Black children also worked in Boer camps. Many had accompanied white families into the camps, where they performed domestic work. There were so many black children in the Bloemfontein camp, for instance, that a special race was organised for them during a camp sports days in 1901. One man remembered a 12-year-old black boy who joined a Boer family in the Merebank camp. He did not receive rations, so Boer children shared their food with him. Other black servants were not so well treated. Lenie Boshoff-Liebenberg referred to an aunt's domestic worker, 'loyal Doortjie', who, because black servants were permitted to leave the camp occasionally, was compelled to smuggle out letters and clothing to a commando nearby. She was caught by a British patrol, imprisoned for three weeks on suspicion of being a spy and died soon after.[37] Although Lenie railed against British cruelty for imprisoning her younger brother, she did not comment on Doortjie's death.

Rebuilding

These examples demonstrate that there was no single childhood experience in the war. Instead, children's experiences of the conflict and the concentration camps were as varied as the children themselves. The daughters of wealthy Boers were allowed unprecedented power, while black children in Boer camps were at the mercy of their employers. Poor, orphaned Boer children ran a higher risk of malnutrition and injury than those surrounded by adults. Boys were more likely to run away; girls kept closer to their families. Some wept at the thought of leaving English-medium schools; others plotted to avenge the deaths of their parents at the hands of the British. Some worked; others played.

When they left the camps in 1902 and 1903, they took with them the trauma, the education and the knowledge they had acquired there. Concentration-camp hospitals were seen as a way of bringing Boers into the

The hostilities over, a Boer family leaves a camp, homeward bound.

civilised fold of the British Empire through medicine. Doctors and administrators argued that hospitals and modern medicine would rid Boers of their superstitious adherence to magic and home remedies. Schools were also a tool for modernisation. Not only did they teach Boer children English, but more Boer children attended school during the conflict than before. Indeed, teachers in the camp schools were astonished to discover children in their late teens learning to read in kindergarten classes.

The Huguenot Seminary received record numbers of applications as the conflict drew to a close. Most of them were from young women who had taught or nursed in the camps and sought formal training to become professional teachers and missionaries in a post-war South Africa. Ironically, the conflict opened up opportunities for such Boer women.

However, the majority of black and Boer children left the camps traumatised, physically and psychologically. Hundreds were sent to orphanages and others returned to devastated farms and homesteads. The significance of the study of children during the Anglo-Boer War becomes particularly clear at this point. The children who left the concentration camps went on to become the adults who supported the nationalist – African and Afrikaner – politics of the early twentieth century. It is possible that they understood the increasingly racialised politics of the twentieth century through the prism of their lives in the concentration camps.

In writing this chapter, the author would like to give grateful thanks to Mimi Syffert and Anneke Schaafsma of Special Collections at Stellenbosch University, and Marlene Schoeman at the Dutch Reformed Church Archive.

In the early 1980s, the historian M.C.E. van Schoor appealed in the national media to individuals who had been in the concentration camps as children to share their experiences with him. This formed part of his research for a book, Kampkinders, 1900–1902: 'n Gedenkboek, *which was published in 1982. Only some of the letters were used in the book, and the entire collection was thereafter donated to the War Museum of the Boer Republics in Bloemfontein. The following excerpts are from this collection.*

Susara Magrieta Susanna Holder (née Coetzee) of the Lichtenburg district was carted off to the Potchefstroom camp with her family as a six-year-old. At Frederikstad the journey had to be continued by train. 'They drove the cattle out of the open railway trucks and put eight families in one truck. It was bitterly cold, and on top of that it started raining. We were getting drenched; my mother was with the weak baby. We didn't have a stitch of dry clothing to put on … The water couldn't drain away fast enough through the holes, as the trucks were still full of dung.' At the camp their misery continued:

> We didn't even have bedding – we slept on some springbok skins on the hard ground … The tent was equally bad, it had only one pair of pegs and just hung slackly. When it rained, the water ran in one side and out the other.
>
> My mother had a very hard time because we cried from hunger. There was one soup kitchen where they boiled soup but when Mom went there, the people were crowding around it so much that she couldn't even get near the soup. Some people fainted because they were almost crushed to death. Then they would tell you that the soup was finished, and you would have to turn back. Late at night when people were asleep, a man would come past and shout loudly that meat had been received. Then people would jump up and run to the butchery. Some got something, but others got nothing.
>
> My mother would queue there from seven in the morning till late in the afternoon. You had to hold the note for the meat up in the air, and the man would randomly take a note here or there. Eventually he would say, 'You can go home now, you'll just have to come back tomorrow.'

Before the war, **Joost Heystek** lived on a farm outside Nylstroom. His family was first held at Nylstroom and then at Irene: 'What do I still remember? Tent wagons with bell tents in between stood in long rows, forming the camp. I recall that almost every day we saw a black coffin standing in some or other wagon tent … On one occasion, a black man walked past a few of us camp boys; he was peeling a peach. When the skin dropped to the ground we rushed forward, snatched it up and divided it into pieces which we guzzled with relish.'

Johanna Elizabeth Opperman (née Van Strÿp) was an orphan who had lived with an uncle and aunt on a farm near the Swaziland border before the war broke out. She was later sent to the Irene camp near Pretoria with a group of orphans. She told how the food they had to eat was 'very poor' – they seldom got meat or vegetables. Firewood was also in short supply so they collected dung to use as fuel. 'In the evening, the candles had to be extinguished at nine o'clock because they were scarce. Regardless of whether you were sick or dying, the candles had to be put out,' she wrote.

An incident I shall never forget was when a train carrying prisoners of war went past the camp. The women were all crying, as they knew that the men were going to be sent away. The men in the trucks, however, were all singing '*Prijs den Heer*' (Praise the Lord) at the top of their voices …

All the men in the camp were 'joiners' [Boers who joined the British forces]. The Boer women were apt

This porcelain doll from 1897 survived the concentration camps and was auctioned by Stephan Welz & Co. in 2013. The unidentified doll's owner made the colourful dress on the right in 1901 while she was interned in a camp as an eleven-year-old.

to make their feelings known about them, and the men had to stay well out of their way.

Sophia Elizabeth Wilhelmina Cronjé (née Van der Merwe) was five when she and her family were taken to the Merebank camp in Natal.

One morning my mother and I went to collect firewood. When a well-known traitor greeted my mother laughingly on our return, she snarled at him: 'You *hendsopper*, you are too cowardly and too rotten to fight for your country – and now you laze around here, guarding women.'

Some of the boys used to hand-walk horses for the English to cool them down and were thus able to boast about the tips they received from the soldiers. One of my aunts disapproved of this; she gave each of them a good hiding and forbade them to do it again.

Hester Schneider (née De la Rey), a niece of General Koos de la Rey, had lived on De la Reyskraal Farm in the Schweizer-Reneke district before she and her family were captured and taken to the Klerksdorp camp. Three of her five sisters died in the camp, and her three brothers also became seriously ill.

The boys had measles and slept on the floor. Then the camp supervisor came and demanded that the flaps of the tent be tied back. The wind blew icily and my mother explained to him about the measles, but he insulted them [her mother and Aunt Kit de Villiers]. Aunt Kit got hold of something to hit him with (I think it was a piece of wood), but he ran away. A certain Bella Rahl caught him and he was given a proper beating. I was very ill myself, suffering from jaundice.

Soon after this incident, a man arrived one morning on a big horse and asked whether my mother and Aunt Kit were the people who had beaten the supervisor. Aunt Kit could speak English well and she explained to him about the children. All he said was: 'Oh well, you'll have to be punished for it.'

Hester and her family, as well as her aunt's family, were then taken to a barbed-wire camp with three tents outside the town. But this punishment was not as harsh as the British camp authorities might have thought.

There was green grass, and *uintjies* [veld bulbs] also grew there. The boys dug up *uintjies* and I ate them. The abattoir was opposite the little camp and when the boys would go there to help with the slaughtering, they got some of the dung-filled intestines that even our dogs refused to eat. My mom would wash the intestines repeatedly. We had a three-legged pot in which she boiled the intestines. Those *uintjies* and intestines saved my life.

P.A. Bornman lived in the Brandfort district and was seven when the war broke out. His family were sent to a concentration camp between Brandfort and Keeromberg. 'The lights in the tents had to be put out at nine o'clock in the evening. If they were still burning after that, the camp police – *hanskakies* [pro-British Boers] – would bang against the tents and shout "lights out". As a joke, my brother Dawid and I banged against the tents early in the evening and shouted "lights out". The people eventually cottoned on to what we were doing. That was the end of this little game.'

CHAPTER SEVEN

Black people and the camps

— BILL NASSON —

PREVIOUS PAGE, MAIN IMAGE Taking a break from the sick, the wounded and the dead: British field ambulance crew in Natal, including a doctor, drivers and orderlies.
SECONDARY IMAGE The cruel shortness of life: In the black camps, too, most of the deaths were those of children.

THIS PAGE Black laundry workers from the Imperial Yeomanry Hospital, Cape Colony

On 22 July 1939, two months before the outbreak of World War II, a local British newspaper published a letter from a wealthy British woman. In her letter to the *Gloucestershire Echo*, Joan Hackett-Dunstone voiced her fears of the consequences of a German invasion of Britain. If that frightening event were to occur, what would be the fate of ordinary civilians in the path of Adolf Hitler's army? Would they be made prisoners and interned in camps? If that were to happen, she questioned what arrangements would be made for households with servants. Would employers be expected to share toilets and sleeping areas with common cleaners and gardeners?

For Hackett-Dunstone the thought of being conquered by so powerful an enemy was alarming. Not only could it mean the end of freedom and liberty, but it could also upset the usual social arrangements between classes.

The servant question

In the Anglo-Boer War, almost four decades earlier, it is likely that many affluent Boer families interned in the concentration camps – established by Hackett-Dunstone's country – would have experienced similar anxiety at the prospect of living alongside domestic servants and black war refugees. However, there were others who were able to share living space quite easily. In her detailed observations of camp life in Bloemfontein, Emily Hobhouse noted that a Boer woman and her children were sharing a tent with their black servant. Such communal living was even more marked in Barberton, where over 100 servants, most with their families, had accompanied their employers into the camp. Hobhouse remarked that there 'appears to be undue familiarity; some natives sleeping, eating and drinking in the same tents as whites'.[1]

It was not only in these camps that the close personal ties between some Boers and their dependent black servants aroused such comment. In Britain's overseas prisoner-of-war camps, republican captives sometimes included trusted commando *agterryers* (personal retainers). Writing to his regimental journal, *The Green Howards Gazette*, from Ceylon in 1901, an officer remarked that Boer prisoners included 'Boer natives' who not only 'conversed in some kind of Dutch', but shared food and accommodation. On the fighting front, too, burghers were seen in commando laagers to 'laugh, talk, eat and joke' with black companions, and there were sightings of *agterryers* who freely 'shared clothing, utensils, rations, drink and songs' with commandos. Shocked by the sight of such mingling, one intelligence officer concluded sarcastically that it was a pity that the Boers had not had the benefit of 'proper training' in how to 'behave like white men'.[2]

ABOVE In addition to handling horses, servicing firearms and setting up camp, personal retainers, or *agterryers*, did the cooking.

OPPOSITE, TOP Buttoned up smartly for duty, however menial the work: *agterryer* captives cleaning a prisoner-of-war camp on St Helena.
BOTTOM Normal domestic life was seemingly uninterrupted: an Afrikaner family with their black servant in the Vredefort camp.

The British had a more aloof style of dominating colonial subjects and were, therefore, surprised by the close nature of paternalistic bonds between some Boer masters and favoured personal servants. Although the loyal black retainers who accompanied commandos were servants, they were included in ways that made them 'invariably more than a servant', as a prominent war historian has suggested.[3] In so doing, many burghers retained the allegiance and obedience of manservants who performed the essential duty of helping to keep them in the field.

In a similar way, some interned Boer women and their families lived alongside known and dependable black servants. Undoubtedly, as chapter two emphasises, the war brought republican women face to face with huge challenges and profound transformations such as new kinds of consciousness and obligations, changing duties, enlarged responsibility, newfound authority as figures of defiant resistance and also a deep fear of the consequences of a loss of command over black men. Nonetheless, the hierarchy was not completely overthrown and some traditional domestic ties remained resilient. As Hobhouse witnessed, in the camps there were Boer households who found ways of keeping familiar

172 THE WAR AT HOME

BLACK PEOPLE AND THE CAMPS

RIGHT Loyal and true: Jan Ruiter, the Griqua servant of Orange Free State leader, Marthinus Steyn

OPPOSITE, TOP A female servant, Tombi, with Mrs Beukes and Mrs Breytenbach at the Volksrust camp.
BOTTOM Many black workers accompanied their employers, such as this respectable-looking family, into the white camps.

black servants under their wing. Remaining with employers was one way for black Africans to survive the war, because their alternative was to forgo shelter, food and income.

Improvised arrangements

By 1901, there were fewer options in the annexed republican territories for black civilians. They were being displaced by the Boer commandos plundering supplies, and they were also being dislodged from rural locations – sometimes even mission stations – by British soldiers intent on denying livestock and crops to the enemy.

At first, men considered to be sufficiently able-bodied to work as labourers were allocated to the closest transport or other field service department in support of the imperial campaign. Their earnings went towards supporting themselves and their numerous refugee dependants, who were being accommodated next to the detention settlements established for the Boers uprooted by the scorched-earth policy. As intensive army operations stripped the countryside of grain and cattle, the number and size of these concentrations of refugees mushroomed, with some black people and Boer women living side by side.

The British military administration had intended to keep Boer and black refugees strictly separate, and the camps were being established as white internment camps. However, this was not strictly adhered to as the need for labour in Boer camps ensured that some Africans were always circulating between segregated settlements. Wives of men who were *agterryers* were often accommodated as family domestic servants in white camps. By the end of 1901, several British army officers had noted sardonically that, no matter how bad the circumstances of the Boer women who had lost their farm livelihood, at least they were not having to manage without personal servants.

On the other hand, the established bonds that bound black servants to Boer domestic life were tested by other enticements and opportunities thrown up by the war. Some women combined daytime work for Boer families with evening chores for the British administration. Others, instead of serving two masters, abandoned Boer households for alternative jobs, such as laundry work for British officers. The camps, originally intended for white people, were soon populated with drifting black refugees, including the dependants of men engaged by the army as labourers, messengers and scouts. In the camps, they also toiled for the imperial war effort, undertaking sanitary and other labour duties, and occasionally even acting as settlement guards – roles that Boer women found especially unnerving.

ABOVE, LEFT AND RIGHT No escaping the impact of British scorched-earth tactics: the possessions of black peasant farmers being incinerated.

OPPOSITE, TOP Local servants of the imperial cause: workers at the Kraai River camp in the north-eastern Cape Colony.
BOTTOM Refugees flee the approaching menace of British columns.

The creation of black camps

As difficult times continued for displaced black people, the need to try to resolve a messy position grew increasingly urgent. The solution, from the first half of 1901, was to provide entirely separate refugee camps to confine black people who were destitute as well as those with livestock who were crossing British lines and entering garrison towns to seek cover from the destructive army campaign. There, they were joined by increasing numbers of black labour tenants (who worked for a farmer in return for access to productive land) and sharecroppers who had been driven off Boer farmlands.

Although some generals had misgivings about making provision near towns for these refugees, the military administration decided it was too risky to turn them away from garrison settlements. It was thought that, if they were sent away, they could end up aligning themselves with republican fighters, who made use of black informants and spies. The other risk was that public opinion could turn against a new occupation regime if people believed that it allowed black people to starve. The British regime preferred to appear humane in its liberal imperialism.

At the same time, as the situation worsened on the Boer civilian front, it became more critical to accommodate black refugees. The British tolerated a small number of black people in white camps as the servants of Boer women, but they found it socially undesirable to permit the growth of large groups on the fringes of these camps. Using the arguments about sanitation that underpinned the rationale for urban segregation at the time, district commissioners declared that concentrations of black African refugees close to white settlements were a health menace to Boer families.

The muddled circumstances of war being what they usually are, the emergence of the first small number of separate black camps was not the result of any well-managed calculation. Instead, refugees were unwittingly choosing the places of their confinement themselves by heading into towns secured by British garrisons. By mid-1901, there were more than 20 500 refugees in larger Orange River Colony camps like Kroonstad, Heilbron and Brandfort, and over half that number in the Transvaal. At this time, black African camps and Boer camps were like two legs of the same body: all were administered by superintendents in charge of white refugees.

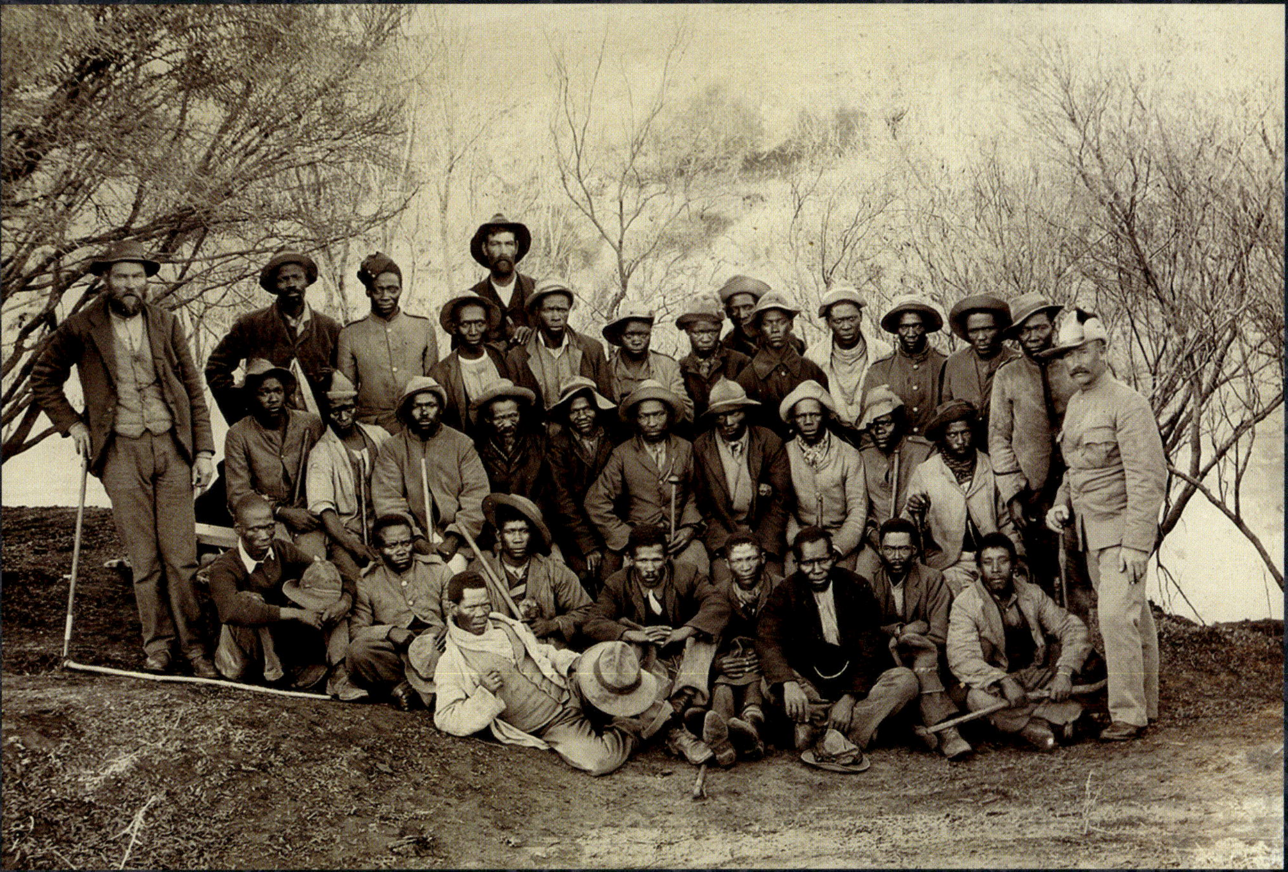

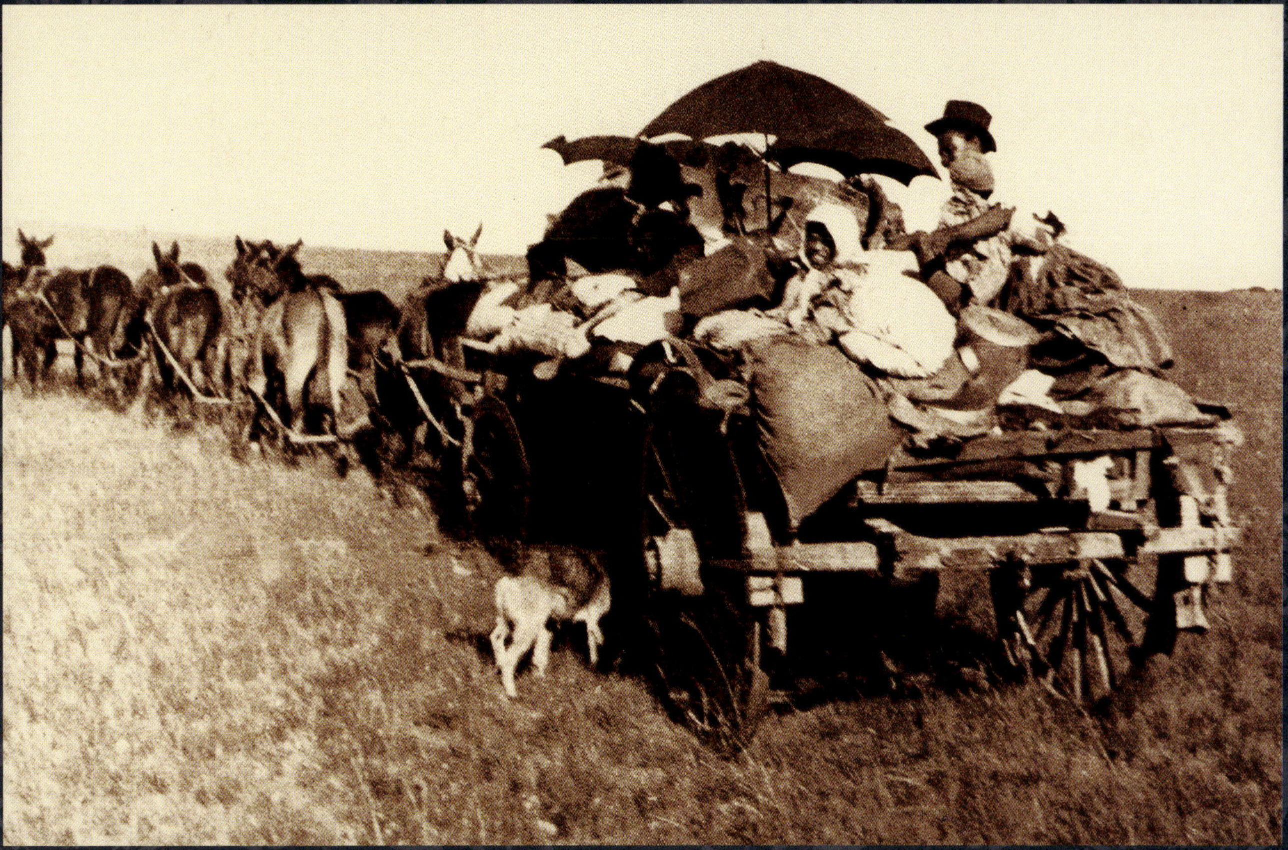

TOP New arrivals settle in to the limited camp facilities.

ABOVE They spied on the Boers: British spies, only known as Charlie, Alfred and Paul, at the Taaibosch camp.

But, as the war progressed and its impact and consequences became apparent, the British were obliged to take stock. It was becoming clear that the existing control of black refugees was inadequate. In some places, living conditions were unacceptable because water was scarce and the only available food was diseased cattle carcasses, rotten porridge and even locusts. With mortality rates mounting daily, the British questioned how these terrible circumstances could be improved. At the same time, Lord Roberts's successor, Field Marshal Lord Kitchener, was swelling the numbers of uprooted people by intensifying the scorched-earth campaign.

In June 1901, the Native Refugee Department was established in the Transvaal in response to these problems, and it soon assumed responsibility for affairs in both annexed states. Although the scale of the black refugee predicament extended beyond the volume of people in concentration camps, over 120 000 people were interned in more than 80 camps in the ex-republics and northern Cape Colony – the majority of whom were women and children. In addition, several thousand black African cultivators and pastoralists from the Highveld were temporarily resettled under supervision on deserted farms and land in the Natal border districts.

The populations of most controlled settlements consisted entirely of black people, although there were camps, such as Mafeking and Brakpan, that had a small population of coloured people. Some of these coloured refugees, like those in the Transvaal under the leadership of Conrad Buys, objected to being accommodated as 'natives'. When entering the Pietersburg camp in 1901, such a group insisted on their citizenship status being recognised as 'coloured *burghers*' because of the implications for various rights, including distribution of rations, schooling for children and freedom for women from enforced labour.

Work and other camp obligations

The formation of a separate administration for these refugee camps went beyond the need to improve the disastrous handling of black people. Camps for black refugees and camps for white Boers were conceived of as entirely different entities, with the former 'primarily farm and labour camps', according to a recent military history of the war.[4] A powerful motive for the full-time native refugee administration was not only that of organising and controlling black Africans, but also a way of tackling one of the key dilemmas of the British campaign – competing demands for black workers.

Earlier in the conflict, the closure of the Witwatersrand mines had prompted many migrant mineworkers to enter military employment. When Johannesburg gold production resumed under British authority, there was, consequently, a serious shortage of labour. In

Black people helping the British effort: a blockhouse construction squad gets acquainted with the railways.

June 1901, Kitchener's solution was to discharge ex-miners from army work so that they could return to the mines. Predictably, that enforced exodus meant that the army would then be short of general workers. Therefore, one of the main responsibilities of the Native Refugee Department was declared to be 'the supply of native labour to the army'.[5]

In that respect, the position of black families in concentration camps was quite distinct from that of Boer families. They were also not conventional war refugees, like the 250 000 republicans in the later Spanish Civil War who fled to France, where they were interned in camps in atrocious conditions and regarded as 'an expensive nuisance'.[6] However many black refugees were seen as a nuisance, a considerable effort was made to ensure they would not be expensive. In 1902 the Native Refugee Department revealed, in its closing financial statement, that the cost of maintaining its camps in the Transvaal had worked out at less than one penny per day for each refugee.

This remarkable economy was achieved by mobilising camp inhabitants to pay for their own upkeep. Their internment was organised not only to ensure that adequate labour would be available for the army, but also so that the camps would be as self-supporting as possible through the cultivation of land in their immediate surroundings. Behind protective lines of armed pickets, fertile zones produced maize and fresh vegetables and supplied firewood, using labour provided mostly by women, children and elderly men, so as not to hamper the labour supply to British forces. The Native Refugee Department's principle of food self-sufficiency reaped additional rewards when camp cultivators produced a surplus of crops like oats and potatoes, because almost a third of the camps' supplies went to the army. In this way, the cultivated patches of camp land became small export farms that fed the imperial army.

BLACK PEOPLE AND THE CAMPS

Major Henri-Gustave Joly de Lotbinière (subsequently Colonel), a Canadian officer of the Royal Engineers, took overall control of black refugees. This was a fitting role for an austere and determined man, who was obsessive about detail, loved the authority to organise things and had never quite outgrown his rural schoolboy passion for trains. In a way, the concentration camps for black people became his unique domain, as he turned the inhabitants into resources to be collected and supplied. The railways that ran inland from the ports facilitated the needs of the British campaign, and refugee settlements were positioned along these lines of rail communication. Thus, refugee labour became part of the war goods capable of being transported easily to bases of army operations, storage depots and other sites.

Refugee workers were paid a fixed wage of one shilling per day with rations (less than the earnings of volunteer black workers in the army) and were rarely able to escape the grip of the camps altogether. They were recruited into military employment for periods of three months at a time and returned to their families at regular intervals, thereby remaining tied to a concentration-camp existence. The number of refugees who were prodded

THE WAR AT HOME

ABOVE British Army wagon drivers enjoying the simple comforts of food and companionship.

OPPOSITE, TOP Cutting the cost of war: trained labourers assembled for the erection of a cheap prefabricated blockhouse designed by Major Spring Rice of the Royal Engineers, a job that took about six hours.
BOTTOM Not only building for Lord Kitchener, but transporting for him too: black army workers supplying equipment and stores to blockhouses.

into army employment increased rapidly, and by the beginning of 1902, over 15 000 camp inhabitants were occupied with various kinds of military work. Their low wages represented another symbol of obligatory servitude. De Lotbinière promised that the Native Refugee Department would mobilise labour for the army and was extremely proud of achieving this goal. He often declared that the supply of workers formed the basis of the organisation of African refugees. And refugee workers were not only used to assist the military. Those men who were too frail or old for heavy labour were given jobs as sanitary workers, watchmen and cultivators in the fields.

When they realised that the Native Refugee Department could provide cost-effective workers and servants, private employers in the vicinity of camps took advantage of this and often secured the services of refugees, both male and female. Some urban households also benefited, and in Johannesburg hundreds of girls and boys were placed in domestic employment by an agency established to recruit and supply child labour from refugee settlements. (This aspect of these children's experience of the war is explored in chapter six.)

Superintendents and officials who ran the camps for black people needed to ensure that they did not become places where refugees could retreat, do nothing and wait for the war to end. In cases where inmates were reluctant to accept work or appeared to have the means of avoiding labour, the favoured solution was manipulation, by threatening to withhold food. Although refugees were encouraged to become self-sufficient, it did not suit the administration if they were *too* autonomous. Therefore, black cultivators who had

BLACK PEOPLE AND THE CAMPS   181

The hands that held the fate of lives: a doctor, nurses and orderlies at the Bloemfontein camp.

retained stores of maize and other grain were permitted to bring in only small quantities – administrators claimed that the rail wagons could not cope with more. This was, however, largely untrue.

Food was also used to pressurise men into accepting military work. Compliant workers and their families were allowed to purchase bags of mealies at a fair market rate. At the same time, less cooperative refugees in the Orange River Colony and Transvaal, who either would not accept work offers or held sufficient cash or goods to enable them to evade employment as labourers, were obliged to pay double the price. So, although there was no policy of actual forced labour, food provided a compelling and convenient form of compulsion.

A condition of crisis

What of conditions in the camps themselves? People were concentrated into hastily improvised and unsanitary camps. They were squeezed into a tangle of makeshift huts or rickety tents made from hessian sacks and patches of canvas, and were not provided with decent nutrition. The consequences were dire, dangerous and life-threatening. More than 10 per cent of all assembled black refugees died. A count of 2 831 deaths in December 1901 'represented a mortality rate of 372 per 1 000 per year, exceeding the highest figure for white deaths recorded in October 1901 at 344 per 1 000 per year'.[7]

In reality, we do not know exactly how many lost their lives, because the records kept of the mortality rate were not accurate. De Lotbinière's small and overstretched staff did not necessarily officially register every death. There was also no tally taken of those who

Living rough: makeshift camp shelters

perished before the formation of the Native Refugee Department or during its early operations. In addition, there were fatalities among the groups in transit to, and between, camps, and the workers recruited from settlements. These deaths were also not reflected in statistical records.

In the 1980s a pioneering account of the fate of black refugees noted a total of '14 154 recorded deaths in the camps',[8] and emphasised the inaccuracy of official figures. Subsequently, as the grim story of the black concentration camps has emerged as a more prominent and publicly represented wartime tragedy – inspiring a centenary commemoration of black African victims – the estimation of human lives lost has been scaled upwards to 'at the very least 20 000 dead'.[9] What is known with absolute certainty is that the largest proportion of deaths occurred among the very young. As was the case with Boer children, black children suffered a mortality rate of over 80 per cent. And this was not the only striking parallel.

Although there were clear differences between the experiences of blacks and whites in the concentration camps – better rations and greater personal freedom for the Boers, for instance – there were also distinct similarities. Camp staff often attributed the high death rates among black African children to the ignorance and neglect of their mothers; and they levelled similar criticism at Boer mothers. In one typical example, in April 1901, Captain A.G. Trollope (chief superintendent of the Orange River Colony camps) claimed that the large number of fatalities in the black African camp at Edenburg was due 'in a very large measure to the bad nursing of the mothers ... Natives do not seem to care for their children till they reach a useful age.'[10]

The cruel, premature deaths of children were due to a lot more than maternal sloppiness. Tents and huts were flimsy and unable to provide adequate protection from extreme weather, and they were placed too close together for the maintenance of proper hygiene. Supplies of roofing and other protective materials were scarce. Fuel supplies were invariably inadequate. Water supply was frequently erratic and, at times, contaminated. Most medical facilities – including hospital care – were rough and rudimentary, and the army doctors attached to the Native Refugee Department did not often visit the camps. Finally, food was a big problem and the health of many refugees, who were already in a weakened state on arrival at the camps, did not improve on a diet lacking in milk and fresh vegetables.

In this unhealthy environment, infectious diseases thrived and vulnerable inmates were infected by epidemics of pneumonia, measles, chickenpox, whooping cough, diphtheria, dysentery, typhoid and other bacterial infections. Further deaths were caused by chronic disorders associated with malnutrition, including debility, diarrhoea and emaciation. De Lotbinière stubbornly reasoned that this terrible toll was beyond prevention and control, based on his belief that black Africans were, by nature, unable to adapt well to abrupt changes and extreme conditions, and that if confronted by unfamiliar food, water and soil, they would struggle to cope.

Some improvement

Human sympathy was also in short supply but this did not mean that no effort was made to improve this harsh environment. By the end of 1901, the Native Refugee Department realised that the camp death rate had got out of hand, but it was brought under control only a couple of months before the end of the war. By then, the deplorable state of white camps had already been tempered due to the influential publicising of camp conditions by the anti-war and humanitarian networks in Britain. Nevertheless, the plight of black refugee families was neither publicised in London, nor was it the topic of public meetings or headlines in the liberal press campaign against the inhumanity of the war.

TOP Keeping the camp fires burning: preparing dung cakes for fuel.

ABOVE A woman with water cans at the Standerton camp

Eventually, at the beginning of 1902, changes were made to improve life expectancy in the camps. Tightly clustered concentration camps were gradually split up into smaller settlements and spread across wider areas, but still kept close to the railway network. This resulted in better sanitation, greater protection against the spread of disease and an increased range of cultivable land for food production within protected camp zones.

A major part of camp reform was the provision of a more varied and nutritious diet for inmates. Camp inhabitants were granted free rations, cows were introduced to provide

The sustaining rituals of ordinary life: a wedding party in wartime finery at a northern Free State camp.

fresh milk, and tinned beef extract, flour and tinned milk were distributed. Petty traders were also permitted daily visits to camps to sell vegetables and fruit. Space opened up for such enterprise and numerous stores were created to sell things classified as 'luxuries' – restricted previously to Boer refugees as a special perk. Black people were then able to purchase items like coffee, tea, sugar, tobacco, candles, blankets and clothing. Absorbed into everyday consumption, these goods comforted refugees, fuelled their endurance of the camps and contributed to a reduction in the death rate.

However, this all came at a cost. Black people spent tens of thousands of pounds on supplementary goods, and the money had to come from somewhere. The need for blankets, sugar and other items encouraged more people to work in the fields, and this stimulated an increase in labour.

Ultimately, efforts by the British administration, and the refugees themselves, to ameliorate the dreadful living conditions had some beneficial effect. But the hidden crisis of the politically quiet black camps rumbled on.

Camp life: Optimistic perceptions

The treatment of interned black refugees was a disastrous consequence of a destructive imperial war. Could this have been predicted and avoided, or at least its calamitous impact diminished? This is the usual question raised about policies in wars that have had devastating consequences for trapped civilians. In the Anglo-Boer War, the partial relief, which came in 1902, was not due to political motive or cautionary warnings. Even when the death toll rose, there were few arguments voiced that Britain was failing in its wartime moral and social duty to ensure the common welfare of those afflicted by the South African campaign.

At the time, commentators on the suffering of concentration-camp inhabitants virtually ignored the predicament of black refugees. It is a well-known fact that Emily Hobhouse never investigated, or even visited, a black concentration camp. In his 1941 account, *The Concentration Camps in South Africa during the Anglo-Boer War of 1899–1902*, writer Napier Devitt remarked on such evasiveness. Although it had black mission church members, the Dutch Reformed Church ignored the losses sustained by black Africans, devoting itself exclusively to a compilation of the lives lost in white camps.

On the odd occasion, critics took some account of the position of black refugees, but this hardly ever extended to the quality of camp administration. Predictably, the staff of the Native Refugee Department presented a glowing picture of black people's gratitude for protection from starvation and assaults by Boer forces. According to G.B. Beak of the Orange River Colony administration, the mellow mood among black Africans was far preferable to the surliness and ungratefulness of the Boers. In his detailed 1906 chronicle, *The Aftermath of War: An Account of the Repatriation of Boers and Natives in the Orange River Colony, 1902–1904*, Beak applauded the stoicism with which Africans accepted the hardships that accompanied war, and their good-natured acceptance of meagre compensation for the unavoidable loss of crops and livestock. Another of the Orange River Colony's superintendents was even more cheerful. Following a camp inspection tour in January 1902, many black Africans were declared to be so content with camp life that they were eager to remain there for the rest of their lives.

The Aborigines' Protection Society in London was not quite as complacent. In the first quarter of 1902, it requested that the colonial office investigate the possibility of raising the standard of living for black refugees in accordance with the levels set for Boer refugees. At the same time, this society noted that the rudimentary nature of black African living was bound to produce an unhealthy environment if large groups were confined in a small area and it would not be easy to remedy this.

Occasionally, a view was presented that the camp experience was a way out of desperate conditions for refugees. In this perception, hopeless women with starving children were begging for admittance to settlements, believing that this was their only chance of survival. A correspondent to the February 1902 issue of *The Foreign Mission Chronicle of the Episcopal Church in Scotland* declared that those who accepted their fate with Christian fortitude would not waste their lives being idle. Instead, with an orderly routine, work prospects for mothers and educational opportunities for children, they would get through hard times and eventually prosper. The writer went on to say that, by dealing them a hard blow, the Anglo-Boer conflict was doing Christian black people an indirect favour.

Visiting Quakers gave a similar message. Reporting on the camps in 1902, representatives of the Society of Friends praised a perceived improvement in health, and more.

OPPOSITE Enduringly resilient and not to be humbled – a woman at the Irene camp.

BELOW The burden of childhood in the camps: young girls carrying dung cakes used for fuel.

Lawrence Richardson and a fellow Quaker, William Alexander, saw the camp existence as a blessing in disguise, because it was enabling the victims of the war to reconstruct their lives in industrious ways. After all, the only way to help people in distress was to let them help themselves. Accordingly, women were being encouraged to cultivate food not only for their own family needs, but also to help feed hungry soldiers. Men had an abundance of jobs from which to choose, and drivers and scouts were earning wages higher than those they had earned in peacetime. Children were not being neglected, as there were now improved prospects of schooling. As Richardson and Alexander saw it, if the war had turned the world upside down, the camps had restored a stable livelihood, possibly even with long-term benefits for those who were experiencing their effects.

In the Cape Colony the view was much the same, except that it was even held by some black African observers themselves. In 1903, the leadership of the South African Native Congress complimented Lord Milner for his commendable handling of the refugee problem, and expressed confidence in the compassion of the imperial government. As the formation of the Union approached later in the decade, leaders of the country's other native congresses – which formed the foundations of the future ANC – paid tribute to Britain's 'able administrators' for their 'great work' in having 'controlled native refugees', and for everything that had been done 'in protecting, housing and feeding them in the camps'.[11]

Of course, this sentiment was in keeping with the climate of the time, when early black African nationalists aligned their loyalty and hopes to the imperial cause in the war. But it is vastly different from the anti-imperialist tone of the ANC during the centenary commemoration, when they denounced the concentration camps as a shared black and Afrikaner atrocity. That irony, evidently, owes more to the perceived nationalist needs of post-apartheid politics than to any unwelcome memory of how historical events were seen and attitudes shaped 100 and more years ago.

Camp life: Critical opinion and resistance

Not all contemporary opinion on the state of the camps was consoling or hopeful. Certain missionary visitors were clearly critical. In 1901 a Transvaal clergyman reported that refugees in Krugersdorp were on their knees, having lost relatives killed by raiding commandos as well as all their possessions. He commented that families had been broken up and marooned in various camps. Women were very worried as they had no knowledge of the whereabouts and safety of their husbands, children, sisters and fathers.

Missionaries of the London-based United Society for the Propagation of the Gospel were equally shocked when they heard first-hand accounts of callousness and brutality. On a visit to the northern Transvaal in September 1901, one of their members, Revd W.H.R. Brown, was accurate in his saddening depiction of what the camps embraced and represented. Not only did they embody extreme poverty, daily deaths and a meagre and uncertain future, but also, far worse, there was knowledge of the underlying rationale for their existence and no political will to do anything about it. 'Between the English and the Dutch they have lost everything,' Brown observed, before concluding bleakly, 'there being no political party interested in their destiny, they "go to the wall", as the weakest are bound to'.[12]

In addition to the few humanitarian sympathisers who spoke for them, the camp inhabitants themselves did not all endure in silence. These displaced civilians were not all helpless victims, resigned to being moved around and accepting whatever was given to them. Invariably, daily endurance involved such approaches as tactical accommodation, willing acquiescence or, at times, resistance.

Some people expressed discontent by deserting. From the end of 1901, several hundred refugees slipped out of camps in the Orange River and Transvaal colonies. However, desertions were comparatively few and this may have been due to the tight supervision of protected zones. But it may also have been partly due to perceptions of little choice – deprivation behind the security of an armed picket line, with some food and shelter, was dreary but tolerable, whereas the thought of risking one's life in the random conditions of guerrilla warfare may have persuaded people to stay.

African dancers entertain inhabitants at the Howick camp in Natal.

Elsewhere, in more direct displays of resentment, disgruntled black refugees assembled to complain of substandard accommodation, shortages of medical supplies and lack of compensation for burnt crops and confiscated livestock. In addition to these widespread grievances, other fluctuating complaints were aired in letters to local magistrates or senior military administrators. These included being overworked, not being allowed to shop in nearby towns, the lack of meat and the monotony of a diet composed of mealie meal (and being obliged to pay for it).

There were also instances of political anger from black refugees who were disgruntled by the increasing awareness that the Boer camps were very different from their own in organisation and provisions. There, for instance, Boers were granted free rations and were provided with better shelter and medical facilities. Having declared themselves loyal followers of the Queen, faithful children of government or English natives, black African objectors were outraged by such injustice. They had been loyal to the empire, yet the Boers, the declared enemy and cause of the war, were the beneficiaries of British generosity and concern.

Repatriation problems

Towards the end of hostilities, the business-like Native Refugee Department commenced the closure of its camps and the repatriation of their inhabitants. Long before then, the administration had anticipated that the speedy dispersal of refugees to farms would boost agricultural recovery and reconstruction of white commercial farming. As the ambitious De Lotbinière boasted, a valuable pool of labour had been conserved for the agricultural industry on the Highveld.

A group of displaced people at a temporary camp, Norvalspont, await their next move.

However, the immediate exodus of families led to many problems. There was not enough transport available and limited grain supplies endangered their food security. Seeds, agricultural tools and draught animals were scarce. Those refugees who possessed military receipts for livestock, which they had been obliged to surrender on their entry to camps, discovered that these were not scrupulously honoured by a system that gave priority to the restocking of white farms. The women had no respite from arduous work, because they found themselves deprived of the strong field-labour skills of men who were waiting to be released from army employment. Furthermore, the rebuilding of wrecked homes by returning families was hampered by material shortages, and there was barely time to create shelter and prepare cultivable land before the expected heavy seasonal rains in 1902.

Nonetheless, the camps were emptied in the latter half of the year, even though the discharge of many army labourers in June 1902 actually increased the number of camp inhabitants briefly as men streamed back to join their families. By the end of that year, almost all refugees from the Transvaal and Orange River Colony camps had been repatriated and given small amounts of money to help them through the initial period (provided by sales from grain depots established by the Native Refugee Department). Meanwhile, labourers with empty pockets were tempted into employment relationships with farmers who were quick to seek labourers in the camps. For some, the release from internment was to precede the deepest destitution imaginable, worsened by the drought in 1902 and 1903. Alarmed magistrates in some districts of both annexed colonies reported near famine conditions by the end of 1902, with people relying on poaching, roots and rats for survival.

The emptying of the camps had not been completely straightforward for the authorities because the more stubborn refugees dragged their feet. In Natal, the Native Refugee Department had given some black people the liberty to cultivate land for themselves, and hundreds of families refused to move until all their crops had been harvested. Others simply stayed in the vicinity permanently, choosing to settle near former camps rather than be repatriated to the former republican territories. There was further resistance from

LEFT Wedding guests Andries, Sarah, Maria, Charlie and Helena looking more glum than festive at the Taaibosch camp.

BELOW Sober and dignified: three other Taaibosch wedding guests

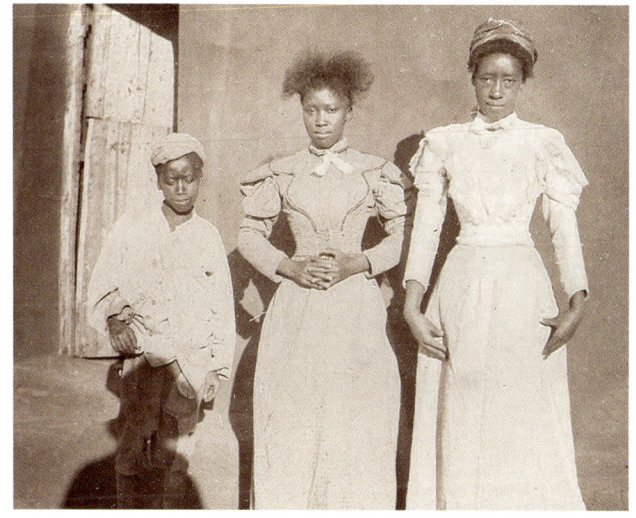

individuals who would not leave until they had been compensated properly for livestock and crop losses, and from families who clung on to settlements in the deluded hope that, by their staying put, the authorities would be persuaded to grant them land – a means of independence.

Finally, rumours of the looming peace troubled the camp inhabitants. After all, many of them had fled from republican commandos earlier in the war. In the immediate aftermath of the peace, many black Africans stayed near former camps for fear of the retribution of returning farmers. Among these people were tenants and workers unwilling to return to landowners because they feared demands for rent or additional labour to compensate for their wartime absence. There was also panic over the prospect of personal reprisals, possibly even execution, for having been loyal to the British. So the most frightened people chose a life camped alongside a railway line, regardless of the cost, until they felt the danger had passed. Although there was no actual basis for such extreme terror, a release from war was not an automatic release from fear.

Writing four years after the end of hostilities, the ever-complacent G.B Beak repeated the admirable accomplishments of the Native Refugee Department. He held that black people left the camps as they had arrived – with few needs, freedom from worry, cheerful and playful, nursed by the Bible and humbly content to accept their lot. In reality, for these victims of scorched earth, the roads home after the signing of the peace agreement were painfully hard and costly. The war had taken its greatest toll in large parts of the former Orange Free State and the southern, central and eastern Transvaal, and those returning to these areas would need immense resilience to build a future after 1902. They would build with few tools. And the future would be without promise.

ABOVE An ageing civilian of the veld with an auxiliary in the British Army in the background

OPPOSITE Black people await their train home at Norvalspont Station after the return of peace.

Separate spheres or shared fate?

For a long time, the traumatic experiences of Boer families in British concentration camps literally became the history of the war, and not only because it was burnt into the memories of Afrikaner people. Modern British, American and other historians of the conflict depict it as a total war, and largely on account of what one historian terms 'the infamous relocation of partisans' families in the concentration camps'.[13]

Created in the shadow of the peace of 1902, the *bittereinder* story of survival and suffering continues to beat away as a chamber in the heart of national historical memory. This story was once an insular political touchstone of immense importance to Afrikaner nationalism, so it is little wonder that its emotional legacy still resonates. An explanation is needed, however, for the belated findings or discoveries of black concentration camps and the accompanying public prominence in more recent years. There is now a new understanding of what the war actually was: it is seen not as an exclusive Anglo-Boer encounter, but as a war involving all South African people, both black and white.

With this bigger picture in mind, the present-day view of wartime civilian life in the early 1900s has come to look very different from the distinct image presented by the Boer War commemorative fever of the past. In other words, after the painful identification of segregated concentration-camp locations since the 1980s (the mere existence of which was not previously mentioned in conventional histories), the wounding experience of removal and internment has become recognised as a common wartime ordeal for the families of black and Afrikaner people alike.

This being the case, it is surprising that current press commentary has stated that the existence of black camps is a recent revelation and that 'historians and scholars are always quick to mention that the conditions at the black concentration camps were not as bleak and oppressive as those in the camps for Afrikaners'.[14] If anything, it has been quite the opposite.

Now we stand, inspired by the song sheet of current politics, in a new resting place for the country's women and children, brought together by shared suffering under the onslaught of an aggressive imperialist war of occupation.

This view of the concentration camps provides a consoling understanding of what happened to all women and children in a war in which the fighting front and the home front were one and the same. After all, the distances that separated black refugee settlements from their white counterparts were being crossed – black African guards, coloured servants and other mobile black labour were communicating with Boer families and they kept each other abreast of their respective fortunes.

Perhaps there has been too much focus on the exceptional plight of Boer women during the Anglo-Boer war. Assuming the truth in this statement, it could also be said that one should not focus too much on the fact that white and black concentration camps were common creations. Above all, they continue to tell their own stories.

The predominant theme of the republican cause, in what was seen as a people's war, was that the camps were created to accommodate the enemy Boer women and their households, who were taken hostage to diminish the assets of Britain's adversaries. On the other hand, those cooped up in black camps were not a civilian enemy. If they, too, bore the brunt of the war's deprivations, it was because they merely got in the way of the scorched-earth campaign. The hungry black women, children and older men who were set to work in the fields were never of politically symbolic consequence. Like the prisoners of war and assembled refugees of World War II and other total wars, they were useful labour for the army administrations that held them under their thumb.

CHAPTER EIGHT

The 'terrible laughter' of the Boers: Humour in the war

— SANDRA SWART —

PREVIOUS PAGE, MAIN IMAGE Hearing it from the horse's mouth: General Christiaan de Wet brings news of the May 1902 Peace of Vereeniging to the Norvalspont camp.
SECONDARY IMAGE Despite deprivation, children continue to be children in the camps.

THIS PAGE Return to ruin: hostilities over, a dejected farmer in front of his home at Reddersburg.

A YOUNG BOER GUERRILLA FIGHTER, Deneys Reitz, described the defeated Boer commandos drifting into the camps in May 1902 as a rabble of 'starving, ragged men, clad in skins or sacking, their bodies covered with sores'.[1] In the aftermath of the Anglo-Boer War, the Afrikaners seemed defeated: the rural economy was shattered, farms had been destroyed and around 27 000 Boer women and children had died in the concentration camps. Yet something strange was happening in this apocalyptic post-war world – Afrikaners were laughing.[2]

British philanthropist Emily Hobhouse, who reported on the outcome of the scorched-earth policy, observed this curious phenomenon. For instance, she wrote about two brothers who had both suffered enormous losses during the war. One 'had seven little mouths to feed. He got seed potatoes … but the drought killed them … He put in a little seed, but till it is ripe he has nothing to live upon. His beautiful house is in ruins, his blue gums all but two cut down, his fruit trees chopped.' Hobhouse continued: 'But how he laughed, and how his brother laughed.'[3]

Hobhouse also observed that 'like all the other burghers [General] de Wet is laughing. If he did not, he says, he should die. It makes him great fun.'[4] In a rural hamlet in the Orange Free State, Hobhouse offered food to a poor man and he said: 'I shall be so glad that I shall laugh without feeling any inclination to laugh.'[5] Hobhouse also said that the Boers in Pretoria 'say little and only laugh'.

She concluded:
There is getting to be something quite terrible to me in this laugh of the Boers which meets me everywhere. It is not all humour, nor all bitter, though partly both; it is more like the laughter of despair. We sit in a row by these stable walls and discuss every project possible and impossible, and then we laugh. Now and again the tears come into the men's eyes, but never into the women's except when they speak of children lost in the camps.[6]

This chapter explores the 'terrible' laughter of the conquered Boers, why they said 'little and only laugh[ed]' and how this laughter has been interpreted by Afrikaner public intellectuals in the decades after the war. Primary evidence of laughter is scarce; laughter fades and records of mirth are not to be found in an archive. But this chapter will explore accounts of the things that made people laugh, their observations on their own laughter and commentary on what was commonly funny – although such information is scarce and recorded only as an afterthought.

ABOVE, LEFT With the gun before he turned to the pen: a young Deneys Reitz, commando and author of the greatest personal narrative of the war, *Commando*. RIGHT About to join the road to normality, a woman with a group of children leaves the Bloemfontein camp after the 1902 peace treaty was signed.

Seriously funny

A story told about laughter is usually a happy one. Laughter is generally viewed as the 'best medicine' and a socially positive force. Nevertheless, sceptics contend that there is something unpleasant behind the smiles. Some argue that laughter arises from a sense of dominance over others and is, therefore, a social correction tool that belittles and helps to control the aberrant. Others argue that laughter is a small bodily rebellion against social constraint.[7] Freud believed that laughter was a channel for nervous energy, allowing the individual to broach otherwise taboo topics like sex and violence. For Freud, a joke was not just a joke.[8]

War chronicles lend support to Freud's theory that laughter can provide catharsis and mental release from suffering. It is evident that the Boers managed to keep joking even during the worst of the war. J.D. Kestell, chaplain to President Steyn and General Christiaan de Wet, observed during a raid in which the men had been told to proceed silently that 'the burghers conversed quite loudly, cracked jokes and laughed in explosive guffaws – for all the world as if they were on some errand which involved no danger'. On another occasion, a low-lying camp was flooded and burghers had to rush to safety: 'This they did laughing and joking, which certainly was a fine proof of the good spirit that prevailed among them, and of the cheerfulness with which they were ready to make any sacrifice for the sake of the great cause.'[9]

Practical jokes became a way of coping with the unwelcome intimacy of commando life and the unremitting stress of guerrilla war. Horseplay was part of commando life.[10] One such example was cited when a man hid the spine of a devil's apple weed underneath a friend's saddle, which caused his horse to buck forcefully when mounted. A different prank was played on General W.J. Kolbe, who was proud of his luxuriant beard. He awoke one morning to find that fellow officers had shaved it off during the night and an amused crowd was waiting for his reaction. *Agterryers*, who sometimes gave clowning performances, were a source of humour, as in the case of General Ben Viljoen's famous *agterryer*, Mooiroos. Shared *grootliegstories* (tall tales) also provided amusement. Another example of a practical joke was when the Du Plessis brothers, who were 'jovial in a grim sort of manner', captured an old male baboon and – each holding one of his hands –

The ruined farmhouse of Jan Gildenhuis in Winburg

walked him on his hind legs to the president saying that 'a new burgher' had joined up. The baboon was so overcome that he meekly allowed his hand to be shaken![11] In fact, it was common to adopt pets as mascots and, like the baboon, they often afforded light relief. In the small commando groups, laughter provided a welcome way to release tension.

Recent studies show that the experience of humour may affect the immune system. Laughter helps stabilise blood pressure, oxygenates the blood, stimulates circulation and produces a feeling of well-being, probably due to endorphin release. In Darwinian terms, those 'with a sense of humour'[12] are able to cope with the sadness of the world with slightly better immune systems. In addition, some experimental studies suggest that humour engenders hope. Reitz recorded that General De la Rey often addressed the men in a 'half-humorous, half-serious manner, and soon he had the men laughing and making light of their misfortunes'.[13]

And laughter certainly did boost morale. This is illustrated by an anecdote told by the Boer combatant Chris Muller:

> Louis Bothma took a position with his heliograph beside a very big rock to protect himself against bullets … While we were still talking, a bomb exploded on the rock. The next moment we were enveloped by a thick cloud of smoke. The general asked … 'Old Chris, are you still alive?' I answered, 'Yes, General, an Englishman isn't allowed to kill me!'[14]

Humour was also a way of boosting the Boers' own confidence and ridiculing the enemy. It was said of Lord Roberts of Kandahar: '*Ja, Roberts fan Kan-da'ar / Is ni Roberts fan Kan-hiir!*' (This joke plays on the Afrikaans words *daar*, meaning there, and *hier*, meaning here. Translated literally, it says: 'Yes, Roberts of Can-there/is not Roberts of Can-here!'.)[15]

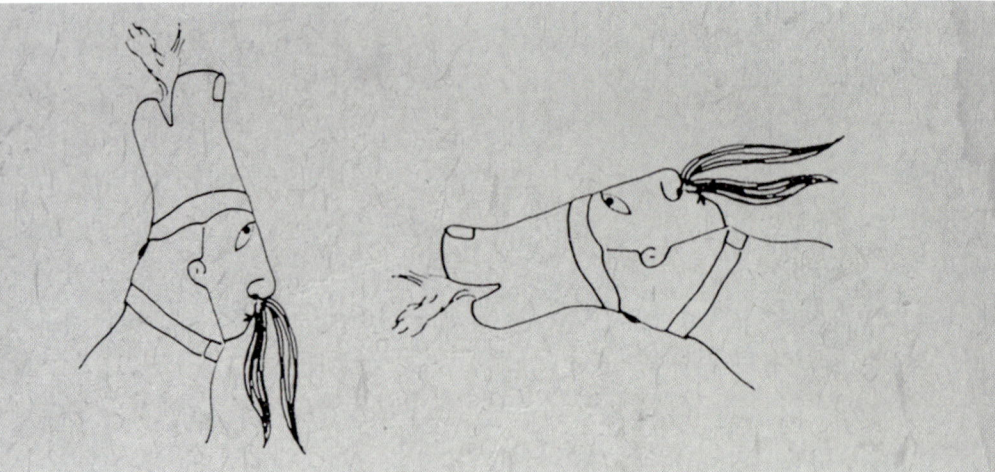

ABOVE LEFT First the Zulus and now the Boers: the slow-moving and champagne-addicted Sir Redvers Buller, nicknamed *Rooivers* (red heifer) by his republican enemies.
RIGHT Buller is lampooned as General Buller the donkey, or the donkey as General Buller

War jokes lifted the spirits of the men, for instance, they referred to martial law as a girl called Martjie Louw. Similarly, a burgher, Aap Geldenhuys, when watching droves of English soldiers march by, made a dry allusion to the second plague of Egypt, 'Dirt turns into lice'.[16] These quips elicited scornful – yet daring – laughter.

When two of his men arrived at Lambert's Bay, General Manie Maritz wrote:

... A British cruiser was anchored near the beach. From pure rowdiness two burghers started shooting at the cruiser with their guns. It wasn't long before the warship's cannons were brought into action and a serious fight ... ensued! The two daredevils had to make a hasty retreat. When they arrived back at their commando, they were two proud fellows with quite a story to tell. 'General,' they asked Maritz, 'has it ever before happened that the entire British navy was challenged by two *Boertjies*?'[17]

General Viljoen commented on the men under him: 'The Afrikander character may be called peculiar in many respects. In moments of reverse, when the future seems dark, one can easily trace its pessimistic tendencies. But once his comrades buried, the wounded attended to, and a moment's rest left him by the enemy, the cheerful part of the Boer nature prevails, and he is full of fun and sport.'[18]

Some jokes were pure silliness. For example, a few English soldiers caught a Boer whom they tried to hurry, but he was slow. The English said, 'We shall have to kill you!' The Boer answered, 'As julle my kielie, dan lag ek my dood.' (If you tickle me, then I'll die laughing.)[19]

Such hilarity (sometimes hysterical laughter) offered an escape from harsh reality. Reitz wrote that, in a particularly heavy assault, he saw his brother 'disappear from sight as a shrapnel shell burst on him, but he rode out laughing, he and his horse uninjured'.[20] When his exhausted commando arrived at the coast, many of the young men had not seen a body of water bigger than 'the dam on their parents' farm'[21]. They rode bareback into the surf, shouting and laughing whenever a rider and his horse were knocked down by the waves. During the battle at Rhenosterkop in November 1900, a Boer soldier noted that the men exchanged jokes and their laughter competed with the sound of the shelling.[22]

Commando humour also offered a form of social control. Mock courts were held, with intentionally outrageous charges, which were greeted 'with laughter and cheering'.[23] In this way, humour conveyed morality and codes of behaviour, and, in so doing, maintained social cohesion. For instance, a few burghers badgered General Viljoen for permission to go home and he was goaded into writing in their passes: 'Permit to go to Johannesburg on account of cowardice, at Government's expense'.[24] Similarly, the populist, but unpopular, Boer prophet, Siener van Rensburg, after recent sightings of a double-tailed comet, had declared that its tail depicted a V for *Vrede*. One night, however, a 'boyish voice from the darkness ahead call[ed] out, "Mijnheer van Rensburg, that letter V up there does not mean *Vrede*, it means *Vlug*" – to the sound of wry laughter in the ranks'.[25]

As well as regulating an internal hierarchy, jokes helped define the boundaries of the community and fostered solidarity. On commando, the jokes called attention to a common identity and provided a sense of belonging. Therefore, the fraternal laughter of insiders also excluded outsiders. Shared jokes created in-group validation and out-group superiority. For example, a practical joke was played on potential *hendsoppers* by Viljoen's officers. Three Boer officers wore as much khaki as they could find, and asked the men if they would like to surrender. They took cattle, sheep, guns and a pony from the would-be *hendsoppers*. The pseudo-colonel mounted his 'big clumsy English horse and rode proudly away' but the horse stumbled over barbed wire and threw its rider. He silenced the teasing of his two 'fellow-Khakis' by saying that the fall had been most fortunate, as the *hendsoppers* were 'now convinced that we are English by the clumsy manner I rode'.[26]

F.W. Reitz, former president of the Orange Free State and wartime state secretary of the South African Republic, was less inclined than his son to make up with the enemy. His son, Deneys Reitz, ended up in the British Army in World War I.

Satirical verse served a similar purpose, rendering the enemy humorous rather than frightening. Deneys's father, State Secretary F.W. Reitz, wrote a poem while in the field about the Boer capture of a naval gun (nicknamed Lady Roberts), which included this representative verse:

> Lord Roberts gave up fighting, he did not care a rap,
> But left his dear old 'Lady', who's fond of mealie-pap.
> Of our dear wives and children he burned the happy homes,
> He likes to worry *Tantes* but fears the sturdy *Ooms*.[27]

The Boers vouchsafed a black humour, which swung between uproarious laughter and bitter empathy; between farce and gallows humour. The death of Queen Victoria in January 1901 offered occasion for this:

> Cousin, cousin, life is miserable. My wife is terribly sick in the concentration camp in Klerksdorp, we've lost some of our best men in battle and now we have to hear that our beloved Queen Victoria has passed away.[28]

Reitz told an anecdote in which humour functioned to resist the enemy's stereotypical view of the Boers, and was arguably an act of self-respect. He once stumbled upon 'two wounded [British] officers … As [he] came up [he] heard one remark, "Here comes a typical young Boer for you."' The officers asked Reitz why the Boers refused to surrender when they were 'bound to lose'. Reitz answered, 'Oh, well, you see, we're like Mr Micawber, we are waiting for something to turn up.' They burst out laughing and one said, 'Didn't I tell you this is a funny country and now here's your typical young Boer quoting Dickens.'[29]

Laughter could, therefore, be a useful tool: to defuse tension, to rebuke an unpopular fellow soldier, to reinforce group identity, to appease a threat and to boost one's confidence. Sometimes, on rare occasions, humour could break down boundaries between

groups, rank levels and even enemy lines. For example, as the war wore on, the Boers needed clothes and often took the uniforms of British prisoners, who were compelled to wear the Boers' tattered discards. In 1902, Louis Slabbert of the Heidelberg Commando noted what he referred to as one of the funniest sights he had ever seen:

> There stood the khakis, with their sunburnt noses and spotty faces, neatly lined up wearing old ragged clothes. In some cases their toes stuck out of broken *velskoene* and in other cases their hair stuck out of the holes in their hats. One of the more comical Tommies grabbed his friend by the shoulder, pretended that he wanted to kick him, then said: 'Come on, get on, you damn Boer!' Both sides burst out laughing at this.[30]

Anecdotes like these, although atypical, reflect shared humanity and mutual empathy. In a parallel vignette, the name 'Lady Roberts' had been chiselled onto a naval gun (the topic of Reitz's satirical verse), which had been captured by Viljoen's commando. His message to General Horace Smith-Dorrien had a jocular tone: 'I have been obliged to expel "The Lady Roberts" [as] an undesirable inhabitant of that place. I am glad to inform you that she seems quite at home in her new surroundings, and pleased with the change of company.' To which the British general responded: 'As the lady you refer to is not accustomed to sleep in the open air, I would recommend you to try flannel next to the skin.'[31]

Helpless laughter?

When the war moved into a phase of uneasy peace, the *bittereinders* continued fighting – with bitter laughter. After the war, the defeated Boers were to become familiar with one comic genre in particular – ridicule. Alfred Milner, British proconsul to South Africa from 1897 to 1905, used a post-war reconstruction administration and anglicisation policy to attempt to transform the republican Afrikaners into English-speaking colonists. There was a general feeling that he wanted to 'wipe out the last trace of Africanderism and damn the consequences'.[32] In December 1900, Milner had notoriously declared that he intended to use the conquest of the republics to expand British culture and restrict Dutch.

Following the Treaty of Vereeniging (31 May 1902), the Boer republics of the Transvaal and the Orange Free State became part of the British Empire. After the war, English became the sole official language and the medium of instruction in schools. The

A British imperialist not known for his compromising character: Sir Alfred Milner, Britain's High Commissioner in South Africa and administrator of the conquered and annexed Boer republics

Camp: Peace Celebrations. 12.

OPPOSITE, TOP Dutifully spreading the word, General de Wet carries the peace terms to another camp crowd.

ABOVE Not necessarily olive branches, but welcoming branches all the same: celebratory arches put up by camp inhabitants to welcome General de Wet

RIGHT General Schalk Burger visiting the Merebank camp near Durban after the end of hostilities

Mr. Schalk Burger informing the terms of surrender at Merebank Burgher Camp on the 7th of June 1902.

THE 'TERRIBLE LAUGHTER' OF THE BOERS: HUMOUR IN THE WAR

Before the war

Almost invisible to history before the great storms arrived: pre-war Boer family life was fundamentally a simple, religious, austere, close-knit and self-consciously respectable rural existence.

future of Dutch and Afrikaans seemed uncertain: the authorities discouraged the use of Dutch and more teachers were brought out from England. The teaching of Dutch had been guaranteed in the peace treaty, but was restricted in practice. The Cape abandoned fluency in Dutch as a prerequisite for entry into the civil service. In the post-war education system, anglicisation was imposed on Afrikaans children. This led to the kind of humour embedded in the very mechanics of social power – the mocking laughter that ensures conformity. A story commonly told by Afrikaners was that the children who spoke more Dutch Afrikaans than the permitted amount had to wear a placard that read: 'I'm a donkey, I spoke Dutch.'

As well as ridiculing the defeated Boers, laughter was used to silence them, to impose discipline and to display social aggression. This may have been the humour of the powerful, but not the *all*-powerful. The Milner regime disparaged those who broke the rules in order to uphold those rules. Yet, although voices were literally silenced, laughter could still be heard. This was the laughter of the powerless, which disguised social critique as comedy. Arguably, this black humour was a grim acknowledgement that the suppressed Boers could still at least laugh.

The laughter of the survivor

This survivalist version of dark humour allowed the preservation of some dignity and the weathering of changes in a profoundly damaged society. Boer combatants and concentration camp inmates suffered from post-traumatic shock after the war. The scorched-earth

policy had left a ruined rural economy, and the social status quo, in terms of class, was in upheaval. As Viljoen observed, 'There is scarcely an Afrikander family without an unhealable wound. Everywhere the traces of the bloody struggle.'[33] One observer recalled:

> I remember that my grandmother chuckled when she told me how, on returning to the farm, Mooifontein, after the war, she and my grandfather found a donkey in Tabakskloof, at the far reaches of the farm … *Oupa* and the donkey pulled a very primitive, damaged plough and she clung desperately to the plough, laughing at herself the whole time (she said). I often heard her say 'all we can do, my child, is laugh' … even speaking of tragic happenings (though she never spoke of her dead children). It is she who said, 'The English aren't such bad people: they just don't know how to run a good concentration camp.'[34]

It can be argued that jokes permitted statements that otherwise would have been socially threatening. Anything said in jest could be denied and justified with the defence 'I was only joking'. American academic Langston Hughes offers a helpful comparison and notes, with 'black tongue in white cheek or vice versa',[35] that African-American slaves used coded humorous language to vent rage. Their stoic laughter masked inner pain and allowed the preservation of outward dignity. Ethnic bonding was reinforced by this shared (yet often desperate) hilarity.

Similarly, political jokes can offer the tellers and listeners alike a brief respite from the realities of everyday life – a moment when they feel that they (rather than the authorities)

This small chain or bracelet was fashioned from the hair of a Mrs S.J. Jooste, who perished in the Merebank camp.

are in control. The political joke, with its incongruities and its mechanisms for making those incongruities appropriate, allows for a different view of reality.

After the war, some jokes may have functioned as veiled resistance and private challenges to the status quo. Through these jokes, a space was created (however small) that the political regime could not penetrate. Any triumphs that emerged from such humour were usually transitory and purely psychological, but the jokes served to maintain self-esteem and morale.

There was challenging humour in many of the writings of the *volkskrywers*, such as C.J. Langenhoven, which involved implicit political commentary. For example, C. Louis Leipoldt commented that he wrote many of the poems in his anthology, *Oom Gert vertel en ander gedigte* (1911), directly after the war, with the 'thunder of English cannons still in his ears'.[36] His bitter irony and lacerating wit were particularly resonant in *Vrede-aand* (Evening of the Peace Treaty):

It's peace time, man; the war is over!
Do you hear the people shouting in the streets?
Can you see, the whole world is upside down?
Come, here's a bottle of sweet wine; let us drink!
Into the sea we let our nation sink;
We have no country any more, we're done for!
It's peace time: let's shout – or are you hoarse?
From laughter? Laugh if you want, because the story's out:
Our nation is gone, we can whistle for it!
Drink, drink your glass! The sun shines through the wine:
Is it too sweet, or does it taste of vinegar? [37]

Such acerbic humour can be interpreted by social historians in two ways. As has been discussed, the jokes may be seen as an unconscious resistance to restraint – allowing social norms to be broken momentarily. Another similar theory suggests that jokes challenge the social order by making the familiar appear unfamiliar. These small rebellions may be protesting against the social order or providence itself. Significantly, joking seems to be more prevalent under totalitarianism than under democracy. Jokes may be understood as small subversive acts and, as George Orwell says, 'every joke is a tiny revolution.'[38]

The counter-argument to this hypothesis is that some jokes offer, not rebellion, but only its illusion, and actually foster further resignation and acquiescence. In a homeostatic system, humour can release tension and, therefore, actually maintain the status quo. Laughter can be a substitute for the political action that could otherwise effect change. Writing about Arab political humour, Iraqi writer and satirist Khalid Kishtainy says that 'people joke about their oppressors, not to overthrow them but to endure them.'[39] It has been said that those who possess guns have no need of jokes. Indeed, political jokes may sometimes be a way of accommodating authoritarianism and assuaging the guilt of the joke-teller in terms of his or her failure to act politically.

If one applies this view, the jokes that 'attacked' the post-war regime were not small rebellions at all. Instead they were crutches for those who did not (or could not) rebel. These jokes enabled the tellers to live more comfortably with their oppression and

After the war

Living psychologically in the shadows of bereavement, loss and the truth of personal survival: for these probable survivors of the camps, their shared traumatic experience of the war added to bonds of kinship and emotion.

troubled consciences. Therefore, this kind of laughter could have been simply a concession in a society that was considered unfair, and even a way of allowing the deaths of fellow ex-combatants (like Hans Lötter and Gideon Scheepers) without precipitating rebellion. In this scenario, gallows humour literally licensed fatalism and inactivity.

An analysis of this short-lived escapism together with the potentially subversive power of laughter, presents us with an understanding of what Emily Hobhouse called the Boers' 'terrible' laughter 'of despair'. F.E.J. 'Fransie' Malherbe, Afrikaans cultural expert, recalled that after the war a Boer was asked how he was by a friend and answered: 'Yes, cousin, my wife and children all died in the concentration camp, my poor livestock died because of drought and the locusts ate all my standing crop, but apart from that, all is well.'[40]

The mirth of a nation?

The strategic focus on the ethnic nature of humour is illustrated in the work of F.E.J. Malherbe. A professor in the Dutch-Afrikaans department at Stellenbosch University from 1930 to 1959, he did much to shape Afrikaans as a written language and promote its cultural side. His doctoral dissertation was entitled *Humor in die algemeen en sy uiting in die Afrikaanse letterkunde* (*Humour in General and its Expression in Afrikaans Literature*).

This chapter showed that a conscious notion of 'the sense of humour'[41] (not considered before the mid-nineteenth century) was emerging as an apparently essential component of a complete person. Similarly, on a larger scale, young nations and nations struggling with identity issues emphasised aspects such as a national sense of humour. For Malherbe, in seeking a modern national character, Afrikanerdom had to define its sense of humour in the *volkstaal*, which C.J. Langenhoven had called 'the expressed soul of our people'.[42]

Malherbe published a series of articles in the *Huisgenoot* magazine in 1934 entitled: 'Does the Afrikaner have a sense of humour?' His central argument was based on the existence of an Afrikaner 'national character', which included a natural and unique sense of humour. Malherbe argued that the Anglo-Boer War had given rise to this form of humour.

He stated that in Afrikaans the greatest humour often arises from sorrow. Using distinctively Afrikaans examples from the war, Malherbe suggested that the nation's 'suffering, our uplifting, glorious grief moved through grief to glory, through irony to humour'.[43] He argued that, in desperate times, if one small thing went right that was seen as reason to smile:

> The racially pure Boer possesses the characteristic of resignation in times of adversity and disaster, illness and death; but also the clear sense of the comical in daily life, and the loving and humorous consideration of values in the great reality that surrounds us ... But the great humour also liberated us from idle wishes and fear, and opened further horizons. Thus a trait of our race developed further.
>
> The highest humour in Afrikaans also arises from sorrow. Yes, where is the secret of our people ... in particular of our farming class, that they do not become despondent over the most dreadful succession of disasters? They always find a joke somewhere in their misery. 'Isn't it droll,' they say, 'that things can go wrong in such a funny fashion?'[44]

Malherbe advocated a hierarchy of humour. His theory was that women had a lesser sense of humour than men because of a lack of intellectual and physical freedom – their work

A stark and sombre resting place: the cemetery at the Bethulie camp in the Orange Free State

'is never done'. He maintained that Afrikaner women permitted themselves only small ironies. Malherbe also believed that they lacked humour because they were *bittereinders* mentally. The ability of women to withstand great hardship during the war had been a popular theme among public intellectuals.

To return to our opening vignette, Reitz's experience of commando laughter resembled guerrilla warfare itself. Success in both arenas depended on travelling lightly over heavy ground, knowing the territory, being able to escape and knowing who your friends were. Laughter was a weapon used for both defence and attack. *Bittereinders* fought the war with a bitter sense of humour. After the war, humour was a grim acknowledgement that the silenced could at least laugh. A funny thing happened on the way to nationhood: with (mother) tongue in cheek, some *taalstryders* (language activists) believed humour was integral to Afrikaner ethnic national identity, but was experienced differently by men and women.

This chapter has explored a historical phenomenon that seems bizarre at first: the laughter of a particular group of men and women in a traumatic war and an ensuing damaged post-war social milieu. From the despairing laughter of the oppressed to the mocking laughter of the oppressor, a century of social history is echoed in the different kinds of Afrikaner laughter and their interpretations. Historians need to learn how to listen. Where there are silences, the sources should be found. Historians could take to heart what Malherbe wrote about the Afrikaner:

> You have to learn to detect humour in the light trembling of the corner of someone's mouth, or the nervous recourse to the bag of tobacco, in the sudden flickering of a dull gaze, in the muttering of thanks after some disaster and set-back, in the resignation when the shadows fall ...[45]

Note: This chapter is drawn from Sandra Swart, '"The terrible laughter of the Afrikaner" – Towards a Social History of Humour', *Journal of Social History*, vol. 42, no. 4, Summer, 2009.

CHAPTER NINE

The Women's Monument: Planning, design and inauguration

— JOHAN VAN ZŸL —

PREVIOUS PAGE First pilgrimage to a place of war memory: the crowd assembles on 16 December 1913 for the unveiling of the Women's Monument.

THIS PAGE Refurbishment carried out at the site of remembrance in 1972

THE ORIGINS OF THE NATIONAL WOMEN'S MONUMENT are closely linked to the events that took place in the post-war South Africa of 1902 and the spirit of the Afrikaners at the time. After the losses they had suffered during the Anglo-Boer War, Afrikaners began mobilising politically with a view to asserting themselves within the constrained parameters of British imperial control.

The erection of this memorial was the first major post-war undertaking to be accomplished on a national level, and it later gave Afrikaners, in both the former Boer republics and the British colonies, a sense of solidarity. Therefore, the monument was a tangible symbol, not only of a nation's profound pain, but also of its resurrection. It indicated that the Afrikaners were slowly but surely regaining their self-respect and pride after the Peace of Vereeniging.

Plans for a monument

During the war, the Free State president, Marthinus Theunis Steyn, had already proposed that the wartime sacrifices of women and children deserved to be commemorated in some way. He had wished to pay tribute to those who had been in the concentration camps as well as the women who had survived in the veld. His decision had been strongly supported by his wife, Rachel Isabella (Tibbie).

However, two months after the signing of the Peace of Vereeniging, which took place on 31 May 1902, Steyn went to Europe to receive treatment for a serious illness that had left him partially paralysed in the last month of the war. This inexplicable condition required intensive medical treatment, and he was able to return to South Africa only in 1905. Soon after his return, he set about realising his ideal, and on 20 July 1906 held a meeting at the house of his brother Jan Steyn. Several prominent Free State Afrikaners attended the meeting, including Abraham Fischer (later prime minister of the Orange River Colony), General J.B.M. Hertzog and Revd C.D. Murray (minister of the Tweetoringkerk in Bloemfontein).

Steyn convinced those present that the tribute should take the form of a monument – something that could capture the nation's imagination – rather than the alternative proposals of a hospital or a children's home. At a subsequent meeting, a steering committee was appointed with Steyn as chairman.[1] This committee believed that the proposal of a monument was a matter of national importance and all Afrikaner leaders should be involved.

RIGHT Men in peacetime in praise of women in wartime: members of the National Women's Monument Commission, including former Orange Free State president, M.T. Steyn and General J.B.M. Hertzog, future prime minister of the Union of South Africa (seated front row, centre right)

BELOW In this 1907 letter to fellow-Afrikaners Marthinus Steyn requests donations from both rich and poor to build the Women's Monument.

Accordingly, a national conference took place on 7 February 1907 in Bloemfontein, attended by the Dutch churches and Afrikaner political organisations, including General Louis Botha's Het Volk (Transvaal), General Hertzog's Orangia-Unie (Free State), Jan Hofmeyr's Afrikanerbond (Cape Colony) and the Het Kongres of Natal. Delegates agreed with Steyn about the need for a worthy memorial in the form of an obelisk or sculpture. It would cost approximately £10 000 to erect a memorial that would depict the 'suffering endured for the fatherland by the Afrikaans woman'[2]. The fund-raising was an ambitious task because of the large sum of money required and because most Afrikaners in the two former Boer republics were impoverished after the war.

It took four years to collect the money. The fund-raising effort included appeals in the press. For instance, President Steyn's plea for contributions was published in the magazine *Die Brandwag*. In addition, hundreds of collection lists were compiled, which the semi-invalid President Steyn signed (with great difficulty, aided by his wife). Commissioners were appointed in each of the four colonies. They divided the colonies into wards, and young girls were appointed in each ward to collect the money. Mrs Steyn also assisted with these efforts because she was responsible for secretarial work relating to the collection lists. In 1908 the poet Totius published a special volume of poetry, *Bij die Monument*, to contribute to the fund-raising.

At the unveiling of the monument in 1913, Steyn would declare that it had been made possible 'not only by the wealth of the wealthy, but especially by the poverty of the poor'. It was an exception to receive contributions in pounds; the Women's Monument came into being by donations of shillings and pennies. The fund-raising went well in the Free State and the Cape Colony, but was slow in the Transvaal.

Although some members of the English-speaking and Jewish communities also contributed to the fund, General Louis Botha had misgivings that the proposed monument might offend English-speaking citizens. Botha, who was involved in the plans for a Union of South Africa, was concerned that it might damage the reconciliation process between English-speaking and Afrikaans-speaking communities. In January 1908 he tried to persuade Steyn to abandon the idea of a monument to women and children in favour of one commemorating Piet Retief, but Steyn rejected this suggestion.

Design and construction

In the meantime, the steering committee had launched a national competition for the monument's design, offering £100 as a prize for the winner. More than 40 designs were received. The design that was eventually chosen was that of an obelisk, 36,5 metres high, ringed by a wall, submitted by sculptor Anton van Wouw and Pretoria architect Frans Soff. However, aspects of their proposed design were modified. For instance, the monument would be placed at the foot of a *koppie* instead of on the summit, and access to the wall around the monument would be via one central set of steps instead of three.

Members of the steering committee had also visited possible sites for the monument. Irene, Vereeniging, Kroonstad, Springfontein and Bloemfontein were all considered. Bloemfontein was finally chosen because the city council had allocated a site south of the city for a public park. It has since been established, from photographs and archaeological remains, that the monument's location had been part of a British military camp during the war.

But the British-controlled Bloemfontein city council did not grant the land for the monument without opposition. There were heated debates, and councillors such as

A poetry collection by Afrikaans writer Totius, sold to raise money for the monument

ABOVE Not everyone's ideal choice as the monument's architectural craftsman: the Dutch-born Afrikaans sculptor, Anton van Wouw

RIGHT Van Wouw's draft design of the monument

Arthur G. Barlow argued that the monument, particularly its side panels, distorted the truth and was intended to aggrieve English-speakers. Because of the controversy, Revd J.D. Kestell advised Steyn to consider towns such as Ficksburg or Ladybrand instead. On 4 November 1911, *The Friend*, a Bloemfontein English-language newspaper criticised council members like Barlow for pettiness. A petition was drawn up containing more than 1 000 signatures in favour of the monument being erected in Bloemfontein.

At a second national conference, held in the Bloemfontein Memorial Hall on 7 July 1911, Steyn gave feedback on the money that had been collected. This amounted to £4 422 from the Free State, £2 807 from the Cape Colony, £2 305 from the Transvaal, £174 from Natal and £71 from overseas. The total amount was £10 236, including interest, but Steyn believed that an additional sum of £5 000 should be raised for the future maintenance of the monument.

It was also decided that the monument needed to be completed in time for the unveiling to take place on 16 December 1913, then called Dingaan's Day. A Bloemfontein building contractor, Medlin and Leham, was given the tender for constructing the monument from sandstone (sourced from the Kroonstad district). According to a contemporary newspaper, it would be the largest monument in South Africa at the time.

Anton van Wouw left for Italy in 1911 to work on the monument's two bas-relief panels and main sculpture group at the studio of Antonio Canova in Rome. (Some of Europe's most famous sculptures were created by Canova's studio.) Van Wouw was in constant contact with Emily Hobhouse, who was also in Rome, for health reasons. She wrote in a letter to Steyn's wife: 'I look forward to seeing Mr van Wouw and give him all the hints and help I can in his efforts to visualise the camps and symbolise all …'[3]

RIGHT Conceived in Mediterranean Europe to be born in South Africa: sculptural work on the central cluster of figures commences in Antonio Canova's studio in Rome.

OPPOSITE, LEFT An ironic legacy of the war: construction of the monument is undertaken by Scottish Bloemfontein firm, Medlin and Leham, with British family connections and a claimed tie to the Crown.

OPPOSITE, RIGHT British philanthropist Emily Hobhouse was a figure synonymous with the Women's Monument.

However, Hobhouse had previously expressed strong views in several letters opposing Van Wouw's selection for such a major commission. In a letter to General Jan Smuts, she argued that the monument '… required real artistic genius for this job, and the poor man is only an inferior though painstaking artist and quite devoid of genius.'[4] She never changed her opinion. She wrote to Smuts that, in her view, the French sculptor Auguste Rodin or the Dutch Pier Pander would have been a better choice: 'I think … Van Wouw as an artist wholly incapable of carrying out worthily such a work as this monument.'[5]

Nevertheless, she assisted Van Wouw with the project and, as a result of her criticism, the sculptures were changed radically. Van Wouw had initially proposed a design of a standing woman with two children seated at her feet. In a letter to Tibbie Steyn dated 12 January 1912, Hobhouse wrote: 'I am in touch with him [Van Wouw] and went to criticise his first clay model at his desire. I did not like it and had to tell him so. He is too easily satisfied and will have, I think, to rub shoulders a bit with the sculptors here …'[6]

In response to her criticism, Van Wouw modified his design and based the new one on Hobhouse's account of a tragic scene she had witnessed at the Springfontein railway station. She had come across a group of destitute women and children who were waiting to be taken to the Springfontein concentration camp after a long journey in open railway carriages. The camp superintendent had refused to accommodate more people because the camp was already overcrowded. There were no tents available and some women and children sought shelter by crawling under the carriages. Others had constructed makeshift shelters by placing sticks in the ground and laying pieces of canvas (scrounged from the British soldiers) over them. Hobhouse had been called to one such shelter to attend to a sick child. She related the scene to Van Wouw:

The mother sat on her little trunk with the child across her knee. She had nothing to give it and the child was sinking fast ... There was nothing to be done and we watched the child draw its last breath in reverent silence. The mother neither moved nor wept. It was her only child. Dry-eyed but deathly white, she sat there motionless, looking not at the child, but far, far away into the depths of grief beyond all tears.[7]

The camp superintendent refused Hobhouse's request that the dying child be given something to alleviate the pain. This scene left an indelible impression in Hobhouse's mind. To her, the entire tragedy of the war was encapsulated in that scene of children's suffering and women's grief.[8]

Apparently Hobhouse closely monitored Van Wouw's progress. She constantly gave him feedback to ensure that he created an image faithful to her description. In a letter to Tibbie Steyn dated 21 March 1912, she wrote that his sculpted child figure appeared to be merely asleep instead of dead. 'He sent for me this week to come and criticise the clay model ... It certainly is an improvement on the small-scale model I saw a couple of months ago, yet very far from what it should be and must be ... The mother seated with the child on her knee is soulless and expresses nothing and the child is comfortably asleep and neither sick nor dead in appearance.'[9]

She suggested that Van Wouw request permission to view the corpse of a child in a morgue and also that he study Michelangelo's *Pietà* sculpture in the Vatican. And Van Wouw followed her advice and incorporated elements of his impressions in his sculpture group. He also modified his original design for the bas-relief on the left-hand side of the monument. The most significant change he made was to replace a seated woman in the centre of the panel with two young girls witnessing someone's death in a tent.

After almost two years, the sculpture group – which is described as one of Anton van Wouw's masterpieces – was finally completed, and in July 1913 the sculptures were

OPPOSITE Made in Italy and ready for shipment: the completed central female figurines of the Women's Monument

BELOW In response to Hobhouse's suggestions, Anton van Wouw modified the placement and representation of his moulded relief to depict women and children witnessing death in a tent.

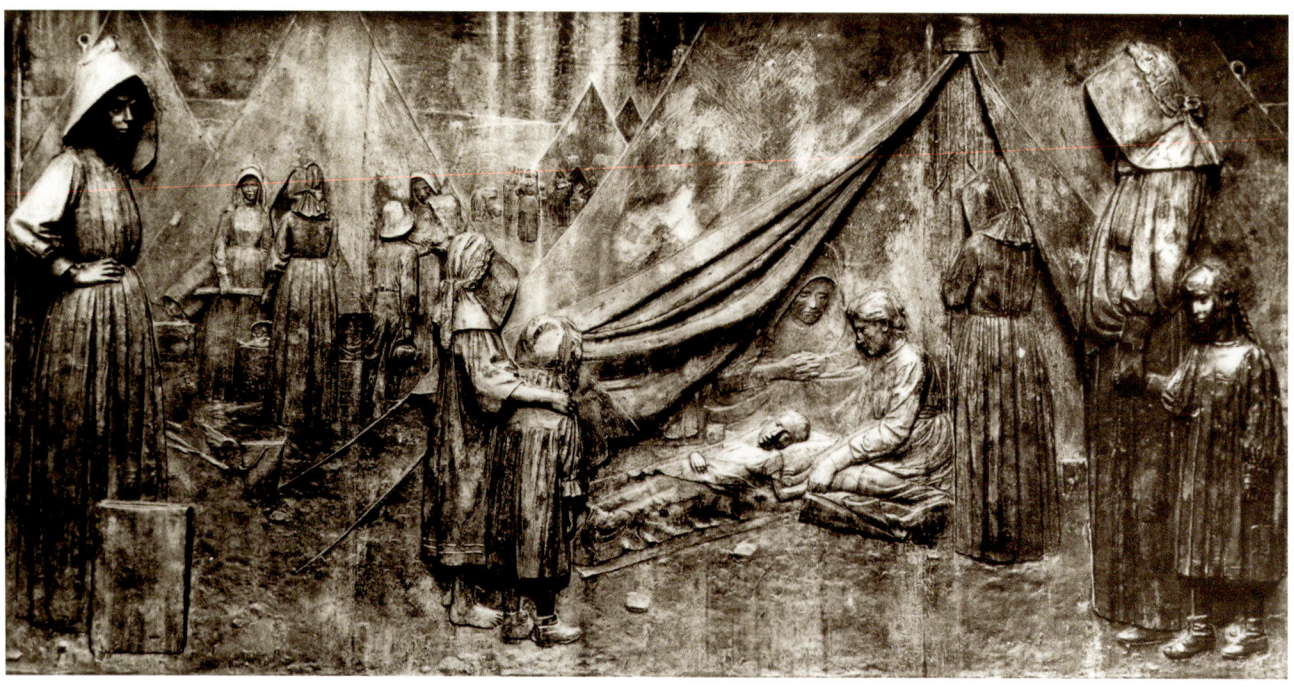

shipped to South Africa, where the construction of the monument was nearing completion. One of the finishing touches made to the monument was the inscription on the pedestal of the sculpture group, formulated by Kestell. Finally, the side panels and main sculpture group were placed in position.

The unveiling

An organising committee was appointed to arrange the unveiling of the monument on 16 December 1913. As recommended by President Steyn and his wife, Hobhouse was invited to perform the unveiling on *Vrouwen-dag*, as the day was dubbed. An ailing Hobhouse arrived from Italy by ship and embarked on the train journey from Cape Town. But she got only as far as Beaufort West, where she was advised to abort the trip because of her deteriorating health. Arrangements for a replacement had to be made quickly, and Tibbie Steyn was chosen.

The festivities commenced two days before the unveiling. Among other events, plays such as *Heldinne van die Oorlog* and *Magrita Prinsloo* were staged at the Grand Theatre in Hanger Street, and choral performances and church services were held in various Dutch churches in the city. Three tented camps known as the Blue, Orange and Green Flag camps were set up on the showgrounds to provide accommodation for the many visitors, and the city council introduced extra tram services to transport them.

On 16 December 1913, the unveiling of the Women's Monument began with a service in the Tweetoringkerk led by the 85-year-old Revd Andrew Murray. This was followed by a procession that included wagons carrying 400 young girls dressed in white, and 1 600 armed, mounted burghers. The procession travelled past Union Jacks flying at half mast.

OPPOSITE There in spirit if not in body . . . Hobhouse was unable to carry out the unveiling through illness; it is undertaken on her behalf by Tibbie Steyn, wife of the former republican president.

BELOW The sacredness of commemoration: the imposing twin towers of the Bloemfontein church in which Dutch Reformed Church dominee Andrew Murray held the inaugurational service for the monument on 16 December 1913.

A message from Pretoria: Prime Minister Hertzog speaks at the opening of The War Museum of the Boer Republics on 30 September 1930.

Shop windows were draped in black in acknowledgement of the devotional atmosphere of the day. The mile-long procession, which also included the vehicles of dignitaries, moved to the site of the monument, where 20 000 people had already assembled, in spite of the oppressive heat. The music corps of the Kimberley Volunteers played Chopin's and Beethoven's funeral marches against the background of a cannon salute that sounded rhythmically from Naval Hill.

Among the guests were Afrikaner leaders from the republican era, such as generals Louis Botha, Christiaan de Wet, Koos de la Rey and J.B.M. Hertzog, and the former Free State presidents Steyn and F.W. Reitz. Although Botha and Smuts had expressed concerns earlier that the Women's Monument might harm the relationship between Afrikaans- and English-speakers, on this historic day political hatchets were buried temporarily.

The proceedings began with a reading from the scriptures. Because of ill-health, President Steyn's speech, which had been handwritten by his wife, was delivered on his behalf by Rocco de Villiers (a former secretary of Steyn and a member of his war staff). In his speech, Steyn emphasised that the monument was not intended to cause anyone pain or to be 'an eternal reproach' but had been placed there out of 'pure piety'. 'If it is sweet for the hero to fight for the fatherland and, laden with glory, to sacrifice himself for freedom, *volk* and fatherland, what reverence is not commanded by the tender woman who, already in the clutches of death herself, sees darling after darling descending into the grave and yet proudly holds her head high, spurring her spouse and sons on the battlefield on not to worry about her but to persevere in the struggle!'[10]

When Tibbie Steyn lowered the cloth that covered the sculpture group and relief panels, a flight of doves was released and the choir sang a hymn. Hobhouse's moving speech (see chapter eleven) was then read on her behalf. After the unveiling, various people, including the consul general of the Netherlands, laid wreaths. Speeches were delivered by several Boer generals, politicians and clergymen, including Botha, De Wet, De la Rey, Revd Willem Postma, Revd A.J. Louw and Professor J.D. du Toit (Totius). The day's proceedings then changed to Dingaan's Day celebrations and various addresses were given, including one by D.F. Malan.

The monument after 1913 and the War Museum of the Boer Republics

After the unveiling, it had to be decided how the monument and site would be maintained in future. This task was entrusted to the National Women's Memorial Commission, which was founded in 1914 with President Steyn as the first chairman. Unfortunately, the archives from 1905 to 1926 pertaining to the monument, which included the architectural plans, have been lost. These records would have made it possible to obtain a more complete picture of the monument's development and the commission's activities during that period.

A prominent war veteran of the old republic: Orange Free State church minister and Afrikaner cultural leader, dominee J.D. Kestell, who was buried at the foot of the Women's Monument in 1941

Later, the Women's Memorial Commission was also responsible for preserving the graves of the people buried there, such as Emily Hobhouse, President Steyn (who died on 28 November 1916) and General De Wet (who died on 3 February 1922). Hobhouse died in July 1926 and her ashes were interred at the monument on 27 October 1926. On 9 February 1941, Revd Kestell was buried at the monument, as was Tibbie Steyn, who died early in January 1955. Mrs Steyn had been opposed to being buried at the monument because she had believed that graves at the site would detract from the monument's original purpose. But, her wishes were ignored and she was laid to rest there. After her funeral, the cemetery within the ring wall of the monument was complete and no further burials took place there.

After the unveiling of the monument, Kestell campaigned for a museum to be built where items from the war that had been donated to the Women's Memorial Commission could be displayed. A large part of the collection consisted of artworks that had been purchased by Nasionale Pers (later to become Naspers, the media company) and presented to the commission.

The cornerstone of the War Museum of the Boer republics was laid in 1926 and it was officially opened by the prime minister, General Hertzog, four years later. The building was later extended twice, in 1954 and 1977. In 2012 the site and museum building were upgraded.

Unfortunately, the sandstone that was used to build the Women's Monument eroded quickly and repairs were already needed by the 1930s. After this the monument underwent frequent restoration – and money for the repairs was collected from the public each

A recent naming of places and counting of their dead: in 1995, marble slabs were laid on which the names of each white concentration camp were inscribed, along with the number of the dead. This was followed in 2010 by the erection of a further monument to mark the dead of both the white and black camps.

time.[11] In the 1970s, the layout of the terrain was also upgraded with the assistance of a landscape architect. Another addition was a sandstone gateway to the site, which was inaugurated on 31 May 1976 by Tibbie Visser, daughter of President Steyn. In 2013 – the centenary of the monument's inauguration – it was renovated once again.

Various commemorations and wreath-laying ceremonies have taken place at the Women's Monument over the decades. The most notable was the celebration of the centenary of the Great Trek in 1938. Other events have included the festival celebrating President Steyn in 1957, the 75th anniversary of the outbreak of the Anglo-Boer War in 1974, and the centenary of the outbreak of the Anglo-Boer War in 1999.

Occasionally, political meetings were also held at the monument. On 20 July 1940, for instance, more than 70 000 people attended a republican protest meeting at the site. This occurred during World War II when the Smuts government came under fire for its support of Britain. The people at the gathering were campaigning for South Africa to become a republic.

In 1982 the monument was declared a national monument. The Women's Memorial Commission decided – controversially – in the early 1980s to have three new sculpture groups added to the monument site. Critics believed that the additional sculptures would be in conflict with the first National Women's Memorial Commission's intention that nothing be erected on the site that might divert the focus from the monument itself. The plans were implemented regardless.

Each sculpture represents a particular aspect of the war. *The Exile* – commemorating the Boers who had been sent to overseas prisoner-of-war camps – was created in 1983 by the sculptor Danie de Jager. Three years later, *Farewell* was unveiled by General Magnus Malan, the chief of the South African Defence Force at the time. It represents a Boer woman saying goodbye to her husband before he goes on commando. *Bittereinder* was unveiled on 31 May 1994, and a clay model was made in preparation for a fourth sculpture, *Agterryer*. The last sculpture was created only in 2013 by Phil Minnaar and placed on the site.

Other additions have been made to the War Museum in the past decade, such as a memorial in 2010 that recognises the suffering of both white and black South Africans in concentration camps, and a monument to commemorate the centenary of the start of the concentration camps. Material from the Bethulie concentration camp was incorporated in this particular monument, because the remains of the camp had to be moved when the Gariep Dam was built. A memorial wall was also built in 2012, bearing the names of all the burghers who died in the Anglo-Boer War.

The appeal of the Women's Monument lies in its simplicity and in the piety it represents. It was the first memorial in the world to commemorate the suffering of women and children in a war. The price paid for this monument was 27 000 white lives lost, but its meaning is universal. It symbolises the suffering of defenceless civilians in war situations and conveys a message with which all of humanity can identify. The Women's Monument is unique not only because it was the first memorial of its kind, but also because it still inspires South Africans in 2013 with its message that survival and victory are possible, no matter what the circumstances may be. It is precisely this message that will encapsulate the monument's significance for South Africa in the next 100 years.

Remembrance not fading away: these photos show the cemetary at the Springfontein camp in the southern Free State before and after its restoration in 2011.

AAN ONZE
HELDINNEN
EN LIEVE KINDEREN
———
"UW WIL GESCHIE..."

CHAPTER TEN

The meaning of the Women's Monument: Then and now

— ALBERT GRUNDLINGH —

PREVIOUS PAGE, MAIN IMAGE For a century, this emotional portrayal of a Boer woman gazing bleakly into the distance, alongside another cradling a dead child, has been the image through which the Women's Monument expresses its meaning to visitors.
SECONDARY IMAGE A stark and lingeringly pastoral place: the monument pictured shortly after its opening, still surrounded by vegetation

THIS PAGE They came to witness: 20 000 people attended the opening of the monument in 1913. Those within its circular wall included the former Orange Free State president, F.W. Reitz, identifiable here by his imposing top hat.

IN HISTORICAL WRITING ABOUT MOST WARS, the focus is usually on the soldiers, and the civilians – particularly women and children – are often the silent victims of such conflicts. However, if one looks at the mortality rate in the Anglo-Boer War, it was undoubtedly a war of women and children. The number of deaths in the white and black concentration camps was considerably greater than the number of men killed in action on both sides. So the war between the Boers and the British was not only waged on the battlefield, but also actively on the home front.

The Anglo-Boer War put Boer women and children in the spotlight and, therefore, their experiences demanded public recognition. After the war, the attention given to the concentration camps and the suffering of the inmates resulted in women and children being seen almost exclusively as the victims of the Anglo-Boer War. The tragic losses left a legacy of bitter memories and mutual recriminations, specifically among Afrikaners, which has dominated much of the academic and popular writing on women and the war.

The impact of the concentration camps was so powerful and pervasive that the main Boer symbol of the war was a memorial for women and children – not for men. It is unusual that this was the primary way of commemorating the war – most war memorials conform to the masculine stereotype of the warrior or hero.

It is also significant that the public was so concerned about the experiences of the women and children in the war that a memorial was erected within a relatively short period of time. The Women's Monument in Bloemfontein was completed less than 11 years after the war; in contrast, the Voortrekker Monument in Pretoria had a more protracted history.

As discussed in chapter nine, the organisational initiative for a memorial came from the former president of the Orange Free State, M.T. Steyn, and his wife, Tibbie. President Steyn received medical treatment in Europe after the Anglo-Boer War, where he further reflected on ways to commemorate the Boer deaths in the concentration camps. Whether or not Europe's rich heritage of monuments acted as additional inspiration is hard to tell in the absence of reliable evidence. However, it is clear that, although Steyn took the organisational lead because of his former political office, his wife did not act as an adjunct. She showed a personal interest in the project because she had lost a number of relatives and friends in the camps. Tibbie Steyn also had a close relationship with Emily Hobhouse, who had acquired prominence through her reports on the British administration's mismanagement of the camps and her efforts to improve the wretched circumstances of the Boer women and children.

When he returned to South Africa, President Steyn began preparations for a suitable memorial. After consultation with various Afrikaner organisations, the decision was taken to build a monument. It was erected approximately three kilometres south of Bloemfontein. The monument is situated among *koppies* against the background of a veld and, therefore, blends in with the natural surroundings. Because the landscape itself becomes part of the monument, this reinforces the idea of the Boer people as a rural nation. Supporters of the project could claim lyrically that the obelisk 'overlooks the surrounding *kopjes* and distant plains, proclaiming its message to the nation with persuasive eloquence'.[1]

A monument with patriarchal ulterior motives?

What was the intended purpose of the monument? According to some present-day interpretations, the monument reflects women's subservience to men and it was erected with patriarchal intentions.

For instance, it has recently been argued that the building of the Women's Monument was a 'male effort to win international sympathy for the nation'.[2] But there is no evidence to back up this claim. It has also been said that excessive emphasis on the women's suffering draws attention away from other dimensions of their experiences. Although the latter statement is true, it is misleading to interpret the post-war focus on women's suffering as men attempting to subordinate women.

In fact, the depiction of suffering in the central sculpture group did not originate from male deliberations, neither was it even the proposal of the male sculptor, Anton van Wouw. It was Emily Hobhouse's idea, based on an incident she had witnessed during the war in Springfontein when she had been asked to visit a sick baby:

> The mother sat on her little trunk with the child across her knee. She had nothing to give it and the child was sinking fast ... There was nothing to be done and we watched the child draw its last breath in reverent silence. The mother neither moved nor wept. It was her only child. Dry-eyed but deathly white, she sat there motionless, looking not at the child but far, far away into the depths of grief beyond all tears. A friend stood behind her who called upon Heaven to witness this tragedy.[3]

TOP Finding inspiration in the Eternal City: Anton van Wouw, monument sculptor and architect, at work in Rome's Canova studio

ABOVE This Van Wouw sculpture failed to win approval and was rejected by the monument organisers.

When Van Wouw was working on the sculpture group in Rome, Hobhouse described this scene to him. She did not have a high regard for Van Wouw as a sculptor and thought that his sculpture failed to do justice to the sad event. She commented that the sculpture of the child should have depicted more accurately the 'aspect of emaciation and death' (also see chapter nine).[4] Therefore, it was a woman, not a man, who chose the specific theme of the monument and a woman who considered its portrayal inadequate in capturing the suffering of Boer women and children.

Given the prominence of the obelisk, some modern critics of the monument have described it as a 'phallic symbol'.[5] This interpretation asserts that the aesthetic ideology of the Women's Monument primarily revolves around its masculinity. One does not want to deny the unintended meanings that monuments can convey, but it is debatable whether such interpretations help us understand what the Women's Monument represented in gender terms at the time.

Although Afrikaner women lived in an overarching patriarchal system during that period, it was a system that also imposed certain obligations on the men. Protection of women was a social and moral imperative. During the war, women and children experienced horrors that the men were unable to prevent or alleviate, and this evoked a strong sense of guilt. President Steyn, who was acutely aware of the ordeals of Boer women and the effects this had on the men on commando, believed that a deep sense of indebtedness was the main incentive for building the monument. He asked, rhetorically, whether it was surprising that the men felt a need to build a memorial for those who had died in the camps.

Therefore, it can reasonably be accepted that the principal motive for the Women's Monument was to give the survivors an opportunity to pay their debts, as it were, to a perished generation. To some leading women of the time, the issue was beyond doubt: they regarded the purpose of the monument as paying tribute first and foremost to women. Tibbie Steyn saw the project as an attempt to place women 'on a high pedestal',[6] while Hobhouse made it very clear that it was essentially a women's monument of which 'all the world's women should be proud'.[7]

These declarations make it difficult to accept the theory of female subservience that some present-day analysts assign to the monument and its symbolism. At the same time, it is possible that the initial symbolism was later extended or that new meanings were introduced due to a changing social and political context.

Even at the time – although it did not necessarily influence the original symbolism of the monument – the predominance of men in the organising committee did lead to some gender-biased oversights. For example, six weeks before the unveiling ceremony, Hobhouse expressed her concern in a letter to Tibbie Steyn that the organising committee might have forgotten to invite the Cape Town women's organisations that had worked hard for the camps.[8]

ABOVE Female at the forefront: Isabella Tibbie Steyn, wife of the Orange Free State president, played a leading role in fundraising and planning.

BELOW Graves of British troops in the Bloemfontein cemetery of earlier Orange Free State leader, President Johannes Brandt. In one of many post-war ironies, the British outpost, which can be glimpsed in the background, is on ground on which the Women's Monument would later be constructed.

Wartime Boer leopards who changed their spots: Generals Louis Botha (top) and Jan Smuts (above), who later became leaders of the Union of South Africa and advocates of Afrikaner-Anglo unity.

RIGHT Publicising the new monument: a Bloemfontein street parade en route to the site

A monument in the name of Afrikaner nationalism?

Another common claim is that the building of the monument was an expression of Afrikaner nationalism. To investigate the validity of this claim, one needs to look at the political undercurrents of the era and the events on the day of the unveiling.

In 1913, the year in which the monument was unveiled, Afrikaner politics was characterised by fissures rather than a sense of unity. There was conflict in Afrikaner ranks about South Africa's relationship with Great Britain and this was reflected in the opposing views of the more practical prime minister Louis Botha and his antagonist, General J.B.M. Hertzog, who was regarded as the main champion of (republican) Afrikaner rights. Matters came to a head when Botha did not choose Hertzog for his cabinet in 1912. In addition, an uneasy relationship existed between Afrikaans- and English-speakers in wider politics. In the typical parlance of the time, the two language communities were described as different races and there was much talk of racial animosity. These developments had a marked impact on the politics that surrounded the building and unveiling of the monument.

Botha (and General Jan Smuts) was central to the efforts to reconcile the divided South African society after the Anglo-Boer War. He was a formidable commander of the Boer forces in the Transvaal during the hostilities, and in the post-war period he emerged as a pragmatic politician. He became premier of the Transvaal Colony in 1907 and the first prime minister of the Union of South Africa in 1910. Botha was concerned about the potentially damaging effects of a commemoration of the concentration camps on reconciliation politics, and, therefore, opposed the idea that political meetings in the Transvaal be used to promote the campaign for the Women's Monument. He also tried, in vain, to derail Steyn's proposal by suggesting a national monument for the Voortrekkers instead. This proposal would have moved the historical focus from a recent and highly emotional war to a more remote and heroic representation of nation building during the Great Trek.

In Bloemfontein, the predominantly English-speaking city council had reservations about the advisability of a monument that could reflect adversely on Great Britain and also, by implication, on those in the Free State capital who had supported the British war

White women in white: members of the choir singing at the 1913 inauguration

effort. It was only after considerable debate in the city council that permission was granted for the monument to be built.

The disagreement between Botha's and Hertzog's supporters, and the apprehensions of white English-speaking South Africans threatened to undermine what was supposed to be a national monument. In November 1913, Coen Brits, a former Boer general in the eastern Transvaal, who planned to travel to Bloemfontein with his previous comrades in arms, recommended to Steyn that the unveiling of the monument be delayed:

> Father is against son, brother against brother, etc. Internal wrangling makes co-operation on a national level impossible ... It is a most inappropriate time to unveil the monument. Would it not be better to postpone proceedings until such time that peace and co-operation have been restored? What I fear is that during the occasion political discussions and speeches may lead to internecine strife and bitterness which would detract from the solemnity of the event.[9]

The unveiling took place on 16 December 1913. The date was significant – it was Dingaan's Day (later the Day of the Vow and currently the Day of Reconciliation), which was the day marking the Voortrekker victory over the Zulu at Blood River (today the Ncome River). Commemorations of this day often carried an ethnic political message. This timing did not reassure those who had misgivings about the Women's Monument. The English-language press expressed regret that this day had been chosen and it was argued that the ceremony could have been held on any other day without lessening the solemnity of the event.

On the day of the unveiling, a crowd of approximately 20 000 people from all over the

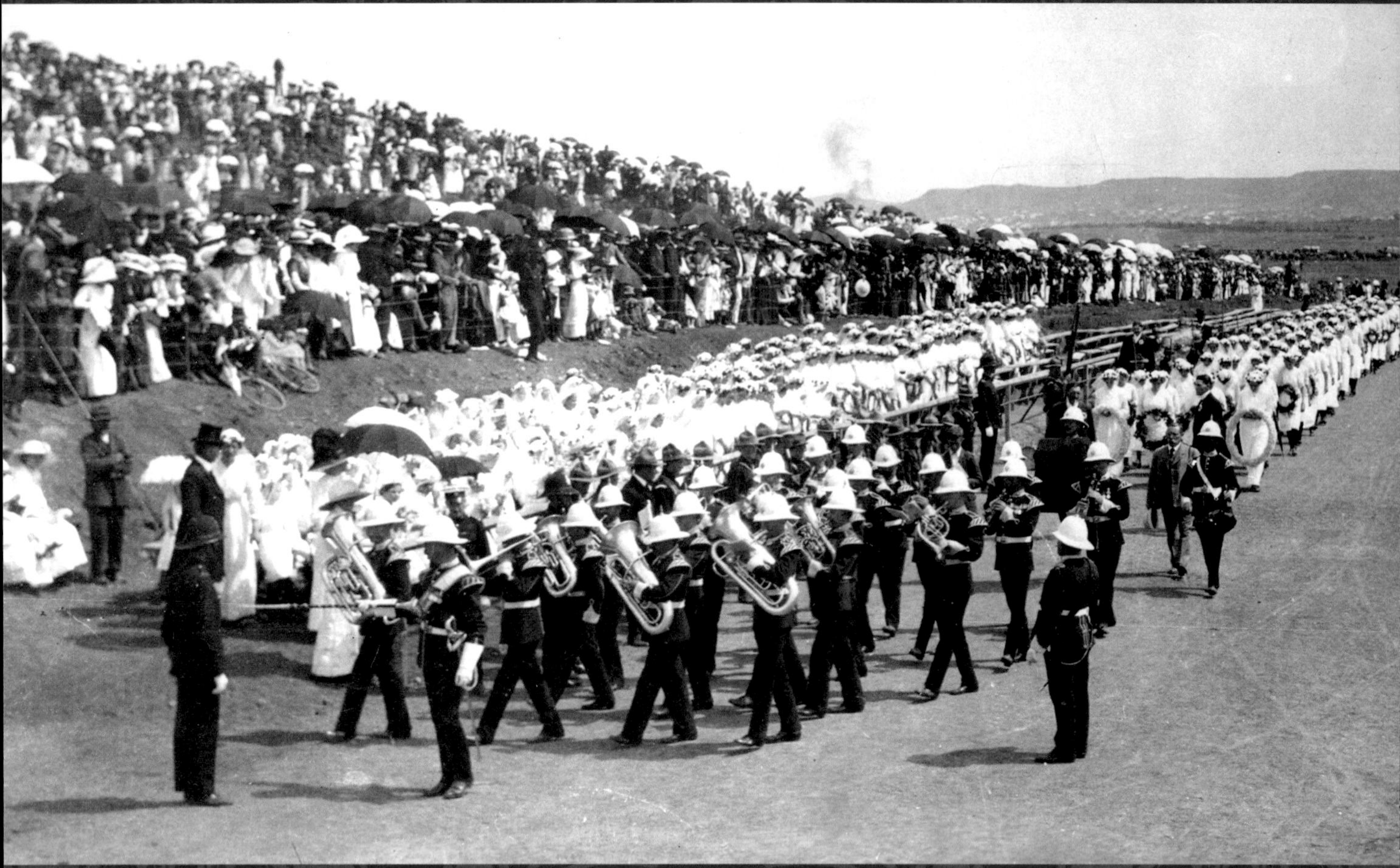

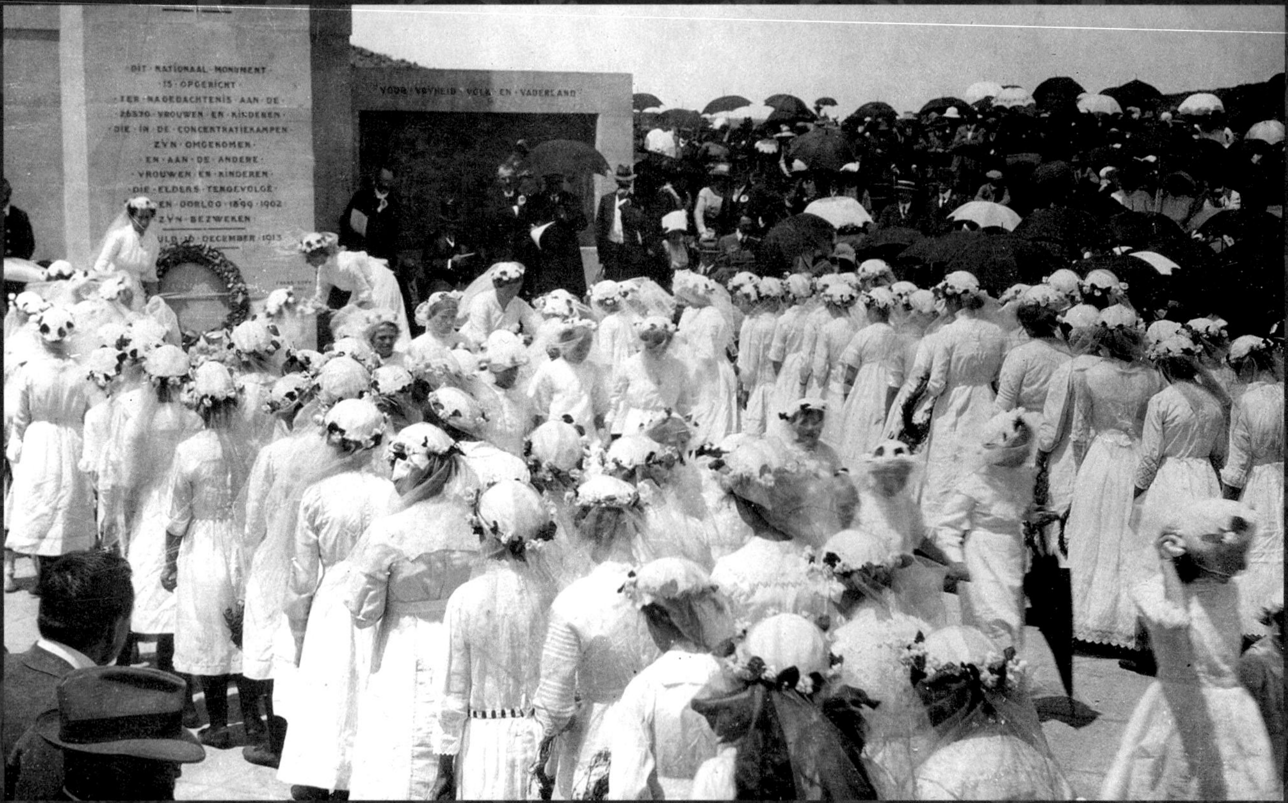
DIT NATIONAAL MONUMENT
IS OPGERICHT
TER NAGEDACHTENIS AAN DE
26370 VROUWEN EN KINDEREN
DIE IN DE CONCENTRATIEKAMPEN
ZYN OMGEKOMEN
EN AAN DE ANDERE
VROUWEN EN KINDEREN
DIE ELDERS TENGEVOLGE
OORLOG 1899 1902
ZYN BEZWEKEN
DECEMBER 1913
VOOR VRYHEID VOLK EN VADERLAND

country gathered at the Women's Monument. A newspaper reporter described the sight as follows:

> Wherever the eye roamed there was nothing but slowly moving or stationary humanity! The hillside seemed as if alive. There was a continually changing pattern in the movement before one's eyes, occasioned by constant streams of newcomers. Denser and denser became the crowd, covering the barrenness of the rocky ground until there was not a bare spot to be seen on either side of the *kopjes* ... The general colour tone was black and white, but here and there bright splashes provided by the sunshades were in evidence ... The ladies who had seats inside the monument were nearly all attired in deep mourning and the men wore the conventional frock coat and top hat.[10]

The atmosphere was solemn and devotional. The tone was set in President Steyn's preamble to the proceedings, printed in the official programme:

> Our hearts will be filled with sadness and a sense of loss. We are after all standing at the grave of thousands of women and children ... Let us exercise the well-known restraint and dignity of the Afrikaner. We are here to mourn the dead, not to honour the living. Let us therefore avoid all applause and rowdiness.[11]

The proceedings were choreographed to meet Steyn's request for calm and pious reflection, and there were no potentially offensive demonstrations. A commando of burghers on horseback led the procession, followed by the Kimberley Volunteer Regiment, representing the former foe. The representation of the enemy in the proceedings symbolised the extent to which the organisers sought to be inclusive. As a climax to the procession, large numbers of women arrived, all wearing white. The crowd was quiet as they made their way to the monument and laid wreaths at the base of the obelisk.[12] This act of respect was intended to convey a spiritual message, not a political one.

The speeches that followed the wreath-laying ceremony complemented the dignified tone of the procession. Steyn's address was read to the crowd by one of his adjutants, because he was too ill to deliver it himself. Steyn emphasised in his speech that the monument was not intended to be a reproach but had been placed there out of 'pure piety'.[13] Botha's speech was conciliatory and he was careful not to promote a political position. He used religious terms in his address, matching the general mood of the proceedings: 'God has not willed that we should exterminate one another. After all the misery and shedding of blood of the past, both races are still here. May we not, must we not, believe that it is His will that we should attempt to take a different path, the path of love and peace?'[14]

Hobhouse's speech, read in her absence because of ill health, also invoked a religious dimension: 'Alongside of the honour we pay the Sainted Dead, forgiveness must find a place. I have read that when Christ said, "Forgive your enemies", it is not only for the

Almost a resurrection, reaching heavenwards: the brochure cover of the inaugural programme.

OPPOSITE, TOP Nothing like the sound of brass: a procession nearing the monument, led by the orchestra of the Kimberley Volunteers.
BOTTOM A group of young women lay wreaths at the foot of the monument.

sake of the enemy He says so, but for one's own sake, "because love is more beautiful than hate".¹⁵ Other Afrikaner leaders, such as D.F. Malan and Revd J.D. Kestell, delivered similar speeches.

However, the speech of Christiaan de Wet, the renowned *bittereinder* general, was a significant exception. According to a reporter from *The Friend* newspaper, De Wet spoke 'from the heart', and he had 'the hearts as well as the ears of his audience'.¹⁶ As a 'rugged, defiant figure', it was reported that 'he stood out among the rest of the ... notable persons in the whole assembly'. De Wet recalled the historical struggles of the Afrikaner and questioned whether the 'progress' that had been made since the Anglo-Boer War was 'progress in the right direction'. His words were enthusiastically received, and Steyn had to ask the crowd to stop cheering.¹⁷

De Wet's popular appeal was perhaps an indicator that, underneath the surface of calm and dignity, the crowd yearned for a more robust political message to assuage their sense

OPPOSITE General Christiaan de Wet, who, unlike most other speakers, delivered a highly political address at the monument's opening ceremony.

BELOW After the fighting, the peace of pilgrimage: a lengthy procession winds its way from Bloemfontein towards the monument.

of injustice. It was a sentiment shared by another prominent *bittereinder* general, C.F. Beyers. General Beyers was unable to attend the unveiling ceremony, but in October 1913 he interpreted the Women's Monument as a 'source of memories', informing the future and signposting the way ahead for a 'free nation'.[18]

On the whole, however, nationalist messages did not dominate the unveiling ceremony. On the contrary, deliberate attempts were made to elevate the occasion to a spiritual level and not to turn it into an Afrikaner political rally promoting ethnic exclusivity. Nevertheless, among Afrikaners, political life and religion were often intertwined, and the memories associated with the Women's Monument evoked deep, unexpressed emotions that could easily be channelled by a nationalist emphasis on common suffering, humiliation and a need for retribution. The reaction to De Wet's speech was a clear indication of this. But these forces had yet to be harnessed effectively; that would happen only in the future.

Conjuring up an earlier past of fortitude and sacrifice: women in Voortrekker costumes at a monument commemoration, possibly on 16 December 1930.

The move towards nationalism

The process of fostering an Afrikaner national consciousness involved hard work in several areas over a number of years. One of the key areas that had to be developed was an Afrikaner literary culture with the capacity and status to convey the aspirations of the *volk* effectively in its own language. Afrikaans was vigorously promoted as a standard spoken and written language, distinct from Dutch, and was officially recognised in 1925, at which point the potential for cultural and political mobilisation increased.

During the 1930s and 1940s, cultural entrepreneurs and politicians attempted to unite a disparate constituency of Afrikaans-speakers, who were divided by class and region, under a single banner of nationalist Afrikanerdom. These developments, which took place within the wider socioeconomic context of increased industrialisation, urbanisation and the erosion of traditional values, led to the need for a 'usable' past.

The growing vitality of the Afrikaans language and the political demands of the time led to the publication of a spate of popular books on the Anglo-Boer War. These generally glorified the Boer generals and *bittereinders* and railed against the injustices of the concentration camps. The hope was expressed that the 'past will contribute to the promotion of and love for the fatherland amongst the younger generation, and that it will help to forge stronger links amongst Afrikaners'.[19]

The ethnic mobilisation of Afrikaans-speakers after the unveiling of the Women's Monument affected the symbolism and meaning assigned to the memorial. Its political message was muted in 1913 but became strident in the 1930s and 1940s. In September 1939, students at Potchefstroom University, who were strongly opposed to South Africa's participation in World War II, clearly reflected this change:

> And even if England today talks sweet, even if she appears as a champion of small nations, we know better. The *Vrouemonument* continually cries out for vengeance! That injustice perpetrated against our nation, that brutality which cries out to heaven. The mark is too deeply branded in our heart; it is too close to our heart ever to forget.[20]

ABOVE LEFT In the 1938 Great Trek commemoration, wagons from throughout the country stopped at the Women's Monument as part of their journey to the north.
RIGHT B.J. Vorster takes his place at the front of the line: following restoration work, in 1974 the prime minister receives a model of the monument.

In addition, increasing numbers of nationalist political rallies were held at the site of the Women's Monument. In 1940, for example, more than 70 000 Afrikaners congregated at the monument to voice their demand for a republican government in South Africa. The occasion resembled one of nationalist mobilisation and National Party leaders, such as Jim Fouché, N.J. van der Merwe and C.R. Swart, urged the crowd to understand and support the historical basis of the need for a republic.

Yet, because the original aim was that the monument should not be used as a political symbol, the Women's Memorial Commission prohibited ceremonies at the foot of the obelisk. As a compromise, it allowed the proceedings to take place a short distance from the group of sculptures. Nevertheless, the Women's Monument could not completely escape Afrikaner nationalism. Cultural entrepreneurs, including ministers and teachers, regularly used the monument as a symbol in nationalist messages. The author Marq de Villiers, who went to school in Bloemfontein during this period, recalls:

> When I was a boy in Bloemfontein we would be taken by bus once a year to the small rise outside town on which stood a simple stone obelisk; there we would be subjected to a memorial service of suffocating boredom and a sermon of interminable length; we were all affected by a desire to disappear *oor die bult* [over the hill]. But on the other hand we all understood why we were there ... We understood viscerally as children that the monument was not merely a stone expression of the evil that outsiders do; it is a symbol of how the *volkseie* [national character] is fundamental to a people's identity: outsiders, people outside the *burgerstand* [middle classes], foreign to the fundamental thought patterns of the people, will always try to do you harm. The only solution is tight solidarity.[21]

Although the Women's Monument would become a symbol of ethnic allegiance over time, it did not attain the same status as the Voortrekker Monument in Pretoria. The cornerstone of the Voortrekker Monument was laid on 16 December 1938 during the centenary celebrations of the Great Trek, when Afrikaners' emotions were heightened. Eleven years later, on

Swallowing a bitter pill: General Piet Cronjé surrenders to Lord Roberts at Paardeberg in February 1900. The nature of the war that followed laid the basis for the Women's Monument.

16 December 1949 (following the victory of the National Party in 1948) the Voortrekker Monument was inaugurated with great fanfare. It was conceived and constructed during an intense nationalist period, and the meaning attributed to it was clear.

On the other hand, the Women's Monument did not have a nationalist intention from the outset, as has been discussed. The monument had to be incorporated into the movement over time – its meaning had to be reassigned. Moreover, the Great Trek represented a successful period in Afrikaner history because independent Boer republics were established in the interior, but the Anglo-Boer War, despite the endurance of the *bittereinders* and the sacrifices of the women, ultimately represented defeat. It signified a period of suffering that was a constant reminder of past grievances and, therefore, did not lend itself to celebration.

The change in the meaning associated with the Women's Monument points to the instability and vulnerability of collective memory, as well as the silences, denials and sublimations that come from trauma. However, aspects like the memories of the war and the deprivations of inmates in the concentration camps have been retained through storytelling and literature. Although memories of the camps were a part of Afrikaner historical consciousness before the 1950s, new generations changed the meaning of what they perceived the Women's Monument to represent. Collective memory takes place in an ever-changing present and is determined by the political and social boundaries of the day.

Ironically, it is often the case that the generation that has experienced social trauma first-hand may be less inclined to react politically, and that the next generation then tries to redress the wrongs of the past. In a general survey of war memories and their impact, it has been found that 'youthful experience of a particular event or change often focuses memories on the direct personal implications of the experience, whereas the attribution of some larger political meaning to the event is more likely to be made by those who did not experience it during their adolescence or early childhood'.[22]

It is significant that the generation that bore the brunt of the Anglo-Boer war generally

Ethnic Afrikaner nationalism riding high: the Voortrekker Monument is inaugurated in Pretoria in 1949, following the ascendancy to political power of the National Party. In its brash evocation of Afrikaner history, it assumes a triumphalist symbolic role, unlike that of the Women's Monument.

did not publicly object to the fact that any political meanings initially attributed to the monument were muted. Although they harboured many bitter feelings about the war, that generation was still in the process of emotional recovery. Moreover, as the ill-considered rebellion of 1914 proved, Afrikaners lacked the capacity to overthrow the new order.

It was a younger generation that reinterpreted the meaning of the monument during the resurgence of Afrikaner nationalism in the 1930s and 1940s. As opposed to the armed resistance of the rebels in 1914, it was also this generation that successfully managed to reclaim constitutionally in 1948 what they had lost in 1902.

The altered political context also changed the emphasis that the Women's Monument was a monument for women. Although the position of women had been the focus during the unveiling of the monument in 1913, subsequent brochures and other material interpreting its symbolism increasingly depicted the role of women as serving male nationalism. It was often no longer a case of honouring women per se, but representing them as silent victims who had sacrificed their lives for freedom and love of the fatherland.

During the era of rampant nationalism, some 40 years after the war, Afrikaner women, often unwittingly, were silenced by the rhetoric of a 'greater cause'. This had the effect of placing them 'into a confinement that suited Afrikaner patriarchy'.[23]

Aesthetically, the genderised ideology of the Women's Monument also changed over time. Initially, no men featured in the group of sculptures and the surrounding area. However, in 1916 Steyn, as the last president of the Orange Free State, was buried at the base of the obelisk. The Women's Monument also became the last resting place of the war hero Christiaan de Wet in 1922, and Revd J.D. Kestell in 1941. These additions meant that the monument became, partially at least, a more inclusive Anglo-Boer War memorial.

Tibbie Steyn felt strongly that the monument should not be turned into a cemetery for well-known Afrikaner men. In 1926, however, Emily Hobhouse's ashes were interred at the foot of the monument. Tibbie Steyn did not want to be buried there herself, but

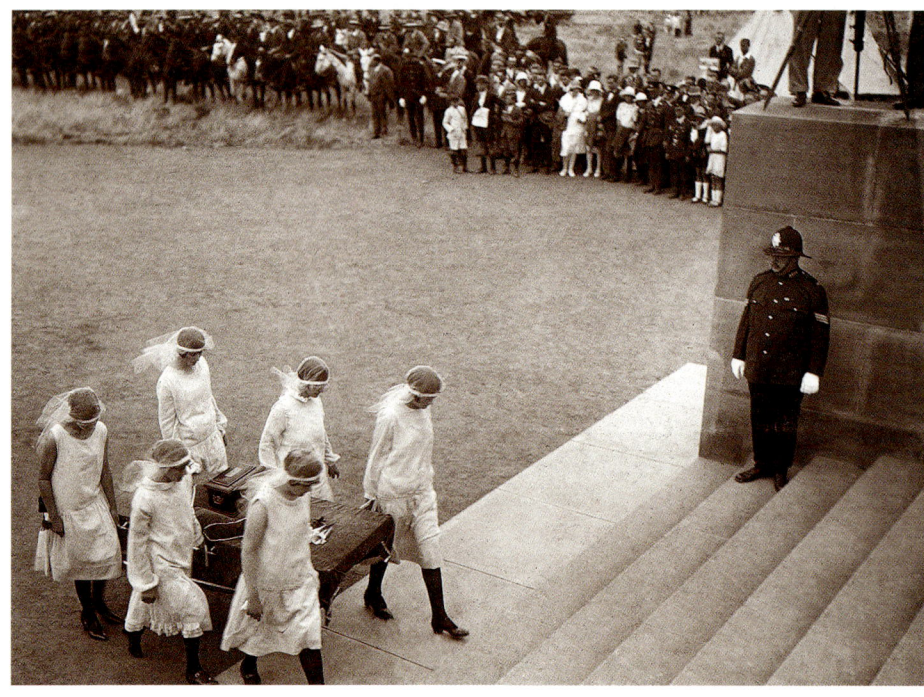

RIGHT The ashes of Emily Hobhouse are buried at the foot of the monument in 1926. Hobhouse and Tibbie Steyn are the only women to have been buried there.

BELOW The procession through Bloemfontein on 27 October 1926, the day on which Hobhouse's ashes were interred

BOTTOM The funeral of President M.T. Steyn at the monument on 3 December 1916, with General Christiaan de Wet delivering a speech.

her wish was ignored and she was laid to rest next to her husband in 1955. D.F. Malan, the National Party prime minister until 1954, argued that Steyn had been the last link with the Boer republics and that the *volk* believed it was symbolically important to bury her among the prominent Afrikaner leaders of a past era. The male nationalism of the time prevailed – even in death.

As Afrikaner nationalism and apartheid developed after 1948, messages and meanings that could contradict this school of thought had to be expunged from the historical record. And so the roles of people like Emily Hobhouse were diminished. In the 1960s, Hobhouse's universal message of womanhood, as expressed in her speech that was read out on her behalf at the unveiling of the Women's Monument, was played down. Moreover, in monument brochures that reproduced Hobhouse's speech of 1913, her reference to the suffering of black people in the camps was omitted. In her speech she had argued that black people had been caught up in a quarrel over which they had no influence. She also expressed the hope that relations would improve in future, with white and black people moving closer together.[24] However, the advent of apartheid and the segregation that preceded it put an end to Hobhouse's ideals.

After the 1960s, the terrain (both physical and cultural) of the Women's Monument gradually changed as it became a more general site commemorating the Anglo-Boer War. Cultural organisations used their resources to add a male presence to the Women's Monument by erecting sculptures commemorating burghers going on commando, *bittereinders* and prisoners of war. Although it may be argued that these sculptures complemented the Women's Monument, this, in itself, is an admission that they moved the focus away from the women and children – 'the Sainted Dead', in Hobhouse's words.

Post-apartheid representation of losses, as the monument acknowledges changed political times; this memorial was erected on the site of the Women's Monument in 2010, with each side acknowledging the respective black and white death toll.

The Women's Monument under a new government

For most of the twentieth century, the meaning given to the Women's Monument and the changing Afrikaner memory of the Anglo-Boer War occurred under white governments and white patronage. The election of a new, predominantly black, government in 1994 created a new political context. Most white people, including many of the cultural entrepreneurs and custodians of war memories, had not foreseen this. Consequently, the centenary commemorations of the war, which took place between 1999 and 2002, required a great deal of cultural mediation.

It became necessary to integrate black people's claims and perspectives, which had been officially neglected for so long, into a fairly unreceptive, inflexible historical and cultural context. It was questioned how best to commemorate the approximately 20 000 black people who had died in the black concentration camps during the war. A modest memorial indicating the number of black and white deaths in the camps was erected on the site of the Women's Monument in 2010, but the intention was not to commemorate the deaths of black women as such.

In 2006 Pallo Jordan, the minister of arts and culture at the time, campaigned for greater recognition of the black women who had died in the Anglo-Boer War. It was proposed that an altered replica of the Women's Monument could be erected in the former Strijdom Square in Pretoria. Another addition to the existing site in Bloemfontein was also considered. The latter proposal would have been an encroachment on the historically based nature of the monument. The Women's Monument has, after all, become one of the most iconic Afrikaner memorial sites (second only to the Voortrekker Monument in Pretoria).

Although nothing came of these plans, many important questions and conflicting arguments were raised. On the one hand, it can be contended that such sites undergo permutations over time regardless, and that the original meanings given to memorials must change according to the political or social context. For example, male heroes of the Anglo-Boer War were later buried at the Women's Monument and three sculptures commemorating burghers erected at the site, even though the monument was initially regarded as sacred ground to be dedicated exclusively to the deceased heroines of the war. In 2013 a fourth male figure, a statue of a black mounted attendant, or *agterryer*, was added. It can be argued that the commemoration of black women at the Women's Monument would support Hobhouse's message of shared pain, universal humanity and the need for greater mutual understanding between white and black people. On the other hand, there are misgivings about the historical accuracy of an adapted monument. The statue of the *agterryer* could be seen as an expression of the comradeship (albeit of a paternal nature) between the burghers and their *agterryers*. There is historical evidence that a close bond existed between them

LEFT AND BELOW Finally brought forward from the rear: in 2013 a statue of a black mounted servant or personal retainer, *Die Agterryer*, is added to the monument display to acknowledge the role such men played in the life of Boer commandos.

in many cases, forged in the face of wartime mortal danger. But the same does not apply in the case of black and white women. Although there was considerable interaction between some white and black women, there is little evidence to suggest that their relationship was on the same level as that of burgher and *agterryer*.

In addition, it can be argued that a monument will only appeal to a community if it evokes spontaneous sympathy and inner conviction. In South Africa, black women's hardships during the Anglo-Boer War have not featured prominently in general historical accounts. The tribulations of segregation and apartheid have overshadowed earlier historical experiences. It is also debatable whether such a memorial to black women or an addition to the existing monument would not merely be seen as an afterthought, perhaps resulting in black women once again coming off second best.

At the root of the issue is the question of the mutating meanings that are assigned to monuments. After the erection of a monument, it is still possible to maintain an undiluted meaning or message – for a while. But when society changes – and since 1994 the South African context has changed dramatically – other considerations come to the fore and adjustments are made accordingly. Such adjustments may have the aim of appealing to a broader society, but may also simultaneously lead to a decrease in the intensity with which the monument is perceived because the new target audience does not share the experiences of the original audience.

In a historically divided country such as South Africa, it is inevitable that the meanings of monuments will change over time. But if the changes are so drastic that the original audience can no longer identify with them, it could result in a monument being stripped of its symbolic value. Regardless of what happens in 2013 with the centenary of the erection of the Woman's Monument, one can, nonetheless, look back on a successful preservation project that has already weathered several political storms.

OPPOSITE Men of war get their commemoration. Between 1983 and 1994, to considerable controversy, three figures were erected in the grounds of the Women's Monument to portray male involvement in the hostilities – the top statue displays a departure from home; bottom left, a man and boy from the 1971 film, *Die Banneling*; and bottom right, the last-ditch, defiant *Die Bittereinder*.

THE MEANING OF THE WOMEN'S MONUMENT: THEN AND NOW

CHAPTER ELEVEN

In Emily Hobhouse's words

— ALBERT GRUNDLINGH —

PREVIOUS PAGE, MAIN IMAGE Emily Hobhouse: British pro-Boer humanitarian yet still a woman of the empire.
SECONDARY IMAGE A 1976 South African Post Office special commemorative issue to mark the 50th anniversary of the death of Emily Hobhouse, or the 'Angel of Mercy', the name bestowed on her by grateful Boer women.
THIS PAGE The misery of the big freeze of 1901, even in the Cape – the Aliwal North camp in June

Although directed at a receptive Boer audience, Emily Hobhouse's speech, which was delivered at the unveiling of the Women's Monument on 16 December 1913, drew on grandiose notions of and cultural references to Britain as an imperial power – albeit one that had erred in its conduct. Hobhouse's speech, despite all its sympathies for the Boers, was first and foremost that of a middle-class British woman of the empire.

This historical context is important for understanding the wide sweep of her presentation and her, at times, prophetic statements. She had a literary background and was prone to serious reflection on human justice and the sanctity of life, and, therefore, her invocations had a universal tone to them, precisely because they echoed the conflicting elements of an imperial world view. In a sense, Hobhouse regarded the war of 1899 to 1902 as a testing ground for the extent to which British values and notions of justice and civilisation would fare under duress. Her yardstick was a universal one. Despite her full immersion in white camp life during the war, South Africa happened to be the setting in which wider concerns could be gauged.

Equally, for all its universality, her speech did speak in uncanny ways to the unique South African situation. In the context of the time, the most obvious example is her call for more harmonious relations between white and black people. Drawing on the American example of President Abraham Lincoln's 1861 to 1865 campaign to outlaw slavery, she sought to drive home the idea that freedom is indivisible and cannot be claimed by one group only. Of course, white South Africans in 1913, and for many decades after, were disinclined to embrace such lofty notions of a common humanity. Equally striking is the prominence Hobhouse gave to women's rights, reflecting her suffragette inclinations in Britain. She drew an analogy between war and full citizenship for males, effectively destroying the argument that citizenship can be bestowed only on men because only men are involved in fighting for the fatherland. The events of the war of 1899 to 1902, from which women could not escape, provided her with a perfect foil. Hobhouse expanded on this by emphasising the universality of women's rights and sought to endow the monument with the gravitas of a 'world monument' for women. It was a noble idea at the time, but not one that allowed for less ambitious and more parochial local imperatives.

Finally, one should perhaps be wary of drawing messages from her speech that are taken out of their historical context. Nonetheless, and from the perspective of South Africa in 2013, there is another often-overlooked dimension of her address. Hobhouse came from a liberal sociopolitical background and this was reflected in her admonishment early in her speech about the pitfalls of unbridled prosperity and that 'too often great national prosperity is accompanied by deterioration of national character'. She may have been referring to the capitalists who had benefited from the war. But it is still tempting to ask whether her warning may also apply to those political and economic elites in South Africa today who place material well-being above all else.

Emily Hobhouse's speech delivered at the inauguration of the Women's Monument[1]

Women's Day, December 16, 1913.

'Would ye be wise, ye cities, fly from war!
Yet if war come, there is a crown in death
For her that striveth well and perisheth
Unstained'.

Euripides *The Trojan Women*,
Translated Gilbert Murray.

Friends,

From far and near we are gathered today to commemorate those who suffered bravely and died nobly in the past.

Of old a great man said: 'Acts deserve acts, and not words in their honour,' and this is true. Yet having come so far at your request to share in this solemn dedication, and having been most closely bound with the last hours of their lives, I feel constrained to offer my tribute to the memory of those women and those little children who perished in the Concentration Camps.

Many of them it was my privilege to know. How strange a thought that from their memory today flows a more vital influence for good than can be found amongst those who have lived and prospered. In this way, perhaps, is the prophetic vision fulfilled: 'Refrain thy voice from weeping and thine eyes from tears, they shall come again from the land of the enemy; thy children shall come again to their own border'.

Do we not in a very real sense meet them again this day?

Yet another thought urges me to offer this tribute of words.

From ancient times men have pronounced eulogies over the graves of their fellow-men who had fallen for their country. Today, I think for the first time, a woman is chosen to make the Commemorative Speech over the National Dead – not soldiers – but women – who gave their lives for their country.

My Friends, this day, this Vrouwen-Dag [Women's Day] is *Good.* Like the Sabbath in the week, it breaks into the hurrying years, and in the pause, the past can calmly be recalled, its inspiration breathed afresh, its lessons conned once more.

Let us take this moment to consider where we now stand and what these lessons are.

You are gathered here from all parts to consecrate this spot to women and children who were stripped of all – I say it advisedly – of all. Husbands and sons, houses and lands, flocks and herds, household goods and even clothing. Denuded, it was good to watch how yet they 'possessed their souls'. 'It is tragic', says a writer, 'how few people ever possess their souls before they die'. That these did I know, because I saw. I bridge in mind the years, the thirteen years, and move once more amid the tents that whitened the hillside. Torn from familiar simple life, plunged into sickness and destitution, surrounded by strangers, were those poor souls – stripped bare. The sight was one to call forth pity, yet pity did not predominate. Quite other feelings swallowed that. Even throughout the deepest misery the greater pity was needed elsewhere. 'Christ,' I have read, 'had pity for the poor, the lowly, the imprisoned, the suffering and so have we, but remember that He had far more pity for the rich, the hard, those who are slaves to their goods, who wear soft raiment, and live in kings' houses. To Him riches and pleasures seemed greater tragedies than poverty and sorrow'. So, as we turn our minds back thirteen years to dwell on the stormy past, pity enters in, but whom is it that we pity?

Surely, had you watched the inward and spiritual graces that shone forth from that outward and visible squalor you yourselves might have felt that it was not the captives in those foul camps that were most in need of pity. The rich and highly-placed, the financiers who wanted war, the incompetent statesmen who were their tools, the men who sat in the seats of the mighty, the blundering politicians of that dark story – all the miserable authorities incapable of dealing with the terrible conditions they themselves had brought about – these needed and still need our deeper pity. That vast tragedy as it rolled through your land upon its bloody way, came at length face to face with the great array of the women and children – the weak and the young. Wholly innocent of the war, yet called upon to bear its brunt, nobly they rose to meet the trial that awaited them. Sympathy indeed they craved and did receive, but they towered above our pity.

And so today. What gave the impetus to this movement? What stirred you to gather pence for this monument? What brought you here from far and wide? It was not pity, it was Honour.

Yet if you have pity and to spare, give it even now to those, who, still alive, must ever carry in their hearts the heavy memories of the blundering wrong by which they wrought that war. You and I are here today filled only with honour for those their heroic and innocent victims who passed through the fire.

For this monument is a symbol.

Far away in Rome I have been privileged to watch its creation. I noted its conception in the Sculptor's thought, I saw its first issue in the common clay; moulded by his hand, it passed into the pure white plaster; at length, chastened to his mind and (meet) for the supreme ordeal it was cast into the pit of burning metal whence issued the perfected work.

Even so did Destiny, the mighty Sculptor – like clay in his hands – take those simple women and children from their quiet homes, mould and chasten them through the successive stages of their suffering, till at length, purified and perfected to the Master-mind by the fierce fire of their trial, they passed from human sight to live forever a sacred memory in your land.

Their spirit which we feel so near to us today warns ever, 'Beware lest you forget what caused that struggle in the past. We died without a murmur to bear our part if saving our country from those who loved her not but only desired her riches. Do not confuse the issues and join hands with those who look on her with eyes of greed and not with eyes of love.'

It is not the glory of those weak sufferers to have laid down this principle. In this South Africa of ours true patriotism lies in the unity of those who 'live *in* her and *love* her as opposed to those who live *on* her but *out* of her. The Patriots and the Parasites.

This issue, though fought out of old, is ever with you, it is alive today; voices of the dead call to you, their spirits lay a restraining hold upon you as they plead: 'Here is the true division beside which all other cleavages are meaningless.'

There can be no permanent separation betwixt those who *love* our country, live *in* her and are bound up *with* her. At bottom such are one.

Alongside of the honour we pay the Sainted Dead, forgiveness must find a place. I have read that when Christ said, 'Forgive your enemies', it is not only for the sake of the enemy He says so, but for one's own sake, 'because love is more beautiful than hate.' Surely your dead with the wisdom that now is theirs, know this. To harbour hate is fatal to your own self-development, it makes a flaw, for hatred like rust, eats into the soul of a nation as of an individual.

As your tribute to the dead, bury unforgiveness and bitterness at the foot of this monument forever. Instead, forgive for you can afford it, the rich who were greedy of more riches, the statesmen who could not guide affairs, the bad generalship that warred on weaklings and babes – forgive – because so only can you rise to full nobility of character and a broad and noble national life.

For what really matters is *character*. History clearly teaches this.

In the present day, minds are strangely confused, eyes are blinded, and it is the almost universal idea that the all-important thing for a country is Material Prosperity. It is false.

Noble Character forms a great nation. Statesmen who aim at material prosperity as if it were an end in itself, forget or have not recognised, that too often great national prosperity is accompanied by deterioration of national character and the highest well-being of the people.

For it is not the rich and prosperous who matter most, but you who live the simplest lives, and upon whom in the last resort, if trial comes, falls the test of the national character.

This thought ennobles the humblest life. The dead we now honour met that test and did not shrink. They died for freedom, they clung to it with unfaltering trust that God would make it the heritage of their children. The years have brought changes they little dreamed, but South Africa is one and it is free. Its freedom is based on all they did; they suffered; they died; they could do no more. The supreme offering was made, the supreme price paid. Their sacrifice still bears fruit. Even could the graves open and give up their dead, we would not wish those women back, nor have them relinquish the great position they have won. Not even the children would we recall, the children, who – counting the vanished years –, would stand before us now, some 20, 000 youths and maidens, fair and comely, – a noble array – peopling the too solitary veld. For who does not feel their spirit move amongst us here today? Who fails to recognise the noble example by which they still live?

In this vast throng can there be found one unresponsive soul? One heart that will not go hence filled with high resolve to live more worthy of the dead?

Emily Hobhouse as an unofficial British war artist: 1903 watercolour images of devastation in the former republics, portraying the Middelburg concentration camp cemetery, the ruined church at Lindley, and a ravaged farmhouse west of Bloemfontein

253

My Friends, memories and emotions throng. Thirteen years have passed since under the burning January sun I trudged daily forth from your wiregirt town to that kopje of many tears. Daily in that camp, as later in others, I moved from tent to tent, witness of untold sufferings, yet marvelling ever at the lofty spirit which animated the childhood as well as the motherhood of your land. So quickly does suffering educate, that even children of quite tender years shared the spirit of the struggle, and sick, hungry, naked or dying prayed ever for 'no surrender'.

Think what it meant for an Englishwoman to watch such things.

Did you ever ask yourselves why I came to your aid in those dark days of strife? I had never seen your country nor ever known anyone of you. Hence it was no personal link that brought me hither. Neither did political sympathy of any kind prompt my journey.

I came – quite simply – in obedience to the solidarity of our womanhood and to those nobler traditions of English life in which I was nurtured and which by long inheritance are mine.

For when Society is shaken to its foundations, then *deep* calleth unto *deep*, the underlying oneness of our nature appears, we learn that 'all the world is kin'.

And surely, the honour of a country is not determined by the blundering acts of some passing administration or weak generalship, but lies in the sum-total of her best traditions which the people at large will rise up to maintain.

Even as the noblest men are ever ready to admit and remedy an error, so England, as soon as she was convinced of the wrong being done in her name to the weak and defenceless, confessed it in very deed, and by thorough reformation of those camps, rendered them fit for human habitation.

Thus she atoned.

I stand here as an Englishwoman, and I am confident that all that is best and most humane in England is with you also in heart to-day. Reverent sympathy is felt with you in this Commemoration and in your desire to accord full honour to your Dead.

You and I were linked together by the strange decrees of fate at that dark hour; we stand now face to face for the last time.

One thing I would ask of you.

When you remember the ill done, remember also the atonement made.

Dwell also upon all you have gained through this great episode, in the legacy left you by the Dead.

Let me explain. It is not mainly sorrow that fills your heart today; time has already softened personal grief. Therefore many may and do say it is useless to perpetuate as we do today memories so drear. But these very memories are needful because they embody that precious legacy from the past. My own face now is turned towards the West, and soon each one of us who witnessed the sufferings of the Concentration Camps will have passed to our own rest; but so long as we who saw those things still live, they will live within us, not as memories of sorrow, but of *heroic inspiration*. For what never dies and never should die is a great example. True is it of your dead that which Pericles said of his countrymen 'The grandest of all sepulchres they have, not that in which mortal bones are laid, but a home in the minds of men; their story lives on far away, without visible symbol, woven into the stuff of other men's lives.'

Your visible monument will serve to this great end – becoming an inspiration to all South Africans and to the women in particular. Generation after generation it will stand here pressing home in silent eloquence these great thoughts – In your hands and those of your children lie the power and freedom won; you must not merely maintain but increase the sacred gift. Be merciful towards the weak, the down-trodden, the stranger. Do not open your gates to those worst foes of freedom – tyranny and selfishness. Are not these the withholding from others in your control, the very liberties and rights which you have valued and won for yourselves? So will the monument speak to you.

Many nations have foundered on this rock. We in England are ourselves still but dunces in the great world-school, our leaders still struggling with the unlearned lesson, that liberty is the equal right and heritage of every child of man, without distinction of race, colour or sex. A community that lacks the courage to found its citizenship on this broad base, becomes 'a city divided against itself, which cannot stand'.

Lay hold of and cherish this ideal of liberty then 'should your statesmen be hostile or coldly neutral, should your rich men be corrupt, should your press which ought to instruct and defend the liberties of all sections of the people, only betray – never mind – they do not constitute the nation. "The nation", said John Bright, "is in the cottage".'

You are the nation, you whom I see here today, you, most of whom live in remote villages and silent farms leading simple hard-working lives. You are your nation's very soul and on you lies the responsibility of maintaining her ideals by the perfecting of your own character.

The old watchword Liberty, Fraternity, Equality cries from the tomb; what these women, so simple that they did not know that they were heroines, valued and died for, *all other human beings desire with equal fervour.* Should not the justice and liberties you love so well, extend to all within your borders? The old Greeks taught that not until power was given to men could it be known what was in them.

The testing time now has come to you.

For ponder a moment.

We meet on Dingaan's Day, your memorial of victory over a barbarous race. We too, the great civilised nations of the world, are still but barbarians in our degree, so long as we continue to spend vast sums in killing or planning to kill each other for greed of land and gold. Does not justice bid us remember today how many thousands of the dark race perished also in Concentration Camps in a quarrel that was not theirs? Did they not thus redeem the past? Was it not an instance of that community of interest, which binding all in one, roots out racial animosity? And may it not come about that the associations linked with this day will change, merging into nobler thoughts as year by year you celebrate the more inspiring 'Vrouwen-Dag' we now inaugurate? The plea of Abraham Lincoln for the black comes echoing back to me, 'They will probably help you in some trying time to come to keep the jewel of liberty in the family of freedom.'

Still more intimately will this Monument speak to the womanhood of South Africa, and beyond to a yet wider range.

To you, women, it should cry ever, 'Go back, go back, to simpler lives, to nobler principles; from these martyrs learn the grandeur of character that chooses rather to suffer to the uttermost than to win life by weakness'. Women, high or low, rich or poor, who have met in your thousands to-day; do not go empty away. You cannot be as if these Dead had not died. Your country demands your lives and your powers in another way. As the national life broadens, difficulties appear little dreamed of in a simpler state. Complicated problems arise which seriously affect the well-being of your sons and daughters. It is for you to think out these problems in your homes, for you to be the purifying element in the body politic, for you to help guide the helm of state.

The Dead have won for you a lofty place in the life of your nation, and the right to a voice in her counsels. From this sacred duty you surely dare not flinch. No one is too humble or unknown; each one counts.

For remember, these dead women were not great as the world counts greatness; some of them were quite poor women who had laboured much. Yet they have become a moral force in your land. They will enrich your history. As the diamonds and the gold glitter in the bedrock of your soil, so their stories written or handed down, will shine like jewels in the dark annals of that time.

And their influence will travel further. They have shown *the world* that never again can it be said that a woman deserves no rights as Citizen because she takes no part in war. This statue stands as a denial of that assertion. Women in equal numbers to the men earned the right to such words as the famous Athenian uttered at the grave of his soldiers: 'They gave their bodies to the commonwealth receiving each for her own memory, praise that will never die'.

Nay, more – for they gave themselves, not borne on by the excitement and joy of active battle, as men do; but passively, with open eyes, in the long-drawn agony of painful months and days.

My Friends, throughout the world the Woman's day approaches; her era dawns. Proudly I unveil this Monument to the brave South African women, who, sharing the danger that beset their land and dying for it, affirmed for all times and for all peoples the power of Woman to sacrifice life and more than life for the common weal.

This is your South African Monument; but it is more; for 'their story is not graven only on stone, over their native earth.'

We claim it as a WORLD-MONUMENT, of which, all the World's Women should be proud; for your dead by their brave simplicity have spoken to Universal Womanhood, and henceforth they are 'woven into the stuff' of every woman's life.

EMILY HOBHOUSE

End notes

FOREWORD
1. Arendt, H: 'Les techniques de la science sociale et l'étude des camps de concentration' (1950), republished in Arendt, H: *Les Origines du Totalitarisme*. Quarto, Gallimard, Paris, 1951.
2. American Senate Proceedings, R Proctor, Senate speech, 17 March 1898.
3. *Manchester Guardian*, 8 April 1897; *New York Times*, 18 March 1897.
4. Quoted in Spies, SB: *Methods of Barbarism? Roberts and Kitchener and Civilians in the Boer Republics, 1900–1902*. Human & Rousseau, Cape Town, 1978, p. 149.
5. Nasson, B: *The War for South Africa: The Anglo-Boer War 1899-1902*. Tafelberg, Cape Town, 2010, pp. 265–266.
6. Wilson, J: *C-B: A Life of Sir Henry Campbell-Bannerman*. Constable, London, 1973, p. 349.
7. Veber, J: *L'Assiette au Beurre: Les Camps de Reconcentration au Transvaal*. Gallica BNF, Paris, 1902.

CHAPTER ONE
1. Hyslop, J: 'The invention of the concentration camp: Cuba, Southern Africa, and the Philippines', *South African Historical Journal*, 63:2, 2011 p. 257.
2. Pretorius, F: 'Die lot van die Boerevroue en -kinders' in Pretorius, F (ed.): *Verskroeide Aarde*. Human & Rousseau, Cape Town, 2001, p. 54.
3. Grundlingh, AM: *Die hendsoppers en joiners: Die rasionaal en verskynsel van verraad*. HAUM, Pretoria, 1979, p. 57.
4. Ploeger, J: *Die lotgevalle van die burgerlike bevolking gedurende die Anglo-Boereoorlog, 1899–1902, vol. 4*. Unpublished manuscript, National Archives (Pretoria), 1999, p. 31.
5. Pretorius, F: 'Die lot van die Boerevroue en -kinders' in Pretorius, F (ed.): *Verskroeide Aarde*, p. 57.
6. The quote, which has been translated, can be found in Pretorius, F: *Life on Commando during the Anglo-Boer War, 1899–1902*. Human & Rousseau, Cape Town, 2001, p. 203. For the specific comments by British commanders see Spies, SB: *Methods of Barbarism? Roberts and Kitchener and Civilians in the Boer Republics, January 1900–May 1902*, Human & Rousseau, Cape Town, 1977, pp. 188–189. For a general British view of indigenous groups see Hyam, R: *Empire and Sexuality: the British Experience*, Manchester University Press, Manchester, 1990, p 204.
7. Spies, SB: *Methods of barbarism? Roberts and Kitchener and civilians in the Boer republics, January 1900–May 1902*, Human & Rousseau, Cape Town, 1977, p. 235.
8. Spies, SB: 'Die Haagse Konvensie van 1899 en die Boererepublieke' in Pretorius, F (ed.): *Verskroeide Aarde*, p. 177.
9. Spies, SB: *Methods of barbarism?*, p. 9.

CHAPTER TWO
1. Marquard, L (ed.): *Letters from a Boer Parsonage: Letters of Margaret Marquard during the Boer War*. Purnell, Cape Town, 1967, pp. 76, 83.
2. Rankin, R: *A Subaltern's Letters to His Wife*. Methuen, London, 1901, p. 220.
3. Neethling, HL: *Vergeten?* Nasionale Pers, Cape Town, 1917, p. 34.
4. Hancock, WK and Van der Poel, J (eds.): *Selections from the Smuts Papers: vol. 1 (June 1886–May 1902)*. Cambridge University Press, Cambridge, 1966, p. 469.
5. Ibid., p. 565.
6. Pienaar, P: *With Steyn and De Wet*. Methuen, London, 1902, p. 103.
7. Theal, GM: *The Prospect in South Africa: An interview with Dr Theal*. Vol. 29 of Publications of the South African Conciliation Committee, London, 1900, p. 5.
8. Rankin, R: *A Subaltern's Letters to His Wife*, p. 98.
9. Quoted in Schoeman, K: *In Liefde en Trou*. Human & Rousseau, Cape Town, 1983, p. 40.
10. Amery, LS (ed.): *The Times History of the War in South Africa, 1899–1902 (vol. 4)*. Sampson, Low and Marston, London, 1906, p. 393.

THE HAVENGA REPORT
1. Excerpts from the depositions were translated into English for the purposes of this book.
2. The terminology of the time has been retained for historical accuracy.
3. Le Roux, JH, Coetzer, PW and Marais, AH (eds.): *Generaal J.B.M. Hertzog, Dele I en II*. Perskor Uitgewers, Johannesburg, 1987, p. 38.

CHAPTER THREE
1. Pretorius, F: *Kommandolewe tydens die Anglo-Boereoorlog, 1899–1902*. Human & Rousseau, Cape Town, 1991, p. 366.
2. De la Rey, JE: *A Woman's Wanderings and Trials during the Anglo-Boer War*. T. Fisher Unwin, London, 1903, p. 4.
3. Ibid., p. 15.
4. Ibid., pp. 26–27.
5. Ibid., pp. 30–31.
6. Ibid., p. 87.
7. Claassen, D: 'Genl. Koos de la Rey se kinders se klere uit Union Jack gemaak' in *Vista*, 25 June, 1966, p. 1.
8. De la Rey, JE: *A Woman's Wanderings and Trials during the Anglo-Boer War*, p. 122.
9. Ibid., p. 99.
10. Ibid., p. 90.
11. Ibid., pp. 112–113.
12. Naudé, JF: *Vechten en Vluchten van Beyers en Kemp bokant De Wet*. Nijgh & Van Ditmar, Rotterdam, circa 1903, pp. 331-332.
13. De la Rey, JE: *A Woman's Wanderings and Trials during the Anglo-Boer War*, p. 70.
14. Ibid., p. 136.

CHAPTER FOUR

1. University of London, Streatfield Collection, LSE 2/11, Lucy Deane papers, 23 December 1901.
2. Marquard, L (ed.): *Letters from a Boer Parsonage*, pp. 36–37.
3. Spies, SB: *Methods of Barbarism?*, pp. 117–118; Cd 524, *South Africa. Return of buildings burnt in each month from June 1900 to January 1901*. London, HMSO, 1901.
4. Marquard, L (ed.): *Letters from a Boer Parsonage*, p. 114.
5. FSAR, A 248, Diary of Mrs Bessie Venter (née Grobbelaar). See also ID 97167 on website www2.lib.uct.ac.za/mss/bccd/ and FSAR, SRC 76, Brandfort camp register, p. 275. Quote translated from Afrikaans.
6. Wessels, A (ed.): *Lord Kitchener and the War in South Africa 1899-1902*. Sutton Publishing Ltd, Stroud, 2006, pp. 128–131; FSAR, SRC 5, RC1121, 3 April 1901.
7. Stoler, AL and Cooper, F: 'Between metropole and colony', in Cooper, F and Stoler, AL: *Tensions of Empire: Colonial cultures in a bourgeois world*. University of California Press, Berkeley, 1997, p. 5.
8. Krebs, P: *Gender, Race, and the Writing of Empire: Public discourse and the Boer War*. Cambridge University Press, Cambridge, 1999, p. 71; Harrison, E: 'Women members and witnesses on British government ad hoc committees of inquiry 1850–1930, with special reference to Royal Commissions of Inquiry'. Unpublished doctoral thesis, London School of Economics and Political Science, 1998, p. 163.
9. NASA, DBC 12, WR Tucker to J Maxwell, 23 January 1902; Otto, JC: *Die Konsentrasiekampe*. Protea Boekhuis, Pretoria, 2005, p. 139. These were among the few lines censored from any of the published material on the camps and omitted from the report published in Cd 936, *Further Papers Relating to the Working of the Refugee Camps in South Africa*. London, HMSO, 1902, p. 14.
10. Van Heyningen, E: *The Concentration Camps of the Anglo-Boer War. A social history*. Jacana, Auckland Park, 2013, pp. 234–235.
11. See NASA, A 2030-76, Ploeger Archive for the diary. For the transcribed text see ID 95176 on website www2.lib.uct.ac.za/mss/bccd/; also FSAR, SRC 76, Brandfort camp register, pp. 97, 463.
12. Ibid.
13. FSAR, SRC 24, RC8657, 28 May 1902.
14. Grundlingh, AM: *The Dynamics of Treason. Boer collaboration in the South African War of 1899–1902*. Protea Boekhuis, Pretoria, 2006.
15. Translated from Afrikaans.
16. Fischer, F: *Tant Miem Fischer se Kampdagboek*. Protea Boekhuis, Pretoria, 2000, pp. 89, 91.
17. Wasserman, JM: *The Pinetown Concentration Camp during the Anglo-Boer War (1899–1902)*. Waterman Publishers, Congella, circa 1998, pp. 64–68.
18. Landman, C: *The Piety of Afrikaans Women: Diaries of guilt*. University of South Africa, Pretoria, 1994, pp. 7–93.
19. The literature is extensive. Google 'Victorian deathbed culture', for instance.
20. Lückhoff, AD: *Women's Endurance*. Protea Boekhuis, Pretoria, 2006, p. 90.
21. Email to E van Heyningen, 5 July 2011.
22. FSAR, SRC 20 RC7735, 27 February 1902.
23. NASA, DBC 12, Report on Klerksdorp camp, 14 April 1902.
24. Dampier, H: 'Women's testimonies of the concentration camps of the South African War: 1899–1902 and after'. Unpublished doctoral thesis, University of Newcastle, 2005; Stanley, L: *Mourning Becomes... Post/memory, commemoration and the concentration camps of the South African War*. Manchester University Press, Manchester, 2006; Stanley, L and Dampier, H: 'Cultural entrepreneurs, proto-nationalism and women's testimony writings: from the South African War to 1940', in *Journal of Southern African Studies*, 33, 3, September 2007, pp. 501–519.
25. Riedi, E: 'Teaching Empire: British and Dominion women teachers in the South African War concentration camps', in *English Historical Review*, 120, 489, 2005, pp. 1316–1333.
26. NASA, FK 1050, CO 25144, ORC 25144 [African 693], 23 June 1902, *Report on Civil Admin since Sept 2001*
27. Robertson, W: *Concentration Camps*. Argus, Cape Town, 1901, p. 13.
28. National War Museum: 920 Brink, G.E. Brink, Reminiscences.
29. NASA, DBC 12, Report on Volksrust camp, February 1902; DBC 12, Vereeniging monthly report for January 1902; DBC 14, Vereeniging monthly report for November 1901.
30. War Museum of the Boer Republics, OM 6344.
31. National War Museum: 920 Brink, G.E. Brink, Reminiscences.
32. PAR, A 48, Lily Rose: 'The Hospital' *Nursing Record*, 26 April 1902, p. 56.
33. Hobhouse, EH: *War without Glamour; or, Women's War Experiences Written by Themselves, 1899–1902*. Nasionale Pers, Bloemfontein, 1924, p. 37.

CHAPTER FIVE

1. Hardy, A: *The Epidemic Streets. Infectious disease and the rise of preventive medicine, 1856–1900*. Clarendon, Oxford, 1993, pp. 28-54.
2. FSAR. SRC 133, Pratt Yule report for 1901, pp. 3, 7; SRC 20, RC7715, 14 November 1901.
3. Paul, HW: *Bacchic Medicine: Wine and alcohol therapies from Napoleon to the French paradox*. Rodopi, Amsterdam, 2001, p. 78. For a fuller discussion of this section, see Van Heyningen, E: 'Women and disease: The clash of medical cultures in the concentration camps of the South African War', in Cuthbertson, G, Grundlingh, A and Suttie, M-L (eds.): *Writing a Wider War: Rethinking gender, race, and identity in the South African War, 1899–1902*. Ohio University Press and David Philip, Athens and Cape Town, 2002, pp. 186–212.
4. Ross, J: *A Few Chapters on Public Health, Adapted for South Africa*. Hay, King William's Town, 1887, p. 1.
5. FSAR, SRC 22, RC8123, 3 April 1902; SRC 22, RC8275, 15 April 1902; SRC 22, RC8274, 21 April 1902.
6. South African Academy for Science and Art: *Volksgeneeskuns in Suid-Afrika. 'n Kultuurhistoriese oorsig, benewens 'n uitgebreide versameling boererate*. Protea Boekhuis, Pretoria, 2010.
7. Ibid., p. 345, no. 4676.
8. Ibid., pp. 342–343, no. 4619.
9. Ibid., p. 345, no. 4678. *Wonderessens* is probably *Wonderkroonessens*, also an

ingredient from the *Huis Apotheek* or family medicine chest (gentian violet, widely used as an anti-fungal drug).

10 Gomme, AB: 'Boer folk-medicine and some parallels', in *Folklore*, 13, 1, 25 March 1902, p. 73. Continued in *Folklore*, 13, 2, 24 June 1902, pp. 181–183.

11 Gomme, AB: 'Boer folk-medicine and some parallels', in *Folklore*, 13, 1, 25 March 1902, p.74.

12 Ryan, M: *A History of Organised Pharmacy in South Africa 1885–1950*. The Society for the History of Pharmacy in South Africa, Cape Town, 1978, p. 3; Burrows, EH: *A History of Medicine in South Africa up to the End of the Nineteenth Century*. Balkema, Cape Town, 1958, pp. 190-191. Today these products are manufactured by Lennons of Port Elizabeth and are widely available as a form of alternative medicine. See www.mkem.co.za/c248/Lennon.aspx, accessed 12 February 2013.

13 Spoelstra, B: *Ons Volkslewe: Kultuurhistoriese leesboek*. Van Schaik, Pretoria, 1922, p. 124.

14 FSAR, SRC 15, RC5664, 20 August 1901; SRC 14, RC5260, 16 September 1901; SRC 13, RC4925, 9 September 1901; SRC 13, RC4875, 12 September 1901.

15 'The Hospital' *Nursing Record*, 26 April 1902, p. 56.

CHAPTER SIX

1 Machteld Nel to JP and Lucasiena Schutte, Jacobs Camp, 4 April 1902, Stellenbosch University Special Collections (hereafter SUSC), MS 403 Opperman Collection, 3B1.

2 Philippina Charlotta Nel to JP Schutte, Potchefstroom Camp, 3 July 1901, SUSC, MS 403 Opperman Collection, 3B1.

3 Philippina Charlotta Nel to JP Schutte, Potchefstroom Camp, 3 July and 1 October 1901, SUSC, MS 403 Opperman Collection, 3B1.

4 Figures taken from Mohlamme, JS: 'African refugee camps in the Boer republics', in Pretorius, F (ed.): *Scorched Earth*. Human & Rousseau, Cape Town, 2001, p. 121, and Kessler, SV: 'The Black and Coloured concentration camps', in Pretorius, F (ed.): *Scorched Earth*, p. 150.

5 Hobhouse, E: *Report of a Visit to the Camps of Women and Children in the Cape and Orange River Colonies: To the Committee of the Distress Fund for South African Women and Children*. Friars Printing Association, London, circa 1901, p. 5.

6 Van Bart, M: 'Poppie "oorleef" toe ook konsentrasiekamp', in *Die Burger*, 2 March 2013.

7 Hobhouse, E: *Report of a Visit to the Camps of Women and Children in the Cape and Orange River Colonies*, p. 10.

8 Quoted in Gouws, J: 'Deneys Reitz and Imperial Co-option,' in Van der Vlies, A (ed.): *Print, Text, and Book Cultures in South Africa*. Wits University Press, Johannesburg, 2012, p. 115.

9 Cummings, AM: 'Letter from South Africa', in *The Monthly Record*, December 1899, Dutch Reformed Church Archive, Huguenot Seminary Collection, K-Div 621, p. 9.

10 Ibid.

11 Ibid., April 1901, p. 1.

12 Mackenzie, E: Untitled memoir, SUSC, MS 177 EO Stubbings Collection, 177 (1.2).

13 Cummings, AM: 'Letter from South Africa', in *The Monthly Record*, November 1900, pp. 4–5.

14 Diary of FE Wookey, SUSC, pp. 27–28, MS 141 Wookey Collection.

15 Diary of Lillian Hutton, pp. 149–150, SUSC, MS 81 Hutton Collection.

16 Davey, AM (ed.): *Lawrence Richardson: Selected Correspondence (1902–1903)*. Van Riebeeck Society, Cape Town, 1977, p. 19.

17 Alice Greene to Sir Henry de Villiers, 30 October, year unknown, SUSC, MS 17 Winifred de Villiers Collection, 17/4.

18 Marquard, L (ed.): *Letters from a Boer Parsonage*, 1967, p. 133.

19 Anna Cummings to friends, 7 March 1900, DRCA, HSC, K-Div 605.

20 Van Heerden, P: *Kerssnuitsels*. Tafelberg, Cape Town, 1963, pp. 115–116.

21 Diary of John Fourie, pp. 34–35, SUSC, MS 23 John Fourie Collection, 23/1.

22 Hobhouse, E: *Report of a Visit to the Camps of Women and Children in the Cape and Orange River Colonies*, p. 7.

23 Van Schoor, MCE (ed.): *Kampkinders, 1900–1902: 'n Gedenkboek*. Dreyer-Drukkers en Uitgewers, Bloemfontein, 1982, pp. 14, 23.

24 Warwick, Peter: *Black People and the South African War, 1899–1902*. Cambridge University Press, Cambridge, 1983, p.156.

25 *Notulen der Conferentie van Leeraren, Arbeiders, en Arbeidsters in de Burger-Kampen in Natal gehouden in het Burger-Kamp te Merebank op den 24sten and 25sten Juni 1902*. Hollandsch-Afrikaanshe Uitgevers-Maatschappij, Amsterdam and Cape Town, 1902, p. 20; Neethling, E: *Should we Forget?* HAUM, Cape Town, 1902, pp. 80–81.

26 Van Schoor, MCE (ed.): *Kampkinders 1900–1902*, pp. 32, 39.

27 Boshoff-Liebenberg, L: *Moedersmart en Kinderleed, of 18 Maande in die Konsentrasie Kampe*. Die Noordelike Drukpers Maatskappy, Pretoria, 1921, pp. 65, 78.

28 Marquard, L (ed.): *Letters from a Boer Parsonage*, pp. 106–108.

29 Ibid., p. 117.

30 Van Schoor, MCE (ed.): *Kampkinders 1900–1902*, p. 44.

31 Hobhouse, E: *Report of a Visit to the Camps of Women and Children in the Cape and Orange River Colonies*, pp. 7, 18.

32 Davey, AM (ed.): *Lawrence Richardson: Selected Correspondence (1902–1903)*, p. 70.

33 Riedi, E: 'Teaching Empire' in *English Historical Review*. Vol. 120, no. 489, December 2005, p. 1320.

34 Van Schoor, MCE (ed.): *Kampkinders 1900–1902*, p. 24.

35 *Notulen der Conferentie van Leeraren, Arbeiders, en Arbeidsters in de Burger-Kampen in Natal gehouden in het Burger-Kamp te Merebank op den 24sten and 25sten Juni 1902*, p. 36.

36 Mohlamme, JS: 'African Refugee Camps in the Boer Republics', in Pretorius, F (ed.): *Scorched Earth*, pp. 123–124.

37 Boshoff-Liebenberg, L: *Moedersmart en Kinderleed*, pp. 38–40.

CHAPTER SEVEN

1 Quoted in Warwick, P: *Black People and the South African War, 1899–1902*. Cambridge University Press, Cambridge, 1983, p. 148.

2. *The Green Howards Gazette*, 12, 6 (1901), p.17; *Household Brigade Magazine*, 32, 3 (1901); *Highland Light Infantry Chronicle*, 3/4, 8 (1901), p. 79.
3. Pretorius, F: *The Anglo-Boer War, 1899–1902.* Don Nelson, Cape Town, 1985, p.79.
4. Atwood, R: *Roberts & Kitchener in South Africa, 1900–1902.* Pen & Sword, Barnsley, 2011, p. 252.
5. Quoted in Warwick, P: *Black People and the South African War*, p. 149.
6. Carr, R: *The Spanish Tragedy: The Civil War in perspective.* Phoenix, London, 2000, p. 247.
7. Pretorius, F: *The A to Z of the Anglo-Boer War.* Scarecrow Press, Lanham, MD, 2009, p. 103.
8. Warwick, P: *Black People and the South African War*, p. 151.
9. Kessler, S: 'The Black concentration camps of the Anglo-Boer War, 1899–1902: Shifting the paradigm from sole martyrdom to mutual suffering', in *Historia* vol. 44, no. 1, 1999, p. 118.
10. Quoted in Stanley, L: *Mourning becomes*, pp. 190–191.
11. Quoted in Karis, T and Carter, GM (eds.): *From Protest to Challenge: A Documentary History of African Politics in South Africa, 1882–1921.* Stanford University Press, Stanford, 1972, p. 18.
12. Quoted in Warwick, P: *Black People and the South African War*, p. 156.
13. Townshend, C: 'People's war', in Townshend, C (ed.): *The Oxford History of Modern War.* Oxford University Press, Oxford, 2005, p. 182.
14. Khumalo, F: 'The Boer War's hidden shame', *Sunday Times*, 10 February 2013, p. 7.

CHAPTER EIGHT
1. Reitz, D: *Commando: A Boer journal of the Boer War.* Faber & Faber, London, 1929, p. 309.
2. Ibid., p. 309. Francis Reitz, Deneys's father, was State Secretary of the Transvaal Republic and had handed the British Agent in Pretoria the Boer Ultimatum in October 1899, precipitating war, and was also a signatory at the peace of Vereeniging.
3. See Van Reenen, R (ed.): *Emily Hobhouse: Boer War Letters.* Human & Rousseau, Cape Town, 1984, p. 210.
4. Ibid., pp. 216–217.
5. Ibid., p. 258.
6. Ibid., pp. 210, 216–217, 258, 266.
7. Critchley, S: *On Humour.* Routledge, London, 2002, p. 3. Billig, M: *Laughter and Ridicule: Towards a social critique of humour.* Sage Publications, London, 2005, pp. 65, 96.
8. Bakhtin, M: *Rabelais and His World.* Indiana University Press, Bloomington, 1984. For recent trends see *Humor: International Journal of Humor Research*, Journal for the International Society for Humor Studies.
9. Kestell, JD: *Through Shot and Flame: The adventures and experiences of J. D. Kestell Chaplain to President Steyn and General Christian De Wet.* Methuen & Co, London, 1903, chapter 16.
10. Pretorius, F: 'Humour on commando during the South African War, 1899–1902,' International Society for Humour Studies, Birmingham, 1 August 1995, and Pretorius, F: *Life on Commando during the Anglo-Boer War, 1899–1902.* Human & Rousseau, Cape Town, 1999, p. 120.
11. Le Riche, PJ (ed.): *Memoirs of General Ben Bouwer.* Human Sciences Research Council, Pretoria, 1980, pp. 75, 76–77.
12. Dillon KM, et al.: 'Positive emotional states and enhancement of the immune system,' in *International Journal of Psychiatry in Medicine*, vol. 15, 1985, pp. 13–15; Martin, RA and Dobbin, JP: 'Sense of humor, hassles and immunoglobulin,' in *International Journal of Psychiatry in Medicine*, vol. 18, 1988, pp. 93–105; Cousins, N: 'Why laughter is good medicine,' in Mindess, H and Turek, J (eds.): *The Study of Humor.* Antioch University, Los Angeles, 1979, p. 79.
13. Reitz, D: *Commando*, p. 173.
14. Muller, CH: *Oorlogsherinneringe van Generaal Chris H. Muller.* Nasionale Pers, Cape Town, 1936, p. 97. Translated from Afrikaans.
15. From Malherbe, FEJ: *Humor in die algemeen en sy uiting in die Afrikaanse letterkunde.* Swets & Zeitlinger, Amsterdam, 1924, p. 176.
16. Quoted in Wessels, E: *Kwinkslag: Humor in die Anglo-Boereoorlog, 1899–1902.* JP van der Walt, Pretoria, 1999, p. 86.
17. Quoted in Wessels, E: *Kwinkslag*, p. 322.
18. Viljoen, B: *My Reminiscences of the Anglo-Boer War.* Hood, Douglas and Howard, London, 1902, p. 281.
19. From *De Huisgenoot*, December 1921.
20. Reitz, D: *Commando*, p. 154.
21. Ibid., p. 282.
22. Ibid., pp. 116, 154, 282; Pretorius, F: *Life on Commando*, p. 144.
23. Pretorius, F: *Life on Commando*, p. 121.
24. Viljoen, B: *My Reminiscences of the Anglo-Boer War*, p. 61.
25. Reitz, D: *Commando*, p. 173.
26. Viljoen, B: *My Reminiscences of the Anglo-Boer War*, p. 399.
27. Ibid., p. 300. See also selected verse in Brink, MJ: *Grappige stories en andere versies, vol. IV.* De Bussy, Pretoria, 1921, see for example pp. 51–52.
28. Cited in Wortley, H: 'Die grap in Afrikaans'. Unpublished master's thesis, University of Stellenbosch, 1992, p. 32.
29. Reitz, D: *Commando*, p. 143.
30. Pretorius, F: *Life on Commando*, pp. 72–73. This was later immortalised as a joke, ending in 'Toe die Kakie so wegstap met die flenterpak, gee die Boer hom 'n skoppie agter op sij broek en sê: "Go, you dirty Boor!"' (When the Khaki walked away in the tattered clothes, the Boer kicked him lightly on the behind and said, 'Go, you dirty Boor!') *De Huisgenoot*, April 1919.
31. Viljoen, B: *My Reminiscences of the Anglo-Boer War*, p. 297.
32. Basson, MA: *Die Voertaalvraagstuk in die Transvaalse skoolwese.* University of Pretoria, Pretoria, 1944, p. 46.
33. Viljoen, B: *My Reminiscences of the Anglo-Boer War*, p. 27.
34. Hendrika Cornelia Scott Swart (1939–), personal communication.
35. For discussion see Gordon, DB: 'Humor in African American Discourse: Speaking of Oppression,' in *Journal of Black Studies*, vol. 29, no. 2, 1998, pp. 254–276.
36. Leipoldt, CL: *Oom Gert vertel en ander gedigte.* Nasionale Boekhandel, Cape Town, 1911.
37. Ibid., p. 85. Translated by the author.
38. Orwell, S and Angus, I (eds.): *The Collected Essays, Journalism, and Letters of George Orwell, vol. 3. As I Please, 1943–1945.* Harcourt, Brace & World, New York, 1969, p. 184.
39. Kishtainy, K: *Arab Political Humour.* Quartet Books, London, 1985, pp. 7, 179.

40 See Van Reenen, R: *Emily Hobhouse,* p. 210 and Malherbe, FEJ: *Humor in die Algemeen en sy Uiting in die Afrikaanse Letterkunde,* p. 157. Another interpretation of the Boer's answer could be that the sarcastic response is to convey to the questioner that his initial question was insensitive.
41 Wickberg, D: *The senses of humour: Self and laughter in modern America.* Cornell University Press, Ithaca, 1998, p. 18.
42 Nienaber, PJ: 'The Evolution of Afrikaans as a Literary Language,' in *Lantern,* 8, 8, 4, 1959.
43 Malherbe, FEJ: *Humor in die Algemeen en sy Uiting in die Afrikaanse Letterkunde,* p. 156.
44 Malherbe, FEJ: 'Die Afrikaner en humor,' in *Die Huisgenoot,* June 1934.
45 Malherbe, FEJ: *Humor in die Algemeen en sy Uiting in die Afrikaanse Letterkunde,* p. 165.

CHAPTER NINE

1 Other members of the committee were General JBM Hertzog, Abraham Fischer (later prime minister of the Orange River Colony), Dr WJC (Jack) Brebner, JP Steyl, CG (Charlie) Fichardt, CH Wessels, Dr Stollreither, the Revd CD Murray, the Revd Grosskopf, Gordon Fraser and Rocco de Villiers, as well as AW Mchardy as secretary.
2 Wessels, E and Raath, AWG: *Onthou: Kronieke van vroue- en kinderlyding, 1899–1902. Kraaluitgewers,* Pretoria, 2012, p. 294. 3 FSAR A1561/1/11 eh (Rome), 5 August 1911.
3 3 FSAR A1561/1/17 eh (Rome), 5 August 1911.
4 Truter, E: 'Rachel Isabella Steyn 1905–1955'. Unpublished doctoral thesis, University of Pretoria, 1994, p. 63.
5 Ibid.
6 Terblanche, A: *Emily Hobhouse.* Afrikaanse Pers Boekhandel, Johannesburg, 1948, p. 513.
7 Van Reenen, R (ed.): *Emily Hobhouse: Boer War letters.* Human & Rousseau, Cape Town, 1984, p. 112.
8 Van Reenen, R. *Heldin uit die Vreemde: die verhaal van Emily Hobhouse.* Tafelberg, Cape Town, 1973, p. 104.
9 Terblanche, A: *Emily Hobhouse,* p. 513.
10 Truter, E: 'Rachel Isabella Steyn 1905–1955', p. 68.
11 In 1952 for example souvenirs of the monument and a publication by Dr NJ van der Merwe, son-in-law of President MT Steyn, were put on sale, while an amount of R30 000 for overall restoration was collected in 1972.

CHAPTER TEN

1 Van der Merwe, NJ: *The National Women's Monument.* Publisher unknown, s.a. (the first edition was probably published between 1926 and 1941), p. 17.
2 Landman, C: *The Piety of Afrikaner Women,* pp. 4, 19.
3 Van Reenen, R (ed.): *Emily Hobhouse: Boer War letters.* Human & Rousseau, Cape Town, 1984, p. 112.
4 Letter from Emily Hobhouse to Mrs. Steyn, 5 April 1912, in Van Reenen, R (ed.): *Emily Hobhouse,* pp. 513–514.
5 Cloete, E: 'Afrikaner Identity: Culture, Tradition and Gender', in *Agenda* 13, 1992, p. 15.
6 Kruger, N: *Rachel Isabella Steyn: Presidentsvrou.* Nasionale Pers, Cape Town, 1949, p. 93. Translated from Afrikaans.
7 *The Friend,* 17 December 1913.
8 Letter from Hobhouse to Mrs Steyn, 30 October 1913, in Van Reenen, R (ed.): *Emily Hobhouse,* pp. 395–396.
9 Letter from C Brits to MT Steyn, 3 November 1913, in Free State Archives, MT Steyn Collection, A156/1/1/8.
10 *The Friend,* 17 December 1913.
11 *De Kerkbode,* 18 December 1913 (my translation).
12 *The Friend,* 18 December 1913.
13 Ibid., 17 December 1913.
14 Ibid.
15 Ibid.
16 Ibid.
17 Ibid.
18 Letter from CF Beyers to MT Steyn, 3 October 1913, in Free State Archives, MT Steyn Collection, A156/1/1/8.
19 Raal, R: *Met die Boere in die Veld.* Nasionale Pers, Cape Town, 1937, preface. The Afrikaner literature on the war in the 1930s and 1940s is discussed more extensively in Grundlingh, A: 'War, wordsmiths and the "Volk": Afrikaans historical writing on the Anglo-Boer War of 1899–1902 and the war in Afrikaner nationalist consciousness, 1902–1990', in Lehmann, E and Reckwitz, E (eds.): *Mfecane to Boer War: Versions of South African history.* University of Essen Press, Essen, 1992, pp. 45–47.
20 Quoted in Moodie, D: *The rise of Afrikanerdom: Power, apartheid and Afrikaner civil religion,* University of California Press, Berkeley, 1975, pp. 192-193.
21 De Villiers, M: *White Tribe Dreaming: Apartheid's bitter roots as witnessed by eight generations of an Afrikaner family.* Viking, Toronto, 1989, p. 237.
22 Kammen, M: 'Frames of remembrance', in *History and Theory* 34, no. 3, 1995, p. 255.
23 Cloete, E: 'Frontierswomen as *volksmoeders*: Textual invocations in two centuries of writing'. Unpublished master's thesis, Unisa, 1994, pp. 111–112.
24 Snyman, J: 'Suffering and the politics of memory', in Du Toit, CW (ed.): *New Modes of Thinking on the Eve of a New Century: South African perspectives.* Unisa Press, Pretoria, 1995, pp. 137–138.

CHAPTER ELEVEN

1 "Vrouwen-dag, December 16, 1913." Atlas Printing Works, Cape Town, 1913.

Further reading

CHAPTER ONE

Atwood, R: *Roberts and Kitchener in South Africa, 1900–1902*. Pen and Sword, Barnsley, 2011.

Grundlingh, AM: *Die hendsoppers en joiners: Die rasionaal en verskynsel van verraad*. HAUM, Pretoria, 1979.

Hyam, R: *Empire and Sexuality: The British experience*. Manchester University Press, Manchester, 1990.

Hyslop, J: 'The invention of the concentration camp: Cuba, Southern Africa, and the Philippines', in *South African Historical Journal*, 63:2, 2011.

Nasson, B: *The War for South Africa: The Anglo-Boer War 1899–1902*. Tafelberg, Cape Town, 2010.

Otto, JC: *Die Konsentrasiekampe*. Protea Boekhuis, Pretoria, 2005.

Ploeger, J: *Die Lotgevalle van die Burgerlike Bevolking gedurende die Anglo-Boereoorlog, 1899–1902*. Unpublished manuscript, National Archives, Pretoria, 1999.

Pretorius, F: *Die Anglo-Boereoorlog, 1899–1902*. Protea Boekhuis, Pretoria, 2001.

Pretorius, F: *Life on Commando during the Anglo-Boer War, 1899–1902*. Human & Rousseau, Cape Town, 2001.

Pretorius, F (ed.): *Verskroeide Aarde*. Human & Rousseau, Cape Town, 2001.

Raath, AWG and Wessels, E (eds.): *Onthou! Kronieke van vroue- en kinderlyding, 1899–1902*. Kraal-uitgewers, Centurion, 2012.

Spies, SB: *Methods of Barbarism? Roberts and Kitchener and civilians in the Boer republics, January 1900–May 1902*. Human & Rousseau, Cape Town, 1977.

Surridge, KT: *Managing the South African War, 1899–1902: Politicians vs Generals*. Boydell Press, Woodbridge, 1998.

Van Heyningen, E: *The Concentration Camps of the Anglo-Boer War: A social history*. Jacana, Auckland Park, 2013.

Wessels, A: *Die Anglo-Boereoorlog*. Sunmedia, Bloemfontein, 2011.

CHAPTER TWO

Brink, E: 'Man-made women: gender, class, and the ideology of the *Volksmoeder*', in Walker, C (ed.): *Women and Gender in Southern Africa to 1945*. David Philip, Cape Town, 1990.

De Wet, C: 'Dagboek van Oskar Hintrager', in *Christiaan de Wet Annale (vol. 2)*. War Museum of the Boer Republics, Bloemfontein, 1973.

Elshtain, JB: *Women and War*. Basic Books, New York, 1988.

Headlam, C (ed.): *The Milner Papers: South Africa, 1897–1905 (vol. 1)*. Cassell, London, 1933.

James, D: *The Life of Lord Roberts*. Hollis & Carter, London, 1954.

Oberholster, AG (ed.): *Oorlogsdagboek van Jan F. Celliers, 1899–1902*. Raad vir Geesteswetenskaplike Navorsing, Pretoria, 1978.

Pretorius, F: *Kommandolewe tydens die Anglo-Boereoorlog, 1899–1902*. Human & Rousseau, Cape Town, 1991.

Pretorius, F: 'The White Concentration Camps of the Anglo-Boer War: A Debate without End', in *Historia*, vol. 55, no. 2 (2010).

Schoeman, K (ed.): *Die herinneringe van J.C. de Waal*. Human & Rousseau, Cape Town, 1986.

Spies, SB: 'Women and the War', in Warwick, P (ed.): *The South African War: The Anglo-Boer War, 1899–1902*. Longman, London, 1980.

Theweleit, K: 'The bomb's womb and the genders of war', in Cooke, M and Woollacott, A (eds.): *Gendering War Talk*. Princeton University Press, Princeton, 1993.

THE HAVENGA REPORT

Le Roux, JH, Coetzer, PW and Marais, AH (eds.): *Generaal J.B.M. Hertzog, Dele l en ll*. Perskor, Johannesburg, 1987.

Rompel, F: *Marthinus Theunis Steijn*. Veen, Amsterdam, 1902.

Van Breda, P: *Die politieke loopbaan van N.C. Havenga, 1910–1954*. Unpublished doctoral thesis, Stellenbosch University, 1992.

Van den Heever, CM: *Generaal J.B.M. Herzog*. APB Bookstore, Johannesburg, 1946.

Van Schoor, MCE: *Marthinus Theunis Steyn: 'n Regsman, staatsman en volksman*. Protea Boekhuis, Pretoria, 2009.

CHAPTER THREE

De la Rey, JE: *A Woman's Wanderings and Trials During the Anglo-Boer War*. T. Fisher Unwin, London, 1903.

Marais, P: *Die Vrou in die Anglo-Boereoorlog 1899–1902*. J. P. van der Walt, Pretoria, 1999.

Meintjes, J: *De la Rey – Lion of the West*. Hugh Keartland, Johannesburg, 1966.

Nasson, B: *The War for South Africa: The Anglo-Boer War 1899–1902*. Tafelberg, Cape Town, 2010.

Pakenham, T: *Die Boere-oorlog*. Jonathan Ball, Johannesburg, 1981.

Postma, W: *Die Boervrou: Moeder van haar volk*. Nasionale Pers, Bloemfontein, 1918.

Pretorius, F: *Kommandolewe tydens die Anglo-Boereoorlog, 1899–1902*. Human & Rousseau, Cape Town, 1991.

Rowan, R: *Nonnie de la Rey, 1856–1923*. Unpublished master's thesis, University of Pretoria, 2003.

Stockenström, E: *Die Afrikaanse Vrou: Die vrou in die geskiedenis van die Hollands-Afrikaanse volk, 1568–1918*. Pro Ecclesia, Stellenbosch, 1921.

CHAPTER FOUR

Fischer, M: *Tant Miem Fischer se Kampdagboek*. Protea Boekhuis, Pretoria, 2000.

Hobhouse, E: *The Brunt of the War and Where it Fell*. Methuen, London, 1902.

Lückhoff, AD: *Women's Endurance*. Protea Boekhuis, Pretoria, 2006.

Marquard, L (ed.): *Letters From a Boer Parsonage: Letters of Margaret Marquard during the Boer War*. Purnell, Cape Town, 1967.

Pretorius, F (ed.): *Scorched Earth*. Human & Rousseau, Cape Town, 2001.

Riedi, E: 'Teaching empire: British and dominion women teachers in the South African War concentration camps', in *English Historical Review*, 2005.

Spies, SB: *Methods of Barbarism? Roberts and Kitchener and civilians in the Boer republics, January 1900–May 1902*. Human & Rousseau, Cape Town, 1977.

Van Heyningen, E: *The Concentration Camps of the Anglo-Boer War*.

CHAPTER FIVE

De Villiers, JC: *Healers, Helpers and Hospitals*. Protea Boekhuis, Pretoria, 2008.

Gomme, AB: 'Boer folk-medicine and some parallels' in *Folklore*, 13, 1, 25 March 1902 and *Folklore*, 13, 2, 24 June 1902.

Suid-Afrikaanse Akademie vir Wetenskap en Kuns: *Volksgeneeskuns in Suid-Afrika. 'n Kultuurhistoriese oorsig, benewens 'n uitgebreide versameling boererate*. Protea Boekhuis, Pretoria, 2010.

Van Heyningen, E: 'Medical history and Afrikaner society in the Boer republics at the end of the nineteenth century', in *Kleio*, 37, 2005.

Van Heyningen, E: 'Women and disease: The clash of medical cultures in the concentration camps of the South African War', in Cuthbertson, G, Grundlingh, A and Suttie, M-L (eds.), *Writing a Wider War. Rethinking gender, race, and identity in the South African War, 1899–1902*. Ohio University Press and David Philip, Athens and Cape Town, 2002.

CHAPTER SIX

Bradford, H: 'Gentlemen and Boers: Afrikaner nationalism, gender, and colonial warfare in the South African War', in Cuthbertson, G, Grundlingh, A and Suttie, M-L (eds.): *Writing a Wider War*.

Duff, SE: 'From new women to college girls at the Huguenot Seminary and College, 1895–1910', in *Historia*, vol. 51, no. 1 (May 2006).

Krebs, PM: 'The last of the gentlemen's wars': Women in the Boer War concentration camp controversy,' in *History Workshop*, no. 33 (Spring, 1992).

Mohlamme, JS: 'African refugee camps in the Boer republics' in Pretorius, F (ed.): *Scorched Earth*.

Riedi, E: 'Teaching empire: British and Dominions women teachers in the South African War concentration camps', in *English Historical Review*, vol. 120, no. 489 (December 2005).

Stanley, L: *Mourning Becomes ... Post/memory, commemoration and the concentration camps of the South African War*. Manchester University Press, Manchester, 2006.

Van Heyningen, E: 'A Tool for Modernisation? The Concentration Camps of the South African War, 1900–1902', in *South African Journal of Science*, vol. 106, nos. 5/6 (2010).

Warwick, P: *Black People and the South African War, 1899-1902*. Cambridge University Press, Cambridge, 1983.

CHAPTER SEVEN

Kessler, S: 'The Black concentration camps of the Anglo-Boer War, 1899–1902: Shifting the paradigm from sole martyrdom to mutual suffering', in *Historia*, vol. 44, no. 1 (1999).

Kessler, S: 'The Black and Coloured concentration camps', in F. Pretorius (ed.), *Scorched Earth*.

Kessler, S: *The Black Concentration Camps of the Anglo-Boer War, 1899–1902*. War Museum of the Boer Republics, Bloemfontein, 2012.

Mohlamme, JS: 'African Refugee camps in the Boer Republics'.

Mongalo BE and Du Pisani, K: 'Victims of a White man's war: Blacks in concentration camps during the South African War (1899–1902)', in *Historia*, vol. 44, no. 1 (1999).

Spies, SB: *Methods of Barbarism?*

Stanley, L: *Mourning Becomes*.

Warwick, P: *Black People and the South African War, 1899–1902*.

CHAPTER EIGHT

Bakhtin, M: *Rabelais and His World*. Indiana University Press, Bloomington, 1984.

Billig, M: *Laughter and Ridicule: Towards a social critique of humour*. Sage Publications, London, 2005.

Critchley, S: *On Humour*. Routledge, London, 2002.

Humor: International Journal of Humor Research, Journal for the International Society for Humor Studies.

Kishtainy, K: *Arab Political Humour*. Quartet Books, London, 1985.

Obrdlik, A: 'Gallows humour: A sociological phenomenon,' in *American Journal of Sociology*, vol. 47, no. 5, 1941, pp. 709–716.

Pretorius, F: 'Humour on commando during the South African War, 1899–1902,' International Society for Humour Studies, Birmingham, 1 August 1995.

Pretorius, F: *Life on Commando during the Anglo-Boer War, 1899–1902*. Human & Rousseau, Cape Town, 1999.

Reitz, D: *Commando: A Boer Journal of the Boer War*. Faber & Faber, London, 1929.

Sanders, B: *Sudden Glory: Laughter as subversive history*. Beacon Press, Boston, 1995.

Swart, S: '"The terrible laughter of the Afrikaner": Towards a social history of humour', in *Journal of Social History*, vol. 42, no. 4 (Summer, 2009).

Van Reenen, R (ed.): *Emily Hobhouse: Boer War letters*. Human & Rousseau, Cape Town, 1984.

Viljoen, B: *My Reminiscences of the Anglo-Boer War*. Hood, Douglas, and Howard, London, 1902.

Wessels, E: *Kwinkslag: Humor in die Anglo-Boereoorlog, 1899–1902*. JP van der Walt, Pretoria, 1999.

Wortley, H: 'Die grap in Afrikaans'. Unpublished master's thesis, University of Stellenbosch, 1992.

CHAPTER NINE

Duffey, AE: *Anton van Wouw: The smaller works*. Protea Boekhuis, Pretoria, 2008.

Keet, AD (jr): *Briewe van Anton van Wouw aan AD Keet*. AD Keet-publikasiefonds met steun van Nasionale Pers, Cape Town, 1981.

Kruger, N: *Rachel Isabella Steyn: Presidentsvrou*. Nasionale Pers, Cape Town, 1949.

Raath, AWG and Wessels, E (eds.):

Onthou! Kronieke van vroue- en kinderlyding, 1899–1902. Kraal-uitgewers, Centurion, 2012.

Truter, E: 'Die lewe van Rachel Isabella Steyn in die Oranje-Vrystaat 1865–1905'. Unpublished master's thesis, University of South Africa, 1989.

Truter, E: 'Rachel Isabella Steyn 1905–1955'. Unpublished doctoral thesis, University of Pretoria, 1994.

Van der Merwe, NJ: *Marthinus Theunis Steyn (deel 2)*. De Nationale Pers Beperk, Cape Town, 1921

Van der Merwe, NJ: *The National Women's Monument*. Published by the Monument Commission, s.a. (the first edition was probably published between 1926 and 1941).

Van Reenen, R: *Emily Hobhouse*.

Van Reenen, R: *Heldin uit die Vreemde: Die verhaal van Emily Hobhouse*. Tafelberg, Cape Town, 1970.

Van Schoor, MCE: *Die Nasionale Vrouemonument*. NG Sendingpers, Bloemfontein, 1993.

CHAPTER TEN

Cloete, EL: 'Frontierswomen as Volkmoeders: Textual invocations in two centuries of writing'. Unpublished master's thesis, University of South Africa, 1994.

Hofmeyr, I: 'Building a nation from words: Afrikaans language, literature and ethnic identity, 1902–1924', in Marks, S and Trapido, S (eds.): *The Politics of Race, Class and Nationalism in Twentieth-Century South Africa*. Longman, London, 1987.

Kammen, M: 'Frames of remembrance', in *History and Theory*, vol. 34, no. 3 (1995).

Kruger, N: *Rachel Isabella Steyn*.

Raath, AWG and Wessels, E (eds.): *Onthou! Kronieke van vroue- en kinderlyding, 1899–1902*.

Snyman, J: 'Suffering and the politics of memory', in Du Toit, CW (ed.): *New Modes of Thinking on the Eve of a New Century: South African perspectives*. Unisa Press, Pretoria, 1995.

Van der Merwe, NJ: *Marthinus Theunis Steyn, (deel. 2)*.

Van der Merwe, NJ: *The National Women's Monument*.

Van Schoor, MCE: *Die Nasionale Vrouemonument*. NG Sendingpers, Bloemfontein, 1993.

CHAPTER ELEVEN

Hobhouse, E: *Vrouwen-dag, December 16, 1913*. Atlas Printing Works, Cape Town, 1913. The original document is part of the DF Malan collection in the Africana section of the JS Gericke library at the University of Stellenbosch.

Author biographies

Bill Nasson is a professor of history at the University of Stellenbosch. He is a scholar with interests in war and South African society, and war and British imperialism. His recent publications include *The War for South Africa: The Anglo-Boer War 1899–1902* (2010) and *South Africa at War 1939–1945* (2012).

Albert Grundlingh is chairperson of the history department at the University of Stellenbosch. He specialises in social and cultural history, with a particular interest in war and society as well as sport and society. His major works deal with the so-called *hendsoppers* and joiners during the Anglo-Boer War of 1899–1902, and black South African troops during World War I.

Helen Bradford has lectured in economic history and has been an associate professor in history at the University of Cape Town, where she is currently a research associate of the African Gender Institute. She is the author of *A Taste of Freedom: The ICU in Rural South Africa 1924–1930* (1988).

Zelda Rowan is a manager at Oxford University Press. In 2003 she obtained a master's degree in cultural history with distinction at the University of Pretoria. Her dissertation on Nonnie de la Rey formed the basis of her chapter in this book. She has a special interest in the war experiences of women and children during the Anglo-Boer War.

Elizabeth van Heyningen is an honorary research associate at the University of Cape Town. She is the joint author of *Cape Town: The Making of a City* (1998), *Cape Town in the Twentieth Century* (1999) and *The Cape Doctor in the Nineteenth Century* (2004). Her most recent publication is *The Concentration Camps of the Anglo-Boer War* (2013).

S.E. Duff is a National Research Foundation post-doctoral research fellow at Stellenbosch University. Her project examines the work and influence of the mothercraft movement in twentieth-century South Africa. She is interested in the histories of childhood, medicine and nutrition. She writes about her research and the history and politics of food and eating at www.tangerineandcinnamon.com.

Sandra Swart of the University of Stellenbosch holds a DPhil in modern history and an MSc in environmental management from the University of Oxford. A social and environmental historian of southern Africa, she is the author of *Riding High: Horses, Humans and History in South Africa* (2010).

Johan van Zÿl is the manager of professional services at the War Museum of the Boer Republics in Bloemfontein. He holds a master's degree in history from the University of the Free State, and specialises in the military history and sandstone architecture of the Free State. Because the Women's Monument is made of sandstone, Van Zÿl particularly enjoyed researching the monument for this book.

Acknowledgements

For an edited and illustrated work, this book has been a relatively short time in the making. For that we are especially grateful to Annie Olivier, our publishing editor at Tafelberg. She got the ball rolling, kept the editors and contributors on their toes, and handled organisation and production with exceptional professionalism, providing a rare combination of efficiency, encouragement and good humour.

We would like to thank our contributors for their admirable commitment and promptness in completing their chapters within a very tight deadline. Translators, editors, designers and others involved in this book's complex production process also deserve particular thanks.

Last, thanks goes to the ever-helpful staff of the Anglo-Boer War Museum in Bloemfontein for providing illustrations, and to Bernard du Plessis for permitting the use of material from his rare personal collection on the philatelic history of the war.

Photographic acknowledgements

Africa Media Online: 42-43, 92-93, 110. Alvaro Viljoen: 137 (middle). Annie Olivier: 226, 247. Bernard du Plessis: 155, 272. Brink family: 83. Conrad Bornman: 224, 243-245. Elizabeth van Heyningen: 147 (left). Free State Provincial Archives: 27 (VA03355), 56 (VA01822), 100 (top, VA06535), 115 (top, VA06173; bottom right VA05302), 116 (VA05298, VA05299, VA05300), 118 (bottom, VA06168), 142-143 (VA06533), 151 (VA05305), 159 (VA06529), 160 (top, VA06531), 162 (VA03281), 164 (bottom, VA03246), 165 (VA06571), 166-167 (VA03281), 193 (VA06559), 195 (VA01601), 198 (right), 207 (bottom left, VA07885), 210-211 (VA02118), 231 (bottom, VA01570), 233 (VA02119), 234 (bottom, VA02132), 236-237 (VA03463), 238 (VA00398), 242 (top, VA04938; middle VA05515). Gallo Images: 241. Isaac Alexander Sutherland, courtesy of Pamela Smith: 104, 111 (top), 131, 135 (bottom), 138, 194. J. Celestine Pretorius: 200 (right). National Museum (Bloemfontein), Marelie van Rensburg: 1. Nico Moolman: 139. Pete Bosman: 137 (top). Stephen Welz & Co.: 167. The National Archives of the UK: 8-9 (CO 1069-215-90), 16-17 (CO 1069-215-45), 177 (top, CO 1069-215-89). War Museum of the Boer Republics: front cover image, endpapers, 2-3, 4-5, 6-7, 11, 19, 20, 22, 23, 24-25, 26, 28-29, 30, 33-41, 44-45, 46-55, 57-83, 85-91, 94-99, 100 (bottom), 101-103, 105-109, 111 (bottom),112-114, 115 (bottom left), 117-118 (top), 119-130, 133, 134, 135 (top), 136, 137 (bottom), 140, 141, 144-146, 147 (right), 148-150, 152-154, 156-158, 160 (bottom), 161, 163, 164 (top), 169-176, 177 (bottom), 178-192, 196, 198 (left), 199-200, 201-207, 209, 212-223, 225, 227-231, 232, 234 (top), 235, 237, 239, 240, 242 (bottom), 246, 248-249, 253

Index

A

Abed, Ajam 77–78
Aborigines' Protection Society, London 186
Adcock, Sister 140
Afghanistan 47–48
African-American slaves 205
African National Congress (ANC) 188
Afrikaans language 204, 238
Afrikaner nationalism 43, 68–70, 192, 232–242
Aftermath of War, The 186
agricultural industry 189–190 *see also* cultivation of land
agterryers (personal retainers) 171, 175, 198, 224, 244–245
alcohol 106, 140
Alexander, William 187
Allen, Nurse Madeleine 140
America 27, 47–48, 149
ANC 188
Anglo-Boer War Museum, Bloemfontein 138, 166, 223–225
animal excrement *see* dung
anti-imperialism 61, 188
Arab political humour 206
arson *see* scorched-earth policy

B

baboon 198–199
Bakkes, Sister 140
baptismal records 155
Barberton concentration camp 159–160, 171
Barlow, Arthur G. 216
Barrett, Dr 110–111
Beak, G.B. 186, 191
Bentinck, Inspector W.J. 118
Bethulie concentration camp 109, 110–111, 134, 224
Beyers, General C.F. 237
Bij die Monument 214
biltong 106
births 83, 110, 123–124, 129, 147, 155, 157
bittereinder men 42, 60, 209
bittereinder women 36–37, 42, 61–64, 66–67, 70, 119, 208–209
black people
    agterryers 171, 175, 198, 224, 244–245
    Boers and 57, 60, 62, 64, 83, 171–174
    British army and 77
    children 105, 147, 152
    employment 162–164, 174–175, 178–182
    scorched-earth policy and 48, 178, 193
black refugee camps
    camp life 156, 162–164, 178–189
    children in 147
    closure of 189–191
    creation of 174–178
    deaths in 25, 123, 146, 182–184
    employment 162–164, 174–175, 178–182
    improvements 184–185
    religion in 162
    views on 185–189, 192–193
bleeding 135
Bloemfontein, occupation of 29, 48, 50–51
Bloemfontein camp 31–32, 140, 146, 155, 158, 159–160, 164, 171
Blue Book reports 132, 137
boererate see folk therapies
Boer men *see hendsoppers*; masculinity
Boer women
    bittereinder women 36–37, 42, 61–64, 66–67, 70, 119, 208–209
    black men and 62, 83
    British doctors and 123, 130–141
    employment 111–112
    guerrilla warfare 36, 55, 61–63
    humour 208–209
    image of 89–90
    protests by 66–67
Bornman, P.A. 167
Boshoff-Liebenberg, Isak 157
Boshoff-Liebenberg, Lenie 156–157, 158, 164
Botha, Annie 39
Botha, General Louis 29, 39–40, 214–215, 222–223, 232–233, 235
Bothma, Louis 199
Brabant, General E.Y. 29, 31
Brakpan concentration camp 178
Brandfort concentration camp 102, 110, 112, 118, 176
Brandwag, Die 214
bread 81–82, 89, 103
Brink, Revd D.P.S. 83
Brink, George 117, 119
British doctors *see* doctors in concentration camps
British supremacy 48, 50, 99–101, 171–172 *see also* racial denigration
Brits, Coen 233
Brown, Revd W.H.R. 188
Brugman, Sannie 89
Bruwer, Getruida Jacoba 52
Buller, Lieutenant General Redvers 31
Burgher peace committees 32
Buys, Conrad 178

C

Campbell-Bannerman, Henry 70
camp doctors *see* doctors in concentration camps
candles 84, 166
Canova, Antonio 216
Cardova, Mr 106, 108
Carlyle, Thomas 130
carpentry 104
cattle *see* livestock
Chamberlain, Joseph 48, 97
chickenpox 113, 184
children *see also* education
    black children 105, 147, 152
    chores of 105–106, 159
    diseases 123–124
    experiences in camps 155–164
    'faded flowers' description 132, 146–148
    games 152–153, 159–160
    journeys to camps 157–158
    orphaned children 156, 164, 165, 166
    personal experiences 166–167
    in prisoner-of-war camps 156–157
    toys 146, 153
    after war 164–165
    war experiences 148–155
Chlorodyne 139

cholera 123, 132
Cilliers, Sarie Margariette 52
class differences 60, 158–159, 171–172
cleanliness *see* sanitation
closure of camps 189–191
clothes
    mending and making of 84
    washing of 105
coffee 82, 106
Cole Bowen, Inspector St John 103–104, 106
coloured people 178
Commando 51, 148–149
Concentration Camps in South Africa during the Anglo-Boer War of 1899–1902, The 186
cooking *see* food and drink
Cronjé (née Van der Merwe), Sophia Elizabeth Wilhelmina 167
Cronjé, widow 158
cross-cultural relationships 110
Cuba 26–27, 55
cultivation of land 179, 181–182, 190 *see also* agricultural industry
Cummings, Anna 149

D

daily life in concentration camps 98, 101–119
Deadwood prisoner-of-war camp, St Helena 153
Deane, Lucy 95
deaths
    in 1900 123
    in black refugee camps 25, 123, 146, 182–184
    in Britain 139–140
    causes of 124–129
    in concentration camps 25, 39–42, 108–109, 119, 123–129, 141, 145–146, 229
    in *reconcentrados* 27
De Jager, Danie 224
De Kock, Meyer 32
De Kok, S. 137
De la Rey, Ada 80
De la Rey, Adaan (Adriaan) 77, 78
De la Rey (née Greeff), Jacoba Elizabeth 'Nonnie'
    background of 75
    on concentration camps 81
    in context of time 89–91
    food and drink 81–82, 84
    in Lichtenburg (Oct. 1899 to Nov. 1900) 75–79

Lord Methuen and 78–79, 88–89
    wandering years (Dec. 1900 to May 1902) 75, 79–82, 84–87
    wartime memoir 75, 90–91
De la Rey, Jacobus 77
De la Rey, Jan 86
De la Rey, General Koos 29, 75, 77–78, 81, 86, 88, 199, 222–223
De Lotbinière, Major Henri-Gustave Joly 180–181, 182, 184, 189
desertion, black refugee camps 188 *see also* escape from concentration camps
De Villiers, Jim 154
De Villiers, Kit 167
De Villiers, Marq 239
De Villiers, Rocco 222
Devitt, Napier 186
De Wet, General Christiaan 29, 57, 61–63, 66, 197–198, 222–223, 236–237, 241
diseases
    in black refugee camps 184
    chickenpox 113, 184
    cholera 123, 132
    in concentration camps 95, 113, 123–129
    dysentery 157, 184
    malaria 127
    measles 102, 112, 124–126, 134, 137, 141, 145, 167, 184
    plague 123, 132
    scurvy 127
    smallpox 123, 132
    tuberculosis 123, 129
    typhoid 123, 126–127, 129, 134, 184
    typhus 123
    women's ailments 129
doctors in concentration camps 123, 130–132, 134
domestic employment 162–164, 181
Douglas, General Charles 78
drinking water 84, 103, 157, 184
drinks *see* food and drink
drought (1902/1903) 190
dung 137–138
Du Plessis brothers 198–199
Du Plessis sisters 119
Dutch language 204, 238
Dutch Reformed Church 149, 155, 160, 162, 186
    Tweetoringkerk 220
Du Toit, Professor J.D. (Totius) 214, 223
Dwyer, Captain J. 104
dysentery 157, 184

E

Edenburg camp 183
education
    in black refugee camps 162, 187
    in concentration camps 112, 117, 145, 160–162, 165
    humour and 204
    during war 150–151, 159
    after war 202, 204
Edward VII 101, 160
Elandsfontein Farm 75, 77–79
Eliot, George 130–131
employment
    black people 162–164, 174–175, 178–182
    Boer women 111–112
    for surrendered burghers 31
English as official language 202, 204
enteric *see* typhoid
escape from concentration camps 109–110 *see also* desertion, black refugee camps
excrement *see* dung

F

'faded flowers' description of children 132, 146–147
family ties in concentration camps 109
Farmer, Revd E. 156
Fawcett, Millicent 147
Fawcett Commission 147
Ferreira, Ignatius 77
Fiji 125
firewood *see* fuel for cooking
Fischer, Abraham 213
Fischer, Miem 108
folk therapies 135–138 *see also* medical knowledge of Boers
food and drink
    biltong 106
    in black refugee camps 181–182
    bread 81–82, 89, 103
    coffee 82, 106
    in concentration camps 98, 104–108, 113, 166–167, 184–185
    drinking water 84, 103, 157, 184
    fuel for cooking 84, 106, 166, 184
    ginger beer 108
    maize porridge 82
    shortages 67, 151
Foreign Mission Chronicle of the Episcopal Church in Scotland, The 186
formation of concentration camps 29–34, 43, 64–65, 67–70, 96–101

Fouché, Jim 239
Fouché, Mrs Niel P. 155
Fourie, John 155
Fourie, Piet 157
Fourie family 157
Franks, Dr Kendal 137, 141
Freud, Sigmund 198
Friend, The 216, 236
friends and family ties in concentration camps 109
Froneman, C.C. 52
fuel for cooking 84, 106, 166, 184
fugitive families 75, 84, 86, 98 *see also* De la Rey (née Greeff), Jacoba Elizabeth 'Nonnie'

G
Gariep Dam 224
Geldenhuys, Aap 200
Geldenhuys, Johanna Chatorina 52–53
Geldenhuys, Mrs Jan 158
Geldenhuys, Talita Lootz 52–53
gender bias 67–68, 123, 132
generational differences, *bittereinders* and *hendsoppers* 60–61
ginger beer 108
Gloucestershire Echo 171
goat dung 137
Godfrey's Cordial 139
Goldswain, Jeremiah 135
Gomme, Alice 137
Great Trek 224, 232, 239–240
Greene, Alice 154
Green Howards Gazette, The 171
Grobbelaar, Bessie 98, 106, 109–110, 112
grootliegstories (tall stories) 198
guerrilla warfare 29, 32, 42, 48, 55, 64–65, 70, 209

H
Hackett-Dunstone, Joan 171
Hague Convention 38
Halle medicines 138
Hamilton, Ian 87
Harrismith concentration camp 113
Havenga, Nicholaas Christiaan 'Klasie' 52–53
Havenga Report 52–53
Heidelberg Commando 202
Heilbron concentration camp 140, 176
Heldinne van die Oorlog 220
hendsoppers (surrendered burghers) 29, 32, 48, 55, 60–64, 66, 101–102, 104–105, 167
Hertzog, General J.B.M. 53, 213–214, 222, 223, 232–233

Heystek, Joost 166
Hobhouse, Emily
    black refugee camps 186
    children in camps 159–160
    on Cole Bowen 103
    on daily life in camps 119
    'faded flowers' description of children 132, 146–147
    folk therapies 137, 141
    on humour of Boers 197, 208
    importance of 97
    on servants in camps 171
    speech of 235–236, 242, 249–256
    on suffering in camps 132, 146–147, 155
    Tibbie Steyn and 229
    Women's Monument 216–220, 223, 230–231, 235–236, 241–242
Hofmeyr, Jan 214
Holder (née Coetzee), Susara Magrieta Susanna 138, 166
horseplay *see* humour
horses 50, 65, 78
hospitals 111–112, 132–134, 138, 164–165
housing in concentration camps 104
Howick concentration camp 156, 162
Hughes, Langston 205
Huguenot Seminary and College 149–150, 154, 165
Huis Apotheek 138–139
Huisgenoot 208
Humor in die algemeen en sy uiting in die Afrikaanse letterkunde 208
humour
    Emily Hobhouse on 197, 208
    gender differences 208–209
    helplessness and 202–204
    laughter of survivors 204–208
    nationalism and 208–209
    political jokes 205–208
    reasons for 198–202
Hunter, General Archibald 78
Hunter, Dr John 132
Hutton, Lillian 152
hygiene *see* sanitation
hymns 108, 119

I
Ilbery, Mrs 140
India 48
infectious diseases *see* diseases
interracial relationships *see* cross-cultural relationships
Irene concentration camp 31, 138, 166

J
Jacobs, E.J. 102–104
Jacobs concentration camp 145
'joiners' 166–167
Jordan, Pallo 243
journeys to concentration camps 157–158

K
Kaffirfontein Native Refugee Camp 99
Kampkinders, 1900–1902 166–167
Kemp, General Jan 82, 84
Kestell, Revd J.D. 198, 216, 220, 223, 236, 241
Kilian, M.E. 155
Kimberley, siege of 152
Kimberley concentration camp 132, 147
Kimberley Volunteer Regiment 235
Kingsley, Charles 130
Kishtainy, Khalid 206
Kitchener, Horatio Herbert 32, 36–37, 39–40, 42, 68, 97–99, 178–179
Klerksdorp concentration camp 111, 118, 156, 167
Koen, Mrs 52
Kolbe, General W.J. 198
Kritzinger family 86–87
Kruger, President Paul 61, 63–64, 96, 139, 145
Krugersdorp concentration camp 119, 156, 188

L
Ladies' Committee 95, 100, 103, 139
Lady Roberts (naval gun) 201, 202
Ladysmith, siege of 152, 154
Langenhoven, C.J. 206, 208
latrines 139
laughing *see* humour
laundry 105
Leipoldt, C. Louis 206
Liberal Party 38
libidos of Boer men 36
Lichtenburg district 77–78, 86
Lincoln, President Abraham 249, 255
Lipp, Charles 150
Lipp, Isabella 150
liquor *see* alcohol
Lister, Joseph 131
livestock 31–32, 50, 51
Lloyd George, David 27
location of concentration camps 21, 25
looting 34, 47–51, 55
'looting corps' 105
Lötter, Hans 208
Louw, Revd A.J. 223

Louw, Johanna 110–111
Lückhoff, Revd A.D. 109

M

Mackenzie, Ella 150
Mafeking, siege of 152
Mafeking concentration camp 127, 134, 178
Magrita Prinsloo 220
maize porridge 82
Malan, D.F. 223, 236, 242
Malan, General Magnus 224
malaria 127
Malherbe, F.E.J. 'Fransie' 208–209
Manchester Guardian 47
map of concentration camps 21
Maritz, General Manie 200
Marquard, Margaret 96, 97, 151, 153–154, 157–158
martial law 150, 200
masculinity 47–48, 51, 55–61
maternal care 139–140, 183
McLeod, Nurse 140
measles 102, 112, 124–126, 134, 137, 141, 145, 167, 184
medical knowledge of Boers 134–139, 141
Medlin and Leham 216
Merebank concentration camp 108, 119, 162, 164, 167
Merriman, John 27, 55
Methuen, Lord 78–79, 88–89
Middelburg talks 39–40, 42
Middlemarch 130–131
Midlands Seminary, Graaff-Reinet 159
Mijne Omzwervingen en Beproevingen gedurende den Oorlog 75
military professionalism 25–27
Milner, Lord Alfred 31, 39–40, 42, 97, 100, 145, 161, 188, 202
mineworkers 178–179
Minnaar, Phil 224
Mooiroos 198
mortality rate *see* deaths
Muller, Chris 199
Murray, Revd A.M. 108
Murray, Revd Andrew 220
Murray, Revd C.D. 213
music in concentration camps 118–119

N

Nasionale Pers (later Naspers) 223
Natal government 31
nationalism, Afrikaner *see* Afrikaner nationalism
National Party 239–240
National Scouts 105
National Women's Memorial Commission 223–224, 239
Native Refugee Department 178–179, 181, 184, 186, 189–191
Nel, Machteld 145, 147, 155
Netley Military Hospital, Britain 126
Nevers, Miss 151
Nightingale, Florence 132
nomadic life in veld *see* fugitive families
Norvalspont concentration camp 103, 106, 112, 160
nurses
    Boer women as 111–112, 165
    in concentration camps 100–101, 118, 140–141
    history of 132
Nylstroom concentration camp 166

O

oath of neutrality 29, 31, 48, 66, 67, 102
Oom Gert vertel en ander gedigte 206
opium 139
Opperman (née Van Strÿp), Johanna Elizabeth 138, 166–167
orphaned children 156, 164, 165, 166
Orwell, George 206

P

Paardeberg, Battle of 47
Pander, Pier 217
passes 32, 62, 201
Pasteur, Louis 123, 131
patent medicines 138–139
peace committees 32
peace negotiations 39–40, 42
Peace of Vereeniging 39–40, 202, 213
Pern, Dr Neil 140
pets as mascots 199
Philippines 27
Pinetown concentration camp 108, 162
plague 123, 132
police in concentration camps 104–105
Postma, Revd Willem 90, 223
post-traumatic shock 204–205
Potchefstroom concentration camp 145, 166
Potchefstroom University 238
Poynton Bros 106
pranks *see* humour
Pretoria
    camp in 31
    capture of 29
Prinsloo, General Marthinus 154–155
Prinsloo, S.L. 138
prisoner-of-war camps 153, 156–157, 171
privacy 98
professionalism, military 25–27
protection camps 31–32
psalms 108, 119

Q

Quakers 186–187
Queen Victoria 201

R

racial denigration 36–37, 48, 50, 62, 171–172 *see also* British supremacy
Rahl, Bella 167
rape 51–53
rations 105, 113, 166, 184–185
rebellion of 1914 241
reconcentrados 26–27, 55
refugee camps 32
Reitz, Deneys 51, 148–149, 197, 199–201, 209
Reitz, F.W. 201, 222
religion, importance of 62, 108–109, 162
Report of a Visit to the Camps of Women and Children in the Cape and Orange River Camps 147
Retief, Piet 215
Rheeder, Mieta 110
Rhenosterkop, battle at 200
Rhodesia 48
Richardson, Lawrence 151–152, 153, 154, 160, 187
Rimington's patrol 52–53
Roberts, Lord 29, 31–32, 47–48, 50, 63–66, 70, 97, 199
Robertson, Revd 117
Rodin, Auguste 217
romantic relationships 110
Rose, Lily 112, 119
Ross, A. 52
Ross, Dr John 131
routines in concentration camps 98, 101–119
Rowntree, Joshua 147
Royal Irish 34
Russian military attaché 47

S

salmonella *see* typhoid
sanitation 123, 131–133, 138, 139, 176
Sargant, Edmund Beale 112, 160
satirical verse 201
Scheepers, Gideon 208

Schneider (née De la Rey), Hester 167
schools *see* education
Schutte, J.P. 145
scorched-earth policy
    black people and 48, 178, 193
    camps and 32–35, 38
    guerrilla warfare and 64–65, 68, 70
    impact of 55
    Nonnie de la Rey and 81
    reasons for 42, 47–50, 55, 64–65, 70, 96–97
Scotland 117, 130
scurvy 127
Second World War 117, 193, 224, 238
servants in concentration camps 105, 171–176 *see also* domestic employment
sexual relationships 110
sexual violence *see* rape
Sherman, William 47, 48
shops 106–108, 185
Simson 86
Slabbert, Louis 202
slaves, African-American 205
smallpox 123, 132
Smith-Dorrien, General Horace 202
Smuts, General Jan 56, 57, 65, 222, 232
soap 84
Society of Friends, Britain 147, 152, 186–187
Soff, Frans 215
South African Academy for Science and Art 136
South African Native Congress 188
Spain 26–27, 55, 179
sport 101, 106, 118, 160
starching 84, 98
starvation as weapon 48, 66–67
Steyn, Jan 213
Steyn, President Marthinus Theunis
    grave of 223, 241
    Havenga Report 53
    during war 56, 61, 63, 66
    Women's Monument 213–216, 222–223, 229–231, 235
Steyn, Rachel Isabella (Tibbie) 67, 213–214, 220, 223, 229, 231, 241–242
Stockenström, Eric 90
stores 106–108, 185
Strange, Superintendent 99
Strydom, Pieter Jacobus 102–104, 117, 118
Sudan 48
Suid-Afrikaanse Akademie vir Wetenskap en Kuns 136
Sunday Schools 162
supply crisis, British army 50–51, 55, 64
surrendered burghers *see* hendsoppers
Swart, C.R. 239
Swarts, Lenie 109

T

tall tales (*grootliegstories*) 198
teachers
    American 149
    in concentration camps 112, 140
Theal, George McCall 61
Theron, Lottie 118–119
Times History of the War in South Africa, The 70
toilets 139
Totius 214, 223
toys 146, 153
Treaty of Vereeniging *see* Peace of Vereeniging
Tregardt, Louis 135, 138
Trollope, Captain A.G. 183
tuberculosis 123, 129
Tweebosch, Battle of 88
Tweeriviere, Battle of 77
Tweetoringkerk 220
typhoid 123, 126–127, 129, 134, 184
typhus 123

U

United Society for the Propagation of the Gospel 188
United States of America *see* America

V

Van Breda, Pieter 53
vandalism *see* looting
Van den Berg, Aletta 137
Van den Berg, Mrs A.M. 119
Van den Heever, C.M. 53
Van der Merwe, N.J. 239
Van Heerden, Petronella 154–155
Van Rensburg, Anna 83, 113
Van Rensburg, Nicolaas 83
Van Rensburg, Siener 201
Van Schoor, M.C.E. 166–167
Van Wouw, Anton 215, 216–218, 230
Van Zyl, Lizzie 145
Vereeniging concentration camp 118
Vermaak, Nonnie 109–110
vernielzucht see looting
Victoria, Queen of England 201
Viljoen, General Ben 198, 200–201
Viner-Johnson, Captain Joseph 132
Visser, Tibbie 224
volk see Afrikaner nationalism
Volksgeneeskuns in Suid-Afrika 136–138
Voortman, Dr John Bernard 134
Voortrekker Monument 229, 232, 239–240
Vrede-aand 206

W

War Museum *see* Anglo-Boer War Museum, Bloemfontein
War Office 48, 97, 100, 132
'wasting' condition 123–124, 132
water *see* drinking water
Wellesley College 151
Wellington 149–150
Wentworth concentration camp 162
Wessels, J. 111
Weyler, General Valeriano 26–27, 55
Winburg concentration camp 140
winter of 1901 20, 39–40, 95, 101–102, 129
Woman's Wanderings and Trials during the Anglo-Boer War, A 75
women *see* Boer women
women's ailments 129
Women's Memorial Commission 223–224, 239
Women's Monument
    after 1913 223–225
    Afrikaner nationalism and 232–242
    construction of 216–220
    design of 215–220
    meaning of 213, 245
    under new government 243–245
    opposition to 215–216, 232–233
    patriarchal motives for 230–231, 241
    planning of 213–215, 229–230
    sculptures added 224, 242
    unveiling of 220–223, 233–237
Wookey, F.E. 152
World War II 117, 193, 224, 238

X

Xhosa people 48

Y

Yule, Dr Pratt 112, 127

A blackened corner or a black frame around an envelope served as a warning to the receiver of the correspondence that he or she was to expect news of a death in the family. This letter was sent from the Krugersdorp concentration camp to Jan Willem van der Ryst in the Bellevue camp. Van der Ryst, from Groenfontein farm in the Potchefstroom district, was captured at Paardeberg on 27 February 1900 while serving with the Boven Mooirivier commando. The letter was most probably sent by his wife.